Fighting Back the von Neumann Bottleneck with
Small- and Large-Scale Vector Microprocessors

Matheus Cavalcante

Fighting Back the von Neumann Bottleneck with Small- and Large-Scale Vector Microprocessors

Hartung-Gorre Verlag Konstanz
2023

Reprint of Diss. ETH No. 29310

SERIES IN MICROELECTRONICS   VOLUME 246

edited by   Luca Benini
             Qiuting Huang
             Taekwang Jang
             Mathieu Luisier
             Christoph Studer
             Hua Wang

Bibliographic information published by Die Deutsche National-bibliothek

Die Deutsche Nationalbibliothek lists this publication in the Deutsche National-bibliografie; detailed bibliographic data is available on the Internet at: `http://dnb.dnb.de`

First edition 2023

HARTUNG-GORRE VERLAG KONSTANZ
`http://www.hartung-gorre.de`

ISSN 0936-5362
ISBN-10: 3-86628-801-8
ISBN-13: 978-3-86628-801-0

Acknowledgments

I was never naïve to think that a Ph.D. would be easy. But, with the hindsight of overcoming this academic hurdle, I tenderly appreciate the support and enlightenment that so many people selflessly dedicated to me as critical for a successful thesis. As such, I eagerly take this opportunity to thank them, if only with a few lines of text.

First, Luca, thank you. I will surely look fondly at the years I passed under your supervision. Whether it is for your vast knowledge, your patience and ability to manage such a large research group as clockwork, or the many amazing projects you allowed us to carry, I cannot possibly summarize how much I learned with you in some mere lines. Instead, I take this opportunity to express how I wish I had learned more. Once again, my most sincere thank you.

I sincerely thank Professor Mauro Olivieri for having so promptly agreed to co-referee this thesis and for your very insightful feedback. I will also remember our discussions during the Paris RISC-V Workshop about the intricacies of the Vector Specification as a fellowship token in this rather narrow field of Computer Architecture!

I could not have done my thesis without the support of my many colleagues at IIS. Gianna, Matteo, Samuel—in alphabetic order—it is hard to express how much I appreciated working with you. Whether it is for having taped out a chiplet and an interposer for which I am immensely proud, for having explored the many idiosyncrasies of vector processing while combining bad jokes with bursts of contagious laughter, or for always having gladly discussed how to supervise our Master's Thesis students better while subtly converting me to a latch-partisan, I will never be able to look back into all this without a smile on my face. My warmest hugs and most amiable thank you go to Ale, Andreas,

Cyril, Gianmà, Luca, Marco, Mattia, Manuel, Michael, Moritz, Nils, Patrick, Paul, Tim, Victor, and Yichao, for the time we shared in IIS.

Thank you to Frank and the DZ team for the immense knowledge in everything VLSI-related! Frank, I realized the more time I spent at IIS, the more I found myself teaching my students what you once taught me. Your teachings on how to present my work, be organized, and always-wise ideas on how to design a chip. And you can rest assured that I will propagate your teachings wherever I go!

Thank you to Tommaso for (willingly or not) imprinting the salentine culture on me while teaching me Italian, which turned out to be quite useful! In this vein, thanks to Maxim for our discussions in French and Swiss German, to which I would always look forward. Whether it was for your vast literature knowledge, for teaching me to enjoy your psychedelic rock, for our time trying to make SoCDAML work despite the pandemic, or for being a great friend, you were an absolute IIS highlight.

A grand merci to the many friends I met in Grenoble. To Thiago, the best colocataire I have ever had, and for our many hilarious discussions around the most pleasant and diverse topics. To Luana, thank you for your profound artistic, philosophical, and sociological points of view, which always leave a mark on me and be fundamental in helping me improve. Thank you Valentin for the warm camaraderie during our TPs and for explaining the (apparently) uncountably-many details I missed in the Lord of the Rings series. And trugarez dit Katell, for allowing me to follow Phelma's Master's degree despite my lack of experience in micro-electronics, for introducing me to RISC-V, and for your much-appreciated friendship. I truly would not be here if it were not for your support!

Thanks to my family for their unconditional support and understanding during the many stressful times of my thesis. Despite the large distance between us, you were often the cornerstone of my life. Finally, I dedicate this thesis to my little brother, Heitor. May you once read this thesis and know that I did it for you.

Abstract

In his seminal Turing Award Lecture, Backus discussed the issues stemming from the word-at-a-time style of programming inherited from the von Neumann computer. More than forty years later, in a context where Moore's Law and Dennard's scaling are no longer reliable sources of computer performance and energy efficiency gains, computer architects must be creative to amortize the von Neumann Bottleneck (VNB) associated with fetching and decoding instructions which only keep the datapath busy for a very short period of time.

The strong emergence of embarrassingly-parallel workloads, such as data analytics and machine learning, created a major window of opportunity for architectures that effectively exploit Data Level Parallelism (DLP) to achieve energy efficiency. Unfortunately, no single architecture can effectively answer the increasing computing requirements of all modern workloads. Parallel multi-core computing is the *de facto* standard for exploiting parallelism while keeping a flexible programming model. However, they do not exploit the workload's DLP characteristics and fail to address the VNB effectively.

In this thesis, we will assess architectural models that relax the constraints imposed by the VNB. We will focus on architectures based on a cluster of simple cores sharing low-latency L1 memory. Being on the streaming multiprocessors of Graphics Processing Units (GPUs), large-scale manycore clusters, or the computing cluster of embedded processors, the shared-L1 cluster is a simple albeit ubiquitous architectural element. Therefore, maximizing its efficiency is the key challenge for improving the overall system's energy efficiency.

Vector processors promise to tackle the VNB by amortizing the energy overhead of instruction fetching and decoding over several chunks of data. They also keep the flexibility of being a programmable architecture. With Ara, we exploit vector Single Instruction, Multiple Data (SIMD) on the application-class domain with a large-scale Vector Processing Unit (VPU), which can orchestrate up to 16 double-precision Floating Point Units (FPUs). Ara is part of a larger revival of interest vector architectures after decades of neglect and was one of the first open-source vector processing units based on the RISC-V Vector Extension (RVV) Instruction Set Architecture (ISA). Furthermore, we propose Spatz, a modern, compact vector machine that targets DLP before integrating it into a shared-L1 cluster. According to our mathematical model of the cluster's energy consumption, a very small Vector Register File (VRF) is needed to optimally balance the energy cost due to the traffic between the L0 VRF and the L1 Scratchpad Memory (SPM). Despite using a VRF much smaller than typical vector processors, we achieve state-of-the-art performance.

In the embedded domain, there is rarely the need for large computational units such as double-precision FPUs. However, there is a growing need for flexible edge computation. Instead of replicating the shared-L1 cluster—which usually only scales to the low tens of cores and connecting them with some latency-tolerant interconnect, we tried to push the core count of the cluster to its limit. Our objective with MemPool, a shared-L1 cluster with 256 cores and 1 MiB of L1 memory, is a highly-flexible architecture that can also meet the ever-stricter computational requirements of edge computing.

Unfortunately, MemPool's flexibility has a price, and using scalar cores as its computation units makes the design a prime target for VNB-related limitations. In this thesis, we explore for the first time vector processing as an option to build small and efficient Processing Elements (PEs) for large-scale shared-L1 clusters. As the PE of MemPool, Spatz alleviates its VNB by adding a VRF which acts as an L0 memory level, thereby reducing the traffic on the interconnects.

To summarize, this thesis explores the vector processing abstraction as an answer to the VNB on modern computational systems, from the High-Performance Computing (HPC) to the edge domain. As part of a revival of interest in the vector-SIMD abstraction, our open-sourced accelerators highlight the soundness of the vector approach without resorting to overspecialized computing architectures.

Zusammenfassung

In seiner wegweisenden Turing-Preis-Rede stellte Backus die Probleme vor, die aus dem „Wort für Wort" Programmierstil resultieren, der vom von Neumann-Computer übernommen wurde. Mehr als vierzig Jahre später sind Moores Gesetz und Dennards Skalierung keine zuverlässigen Quellen für Computerleistung und Energieeffizienzgewinne. In diesem Kontext müssen Computerarchitekten kreativ sein, um den von Neumannschen Engpass zu amortisieren, der mit dem Abrufen und Dekodieren von Anweisungen verbunden ist, die den Datenpfad nur für eine sehr kurze Zeit beschäftigen.

Die starke Verbreitung von Arbeitslasten mit extremer Parallelität wie Datenanalyse und maschinelles Lernen hat eine große Chance für Architekturen geschaffen, die Datenparallelität (DLP) effektiv nutzen, um Energieeffizienz zu erreichen. Leider kann keine einzelne Architektur effektiv den steigenden Rechenanforderungen aller modernen Arbeitslasten gerecht werden. Mehrkernprozessoren sind zu einem Quasistandard geworden zur Ausnutzung von Parallelismus unter Beibehaltung eines flexiblen Programmiermodells. Diese Systeme nutzen jedoch keine Datenparallelität aus und können den VNB nicht effektiv bewältigen.

In dieser Dissertation werden wir Architekturmodelle bewerten, die die Beschränkungen des VNB lockern. Wir konzentrieren uns auf Architekturen, die auf einem Cluster einfacher Prozessoren basieren, die sich einen L1-Speicher mit niedriger Latenz teilen. Ob es sich dabei um die Streaming-Multiprozessoren von Grafikprozessoren (GPUs), um viele große Mehrkernclustern oder um den Rechencluster eingebetteter Prozessoren handelt, der gemeinsam genutzten L1 Cluster ist ein einfaches, wenn auch allgegenwärtiges Architekturelement. Daher ist

die Maximierung seiner Effizienz die Schlüsselherausforderung zur
Verbesserung der Energieeffizienz des gesamten Systems.

Vektorprozessoren versprechen, das VNB zu bewältigen, indem sie
den Energieaufwand für das Abrufen und Decodieren von Anweisungen
über mehrere Datenblöcke hinweg amortisieren. Sie behalten auch
die Flexibilität einer programmierbaren Architektur bei. Mit Ara
nutzen wir das vektorielle „Single Instruction, Multiple Data" (SIMD)
Modell im Anwendungsbereich mit einem großen Vektorprozessor,
die bis zu 16 Gleitkommaeinheiten (FPUs) mit doppelter Genauigkeit steuern kann. Ara ist Teil eines größeren Wiederauflebens des
Interesses an Vektorarchitekturen und war eine der ersten Open-Source-
Vektorprozessoren, die auf der RISC-V Vektorbefehlssatzarchitektur
basiert ist. Darüber hinaus schlagen wir Spatz vor, eine moderne,
kompakte Vektormaschine, die auf DLP abzielt, bevor es in einen
gemeinsam genutzten L1-Cluster integriert wird. Gemäß unserem
mathematischen Modell des Energieverbrauchs des Clusters ist eine
sehr kleine Vektorregisterspeicher (VRF) erforderlich, um die Energie-
kosten aufgrund des Datenverkehrs zwischen dem L0 VRF und dem
L1 Speicher optimal auszugleichen. Trotz der Verwendung eines VRF,
der viel kleiner ist als bei typischen Vektorprozessoren, erreichen wir
eine Spitzenleistung auf dem neuesten Stand der Technik.

Im eingebetteten Bereich besteht selten Bedarf an großen Rechenein-
heiten wie Gleitkommaeinheiten mit doppelter Genauigkeit. Es besteht
jedoch zunehmend Bedarf an flexibler Edge Computing. Anstatt den
gemeinsamen L1-Cluster zu replizieren—der normalerweise nur auf
die niedrigen Zehnerkerne skaliert—und sie mit einer latenztoleranten
Verbindung zu verbinden, haben wir versucht, die Kernanzahl des
Clusters an seine Grenzen zu bringen. Unser Ziel mit MemPool, einem
L1-Cluster mit 256 Kernen und 1 MiB L1-Speicher, ist eine hochflexible
Architektur, die auch den immer strengeren Rechenanforderungen des
Edge-Computing erfüllen kann.

Leider hat die Flexibilität von MemPool einen Preis, und die
Verwendung von Skalarprozessoren als Berechnungseinheiten (PEs)
macht das Design anfällig für VNB-bezogene Einschränkungen. In
dieser Dissertation erforschen wir erstmals das Vektormodell als Option,
um kleine und effiziente PEs für große L1 Clusters zu erstellen. Spatz
entlastet das VNB von MemPool, indem es den Verbindungsverkehr
dank der Hinzufügung eines L0-VRF reduziert.

Zusammenfassend untersucht diese Dissertation das Vektormodell als Antwort auf das VNB in modernen Rechensystemen, von Hochleistungsrechnen bis zum Edge-Bereich. Als Teil einer Wiederbelebung des Interesses an der Vektor-SIMD-Abstraktion heben unsere Open-Source-Beschleuniger die Solidität des Vektoransatzes hervor, ohne auf über spezialisierte Rechenarchitekturen zurückgreifen zu müssen.

Résumé

Lors de sa conférence de remise du Prix Turing, Backus a discuté des problèmes issus du style de programmation « mot par mot » hérité de l'architecture de von Neumann. Plus de quarante ans plus tard, dans un contexte où la loi de Moore et les lois d'échelle de Dennard ne sont plus sources fiables de performance et d'efficacité énergétique, les architectes en informatique doivent faire preuve de créativité pour amortir les limitations de l'architecture de von Neumann (VNB), dues au chargement et décodage d'instructions qui n'occupent le chemin de données d'un ordinateur que pendant une courte période de temps.

La forte émergence d'algorithmes au parallélisme extrême, telles que l'analyse de données et l'apprentissage automatique, a créé une opportunité majeure pour les architectures qui exploitent efficacement le parallélisme de données (DLP). Malheureusement, aucune architecture unique ne peut répondre efficacement aux exigences croissantes en matière de calcul de toutes les charges de travail modernes. Les processeurs multi-cœurs sont la norme de facto pour exploiter le parallélisme tout en conservant un modèle de programmation flexible. Cependant, ils n'exploitent pas le parallélisme de données et, par conséquent, ne parviennent pas à traiter le VNB de manière efficace.

Cette thèse évaluera des paradigmes architecturaux qui amenuisent les contraintes imposées par le VNB. Nous nous concentrerons sur des architectures basées sur un cluster informatique de cœurs très simples partageant une mémoire L1 à faible latence. Que ce soit sur les multiprocesseurs de flux des processeurs graphiques, sur des clusters à nombreux cœurs à grande échelle, ou sur des systèmes informatiques embarqués, les clusters à mémoire L1 partagée est un élément architectural simple mais omniprésent. Par conséquent, maximiser son efficacité est le défi clé pour améliorer l'efficacité énergétique de tout le système.

Les processeurs vectoriels promettent de s'attaquer au VNB en amortissant le surcoût énergétique de chargement et décodage des instructions sur des données multiples, tout en gardant la flexibilité d'une architecture programmable. Avec Ara, nous exploitons le modèle de programmation « Single Instruction on Multiple Data » (SIMD) sur le domaine des applications avec une unité de calcul vectoriel (VPU) à grande échelle, qui peut orchestrer jusqu'à 16 unités de calcul en virgule flottante à double précision (FPUs). Ara fait partie d'un plus large renouveau d'intérêt pour les architectures vectorielles après des décennies de négligence et a été l'une des premières unités de traitement vectoriel en open-source basées sur le jeu d'instructions vectoriels RISC-V. De plus, nous proposons Spatz, une unité de calcul vectorielle moderne et compacte qui cible le DLP avant de l'intégrer dans un cluster à mémoire L1 partagée. Selon notre modèle mathématique de la consommation d'énergie du cluster, un très petit banc de registres vectoriels (VRF) est nécessaire pour équilibrer de manière optimale le coût énergétique dû au trafic entre le VRF de niveau L0 et la mémoire L1. Nous obtenons une efficacité élevée malgré un très petit VRF en comparaison avec celui des processeurs vectoriels traditionnels.

Dans le domaine embarqué, il est rarement nécessaire d'avoir des unités de calcul telles que des FPUs à double précision. Cependant, il y a un besoin croissant d'informatique en périphérie flexible. Au lieu de répliquer le cluster à L1 partagée—qui généralement ne s'étend qu'à quelques dizaines de cœurs—et de les connecter avec un réseau tolérant à la latence, nous avons poussé le nombre de cœurs du cluster à ses limites. Notre objectif avec MemPool, un cluster avec 256 cœurs et 1 Mio de mémoire L1, est d'obtenir une architecture hautement flexible qui peut également répondre aux exigences de calcul de plus en plus strictes de l'informatique en périphérie.

La flexibilité de MemPool a un coût, et l'utilisation d'un cœur scalaire comme unité de calcul (PE) en fait une cible privilégiée pour les limitations liées au VNB. Dans cette thèse, nous explorons pour la première fois l'utilisation d'une VPU comme un PE petit et efficace pour des clusters à grande échelle. En tant que PE de MemPool, Spatz soulage son VNB grâce à l'ajout d'un VRF qui agit comme mémoire L0, réduisant ainsi le trafic sur les réseaux de connexion L1 de MemPool.

En résumé, cette thèse explore l'abstraction de calcul vectoriel comme réponse au VNB dans les systèmes de calcul modernes, du domaine haute-performance jusqu'à l'informatique en périphérie. Dans le cadre d'une résurgence de l'intérêt pour l'abstraction vectorielle, nos accélérateurs mettent en évidence la pertinence de l'approche vectorielle sans recourir à des architectures de calcul sur-spécialisées.

Riassunto

Nella sua conferenza di consegna del Premio Turing, Backus ha discusso le problematiche derivanti dallo stile di programmazione «word per word» ereditato dall'architettura di von Neumann. Oltre quarant'anni dopo, in un contesto in cui la Legge di Moore e il scaling di Dennard non sono più fonti affidabili di incremento delle prestazioni e dell'efficienza energetica dei computer, gli architetti informatici devono essere creativi per ammortizzare i limiti dall'architettura di Von Neumann (VNB) associati al recupero e alla decodifica delle istruzioni, che mantengono il data path occupato per un breve periodo di tempo.

Il pressante emergere di applicazioni altamente parallele, come l'analisi dei dati e l'apprendimento automatico, ha creato un'enorme opportunità per architetture che sfruttano in modo efficiente il Parallelismo a livello dei dati (DLP) per raggiungere un'alta efficienza energetica. Purtroppo, non esiste un'unica architettura che riesca a rispondere adeguatamente alle crescenti esigenze di calcolo delle applicazioni moderne. La computazione parallela multi-core è l'architettura standard per sfruttare il parallelismo, mantenendo un modello di programmazione flessibile. Tuttavia, tali architetture non sfruttano il DLP e, di conseguenza, non affrontano in modo efficace il VNB.

In questa tesi, valuteremo modelli architetturali che allentano le limitazioni imposte dal VNB. Più precisamente, ci concentreremo su architetture basate su un cluster di core semplici che condividono memoria L1 a bassa latenza. Sia che si trovino su delle unità di elaborazione grafica, su di cluster manycore su larga scala o su di processori embedded, il cluster con memoria L1 condivisa è un elemento architetturale semplice ma onnipresente. Pertanto, massimizzare la sua efficienza è la sfida chiave per migliorare l'efficienza energetica complessiva del sistema.

Processori vettoriali promettono di gestire il VNB in modo efficace ammortizzando il costo energetico del recupero e della decodifica delle istruzioni su vari elementi di un vettore. Mantengono anche il carattere flessibile delle architetture programmabili. Con Ara, esploriamo l'astrazione «Single Instruction, Multiple Data» (SIMD) vettoriale per costruire un'unità di elaborazione vettoriale (VPU) su larga scala, in grado di orchestrare fino a 16 unità di punto flottante a doppia precisione. Ara fa parte di un rinnovato interesse per le architetture vettoriali dopo decenni di oblio ed è stata una delle prime VPU open-source basate sull'insieme di istruzioni vettoriali RISC-V. Inoltre, proponiamo anche Spatz, un processore vettoriale moderno e compatto che si concentra sull'esplorazione del DLP e lo integriamo in un cluster con memoria L1 condivisa. Secondo il nostro modello di consumo energetico del cluster, è necessario un piccolo file dei registri vettoriali (VRF) per bilanciare in modo ottimale il costo energetico dovuto al traffico tra il VRF di livello L0 e la memoria di livello L1. Nonostante un VRF molto più piccolo rispetto a quelli dei tipici processori vettoriali, Spatz raggiunge un'efficienza energetica all'avanguardia.

Nel dominio embedded, raramente c'è bisogno di unità di calcolo grandi come le FPUs a doppia precisione. Tuttavia, c'è una crescente necessità di edge computing flessibile. Invece di replicare il cluster con memoria L1 condivisa, che di solito si espande solo fino alle decine di core, e connetterli con una rete d'interconnessione a bassa latenza, abbiamo cercato di spingere il numero di core del cluster al limite. Il nostro obiettivo con MemPool, un sistema con 256 core e 1 MiB di memoria L1, è di ottenere un'architettura altamente flessibile che possa anche soddisfare l'esigenze computazionali dell'edge computing.

Purtroppo, la flessibilità di MemPool ha un costo, e l'uso di core scalari come unità di calcolo (PE) lo rende un obiettivo principale per le limitazione legate al VNB. In questa tesi, esploriamo per la prima volta i processori vettoriali come opzione per costruire dei PE piccoli ed efficienti per cluster con memoria L1 condivisa di larga scala. Come PE di MemPool, Spatz allevia il suo VNB attraverso un VRF che funge da memoria L0, riducendo così il traffico di memoria L1.

In sintesi, questa tesi esplora il processamento vettoriale come risposta al VNB nei sistemi di calcolo moderni. Come parte di una rinascita dell'interesse per il calcolo vettoriale SIMD, i nostri acceleratori open source evidenziano la solidità dell'approccio vettoriale senza dover ricorrere ad architetture di calcolo altamente specializzate.

Resumo

Em sua seminal palestra de premiação do Prêmio Turing, Backus discutiu sobre os problemas decorrentes do estilo de computação "palavra-por-palavra" herdado da arquiteture de von Neumann. Mais de quarenta anos depois, em um contexto em que a Lei de Moore e a Escala de Dennard não são mais fontes de ganhos em desempenho computacional e eficiência energética. Portanto, os arquitetos de computadores devem ser criativos para amortizar as limitações da máquina de von Neumann (VNB) decorrente do custo inerente à leitura e decodificação de instruções que mantêm o processador ocupado apenas por um curto período de tempo.

A forte emergência de aplicações com paralelismo extremo, como análise de dados e aprendizado de máquina, criou uma enorme oportunidade para arquiteturas que exploram de forma eficiente o Paralelismo de Dados (DLP) para alcançar alta eficiência energética. Infelizmente, não há uma única arquitetura que consiga responder de maneira adequada às crescentes necessidades de computação de as aplicações modernas. A computação paralela a múltiplos processadores é a arquitetura padrão para explorar o paralelismo, mantendo um modelo de programação flexível. No entanto, tais arquiteturas não exploram o DLP e, como resultado, não lidam com o VNB de maneira efetiva.

Nesta tese, nós avaliaremos modelos arquiteturais que relaxam as limitações impostas pelo VNB. Mais precisamente, nós nos concentraremos em arquiteturas baseadas em um cluster de cores simples compartilhando memória L1 de baixa latência. Seja nas Unidades de Processamento Gráfico, nos clusters manycore de grande escala ou em processadores embarcados, o cluster com memória L1 compartilhada é um elemento arquitetural simples, mas onipresente. Portanto, maximizar sua eficiência é o desafio-chave para melhorar a eficiência energética geral do sistema.

Processadores vetoriais prometem lidar com o VNB de maneira efetiva ao amortizar o custo energético de decodificação de instruções sobre vários elementos de um vetor. Eles também mantêm o caráter flexível de arquiteturas programáveis. Com Ara, nós exploramos a abstração *Single Instruction, Multiple Data* (SIMD) vetorial para construir uma Unidade de Processamento Vetorial (VPU) em grande escala, capaz de orquestrar até 16 Unidades de Ponto Flutuante (FPUs) de dupla precisão. Ara faz parte de um renovado interesse em arquiteturas vetoriais após décadas de esquecimento e foi uma das primeiras unidades de processamento vetorial de código aberto baseadas no conjunto de instruções vetoriais RISC-V. Além disso, propomos também Spatz, uma processador vetorial moderno e compacto que se concentra na exploração do DLP e o integramos a um cluster com memória L1 compartilhada. De acordo com nosso modelo de consumo de energia do cluster, um pequeno arquivo de registro vetorial (VRF) é necessário para equilibrar de forma ideal o custo energético devido ao tráfego entre o VRF de nível L0 e a memória de nível L1. Apesar de um VRF muito menor do que aquele de processadores vetoriais típicos, Spatz alcança uma eficiência energética de última geração.

Aplicações embarcadas raramente precisam de grandes unidades aritméticas tais como FPUs de dupla precisão. No entanto, há uma crescente necessidade de computação de borda flexível. Ao invés de replicar o cluster com memória L1 compartilhada, que normalmente só escala até algumas dezenas de cores, e conectá-los com uma rede de conexão a baixa latência, nós tentamos levar o número de cores dos clusters ao seu limite. Nosso objetivo com MemPool, um sistema com 256 cores e 1 MiB de memória L1, é construir uma arquitetura flexível que possa atender às rigorosas exigências de computação na borda.

Infelizmente, a flexibilidade de MemPool tem um preço, e o uso de cores escalares como suas unidades de cálculo torna o design um alvo principal para o VNB. Nesta tese, nós exploramos pela primeira vez processadores vetoriais como uma opção para construir unidades de computação pequenas e eficientes para clusters com memória L1 compartilhada de grande escala. Como PE do MemPool, Spatz alivia seu VNB através de um VRF que atua como nível de memória L0, reduzindo assim o tráfego de memória L1.

Em suma, esta tese explora o processamento vetorial como uma resposta ao VNB nos sistemas computacionais modernos. Como parte de um ressurgimento do interesse computação SIMD vetorial, nossos aceleradores de código aberto salientam a solidez da abordagem vetorial sem recorrer a arquiteturas de computação superespecializadas.

Contents

Chapter 1

Introduction

Being in the High-Performance Computing (HPC) domain, 5G/6G baseband processing, and embedded systems, the pervasive emergence of Artificial Intelligence (AI) and Machine Learning (ML) applications translates into an explosion of the computational requirements across many application domains. However, there is a growing mismatch between the performance requirements and the power consumption budget. For example, the performance of the fastest supercomputers increases by $10\times$ every five years, while their peak power consumption has stagnated at $30\,\text{MW}$ for the past years. With Moore's Law and Dennard's scaling slowing down, computer architects must strive for innovative architectures that achieve high performance and energy efficiency. This thesis takes the novel approach of re-imagining techniques commonly reserved for HPC architectures and applying them to computational-intensive embedded devices. Such dialogue between different branches of computer architecture leads to many potential collaboration opportunities. More precisely, this work improves high-performance computing units' power, performance, and area through architectural co-optimization, adapting data-parallel architectures to exploit emerging Very-Large-Scale Integration (VLSI) technologies.

1.1 Opportunities and Challenges

1.1.1 High-Performance Computing Architectures

In his seminal Turing Award lecture, Backus discussed the issues stemming from the word-at-a-time style of programming inherited from the von Neumann computer [1]. Almost fifty years later, Moore's Law [2] and Dennard's scaling [3] are no longer reliable sources of performance and energy efficiency gains. Therefore, computer architects must be creative to amortize the von Neumann Bottleneck (VNB) associated with fetching, decoding, and dispatching instructions that only keep the datapath busy for a short time.

Vector processors have long been boasted as one of the most efficient architectures to tackle the VNB. The need for efficient, high-performance computing led to a revival of interest in vector processing. For example, until the past year, the Fugaku [4] vector machine was crowned the world's fastest supercomputer [5]. Furthermore, RISC-V helped reignite interest in vector architectures with the RISC-V Vector Extension (RVV) [6]. In this context, Ara [7] is an open-source RVV-based vector machine with a large Vector Register File (VRF), achieving high scalability and energy efficiency. Furthermore, Ara achieves almost optimal performance for large problems.

There is no panacea for computer architecture, but there is an urgent need for architectures to tackle the heterogeneity and flexibility requirements of modern compute-intensive workloads while meeting strict performance and energy efficiency targets. For example, ML and AI algorithms have been proposed for 5G/6G networks to improve their throughput, coverage, and energy efficiency [8]. However, although the computing needs of baseband stations grow by $10\times$ every three years, their power consumption remains roughly constant. Moreover, 5G/6G solutions are moving away from dedicated Application-Specific Integrated Circuits (ASICs) for baseband processing and towards flexible solutions that shorten their Time-to-Market (TTM) [9]. The need for flexibility motivated Graphics Processing Units (GPUs), which dominate the Top500 list [5]. However, the General-Purpose computing on Graphics Processing Units (GP-GPU) programming model sacrifices efficiency for flexibility, and supercomputers based on GPUs are less dominant in the energy efficiency race [10] than in raw performance [5].

HPC architectures arrive at their crossroads, and no obvious solution can balance today's embarrassingly-parallel workloads' performance, efficiency, and flexibility needs. Nevertheless, there is much to learn from the shortcomings of vector, GP-GPU, and systolic architectures. In this vein, novel computer architectures combine performance, flexibility, and efficiency by re-imagining the control path and optimizing the data movement of the current HPC solutions.

1.1.2 Energy-Efficient Edge Computation

There is an ever-increasing need for computing on edge devices, bringing the computation closer to the source of data, as a way to tackle the shortcomings of cloud computing (e.g., bandwidth, latency, and privacy). In addition, AI and ML massively-parallel applications now power almost all smart edge devices, disrupting a market that was used to extremely tight power budgets but not to such computing-intensive workloads. Fortunately, HPC architectures have dealt with those contradictory requirements for the past decade. In this vein, this thesis defies common architectures for edge computing by applying techniques conceived for the HPC domain to embedded devices. This line of research is twofold, following novel architectural and emerging VLSI physical solutions for the edge domain.

Architecturally, vector processors are a straightforward solution to meet the smart edge devices' computing and efficiency demands. However, due to their historical association with supercomputers, vector processors typically include many microarchitectural tricks to exploit Instruction Level Parallelism (ILP), e.g., renaming, speculation, out-of-order execution, and branch prediction. However, the defining characteristic of a vector processor is not ILP but Data Level Parallelism (DLP). This key observation motivates the design of streamlined vector cores that exploit DLP.

Spatz [11] is an RVV-based vector processor engineered as a small and efficient Processing Element (PE) for embedded multicore clusters. The vector abstraction relaxes the VNB due to the instruction fetch and dispatching by the scalar cores. Moreover, Spatz' small latch-based VRF acts as an L0 Scratchpad Memory (SPM). Unlike typical vector architectures that target ultra-long vectors [7], [12], Spatz' VRF was designed to be small and efficient, optimizing the critical issue of data movement between the VRF and the costly L1 memory [13]. Furthermore, Spatz was integrated within MemPool [14], a large-scale manycore 32-bit system. The hybrid vector-manycore abstraction allowed MemPool to utilize its functional units fully and more than doubled its energy efficiency.

1.1.3   Emerging VLSI Technologies

The many technological challenges in implementing Extreme Ultraviolet Lithography (EUV) slowed the scaling of cutting-edge Complementary Metal-Oxide-Semiconductor (CMOS) technologies. While silicon foundries struggled to adopt EUV, immersion lithography solutions were pushed to their absolute limit past 20 nm nodes through double or even triple patterning to produce the smallest technology features. Unfortunately, this cutting-edge manufacturing process comes with a high cost. Multiple patterning poses challenges to standard-cell design, creates routability issues, and is a major contributor to the cost of chips due to the increased number of lithography masks. Non-recurring expenses almost double when transitioning to a more advanced technology node [15]. Despite the high costs, many companies keep investing in in-house ASIC solutions, such as Google [16], Tesla [17], and Apple [18].

The disaggregation of monolithic chips into Multi-Chip Modules (MCMs) allowed Systems-on-Chip (SoCs) to keep up with Moore's Law [19]. Through Two-and-a-Half-Dimensional Integrated Circuits (2.5DICs), multiple chiplets are stacked on top of an organic package substrate or silicon interposer that interconnects them. MCMs allow for heterogeneity in the chiplets' technologies, improved yield, and the potential for reusing chiplets in different products, reducing their engineering cost. In addition, MCMs have the potential to popularize the production of cutting-edge designs by diluting the cost of the chiplets over a much cheaper silicon interposer. In this context, 2.5DIC integration is a popular solution, and the major Electronic Design Automation (EDA) vendors acknowledged it through the inclusion of 2.5DIC support in their tool suites [20], [21].

Further gains can be attained through vertical integration, which promises to address the scaling problems of the traditional Two-Dimensional Integrated Circuit (2DIC) integration foreseen by Moore's

Law [22]. Three-Dimensional Integrated Circuits (3DICs) promise better Power, Performance, and Area (PPA) than 2DIC and 2.5DIC counterparts thanks to a drastic reduction of the interconnect lengths, particularly of long global interconnects while enabling a smaller form factor by adding the third dimension [23], [24].

Emerging VLSI techniques powered by advanced interconnects, such as 3DICs with Cu–Cu Hybrid Bonding (HB) and silicon photonics applied to ultra-fast optical backplanes, promise a true revolution in VLSI. However, the data model is a major factor preventing the widespread adoption of 3DIC. EDA tools cannot handle tightly-interconnected 3DICs, and MCM flows circumvent the issue by implementing each die separately [25] or by "tricking" the EDA tool into seeing the two dies as a single metal stack [26]. Vertical integration led to large PPA gains on large-scale computational-intensive systems [25], [27]. For example, we explored the impacts of 3DIC integration with MemPool, our scaled-up shared-L1 cluster with 256 cores and 1 MiB of L1 SPM accessible from all cores within five cycles of zero-load latency. A memory-on-logic 3D implementation of MemPool relaxed its routing congestion, improved its operating frequency, and reduced its footprint while packing 4× more L1 SPM than its 2DIC counterpart [28].

Despite the obvious gains promised by advanced packaging, more work must be done on co-optimizing computer architectures to such emerging technologies. The limited EDA support acts as a gap between architects and physical designers, preventing bridging the gap between computer architecture and circuit design with cutting-edge CMOS technologies by aggressively designing architectures that exploit emerging VLSI technologies. For example, actively exploiting the vertical stacking of dies on top of each other and the possibility of high-bandwidth, low-power optical links between dies requires a shift in how computer architects see their systems. This research has the potential to shape computer architectures in a post-Moore world—dominated by pervasive embarrassingly-parallel workloads under tight power consumption limits—through its interfacing of innovative computing architectures and cutting-edge VLSI technologies.

1.2   Contributions

This thesis focuses on many aspects of the current challenges in computer architecture. We strive to meet high computing performance targets under stringent power consumption budgets on the HPC and embedded domain. The most important contributions of this thesis can be summarized as follows:

1. An analysis of intrinsic limitations of modern vector processors, with insights into the conditions needed for a vector processor to achieve high performance and energy efficiency. This analysis was done with an open-source, high-performance, parametric, scalable RISC-V-based vector processor [7]. Its implementation is also a proxy for evaluating modern vector Instruction Set Architectures (ISAs), particularly regarding which vector instructions are taxing on the system's energy efficiency [29][1].

2. An evaluation of the performance, energy efficiency, and implementation feasibility of the shared-L1 cluster architectural template, which comprises a set of PEs sharing access to some low-latency, high-bandwidth L1 SPM as a function of the size of the PE's L0 memory [30]. Furthermore, we depart from classical vector processors, typically associated with supercomputers, and propose an embedded, compact, energy-efficient vector processor as the PE of a shared-L1 cluster. With this PE, we improve the state-of-the-art computing clusters' performance, area efficiency, and energy efficiency.

3. An analysis of the cost associated with scaling up the shared-L1 cluster—which usually only scales to the low tens of cores—to the hundreds of cores. We designed a hierarchical interconnection network topology that connects 256 cores in a Non-Uniform Memory Access (NUMA) memory organization with very strict latency constraints and tackled the challenges related to the physical implementation of large designs in a modern technology

---

[1]Joint work with Matteo Perotti. I am responsible for the ground work on this vector processor, while Mr. Perotti extended the unit to a full ISA support and analyzed its implications on the baseline unit.

node [14][2]. Furthermore, we also co-optimized the scaled-up shared-L1 cluster with emerging VLSI technologies such as 3DICs [28], exploiting the PPA gains and the cost impact of vertical integration on such a common architectural template.

4. The deployment of our compact Vector Processing Unit (VPU) as the PE of our scaled-up shared-L1 cluster. We investigated how large the PE of a shared-L1 cluster should be, and exploited the PE's VRF to reduce the traffic through the costly L1 interconnect. Our implementation trades off a moderate area increase against impressive gains in energy efficiency, while reaching much higher utilization of the PE's Functional Units (FUs) than the scalar equivalent shared-L1 cluster [11].

1.3 List of Publications

Most of the material covered in this thesis have been published in the following conference and journal papers:

[7] M. Cavalcante, F. Schuiki, F. Zaruba, and L. Benini, "Ara: A 1-GHz+ scalable and energy-efficient RISC-V vector processor with multiprecision floating-point support in 22-nm FD-SOI," *IEEE Transactions on Very Large Scale Integration (VLSI) Systems*, vol. 28, no. 2, pp. 530–543, 2020.

[14] M. Cavalcante, S. Riedel, A. Pullini, and L. Benini, "MemPool: A shared-L1 memory many-core cluster with a low-latency interconnect," in *Proceedings of the 2021 Design, Automation, & Test in Europe Conference & Exhibition (DATE)*, Grenoble, France: IEEE, Mar. 2021, pp. 701–706.

[28] M. Cavalcante, A. Agnesina, S. Riedel, M. Brunion, A. García-Ortiz, D. Milojevic, F. Catthoor, S.-K. Lim, and L. Benini, "MemPool-3D: Boosting performance and efficiency of shared-L1 memory many-core clusters with 3D integration," in *Proceedings of the 2022 Design, Automation & Test in Europe Conference*

---

[2]Joint work with Samuel Riedel. Mr. Riedel focused on programmability aspects, while I focused on the interconnect analysis and physical implementation.

& Exhibition (DATE), Antwerp, Belgium: IEEE, Mar. 2022, pp. 394–399.

[29]   M. Perotti, M. Cavalcante, N. Wistoff, R. Andri, L. Cavigelli, and L. Benini, "A 'new Ara' for vector computing: An open source highly efficient RISC-V V 1.0 vector processor design," in *Proceedings of the 33rd IEEE International Conference on Application-specific Systems, Architectures and Processors*, Gothenburg, Sweden: IEEE, Jul. 2022.

[30]   G. Paulin, M. Cavalcante, P. Scheffler, L. Bertaccini, Y. Zhang, F. Gürkaynak, and L. Benini, "Soft tiles: Capturing physical implementation flexibility for tightly-coupled parallel processing clusters," in *Proceedings of the IEEE Computer Society Annual Symposium on VLSI 2022*, Pafos, Cyprus: IEEE, Jul. 2022.

[11]   M. Cavalcante, D. Wüthrich, M. Perotti, S. Riedel, and L. Benini, "Spatz: A compact vector processing unit for high-performance and energy-efficient shared-L1 clusters," in *Proceedings of the 41st International Conference on Computer-Aided Design*, San Diego, CA, USA: IEEE/Association for Computing Machinery, Oct. 2022.

The following publications with contributions by the author provide additional evidence and insights, and are covered in part by this thesis:

[31]   M. Cavalcante, A. Kurth, F. Schuiki, and L. Benini, "Design of an open-source bridge between non-coherent burst-based and coherent cache-line-based memory systems," in *Proceedings of the 17th ACM International Conference on Computing Frontiers*, (Catania, Italy), ser. CF '20, New York, NY, USA: Association for Computing Machinery, 2020, pp. 81–88.

[32]   A. Kurth, W. Rönninger, T. Benz, M. Cavalcante, F. Schuiki, F. Zaruba, and L. Benini, "An Open-Source Platform for High-Performance Non-Coherent On-Chip Communication," *IEEE Transactions on Computers*, pp. 1794–1809, 2021.

[25]   A. Agnesina, M. Brunion, A. García-Ortiz, F. Catthoor, D. Milojevic, M. Komalan, M. Cavalcante, S. Riedel, L. Benini, and S.-K.

Lim, "Hier-3D: A hierarchical physical design methodology for face-to-face-bonded 3D ICs," in *Proceedings of the ACM/IEEE International Symposium on Low Power Electronics and Design*, ser. ISLPED '22, Boston, MA, USA: Association for Computing Machinery, 2022.

[33] S. Riedel, G. H. Khov, S. Mazzola, M. Cavalcante, R. Andri, and L. Benini, "MemPool meets systolic: Flexible systolic computation in a large shared-memory processor cluster," in *Proceedings of the 2023 Design, Automation & Test in Europe Conference & Exhibition (DATE)*, Antwerp, Belgium: IEEE, Mar. 2023.

[34] P. Iff, M. Besta, M. Cavalcante, T. Fischer, L. Benini, and T. Hoefler, "Sparse hamming graph: A customizable network-on-chip topology," in *Proceedings of the 60th Design Automation Conference*, ser. DAC '23, San Francisco, CA, USA: Association for Computing Machinery, Jun. 2023.

[35] P. Iff, M. Besta, M. Cavalcante, T. Fischer, L. Benini, and T. Hoefler, "HexaMesh: Scaling to hundreds of chiplets with an optimized chiplet arrangement," in *Proceedings of the 60th Design Automation Conference*, ser. DAC '23, San Francisco, CA, USA: Association for Computing Machinery, Jun. 2023.

[36] V. Jain, M. Cavalcante, N. Bruschi, M. Rogenmoser, T. Benz, A. Kurth, D. Rossi, L. Benini, and M. Verhelst, "PATRONoC: Parallel AXI transport reducing overhead for networks-on-chip targeting multi-accelerator DNN platforms at the edge," in *Proceedings of the 60th Design Automation Conference*, ser. DAC '23, San Francisco, CA, USA: Association for Computing Machinery, Jun. 2023.

[37] M. Perotti, M. Cavalcante, A. Ottaviano, J. Liu, and L. Benini, "Yun: An open-source, 64-bit RISC-V-Based vector processor with multi-precision integer and floating-point support in 65-nm CMOS," *IEEE Transactions on Circuits and Systems II: Express Briefs*, 2023.

1.4   Thesis Organization

Figure 1.1 shows the dependency graph of the remaining chapters of
this thesis, highlighting their dependencies. Most of this work has
been previously published journal or conference papers.

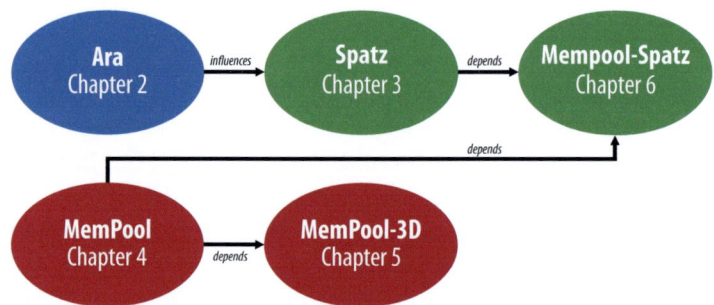

Figure 1.1: Thesis overview and dependencies between chapters.

Chapter 2: This chapter explores vector processing with **Ara**, a
   modern application-class 64-bit vector processor based on the
   RVV ISA. Ara tackles the VNB by amortizing its scalar core's
   instruction fetching and decoding cost. In that chapter, we also
   analyze the shortcomings of coupling an in-order non-speculative
   vector accelerator and a scalar in-order core. Namely, for small
   problems, we note a performance drop as the vector unit waits
   for the scalar core to dispatch instructions.

Chapter 3: Instead of tackling the VNB by amortizing the instruction
   fetching cost, we can also maximize the core's compute/control
   area ratio. In this scenario, vectors much shorter than Ara's and
   other common vector units are enough to maximize the energy
   efficiency of our computing tile. In Chapter 3, we develop a
   model for the energy efficiency of a shared-L1 computing cluster
   as a function of the size of the L0 VRF. Furthermore, we present
   Spatz, a compact 64-bit embedded vector unit based on the
   RVV ISA. Unlike Ara, conceived as an application-class VPU,
   Spatz is an embedded VPU whose VRF is extremely small,

allowing for a lean architecture that focuses solely on exploiting DLP. Using Spatz as the PE of our shared-L1 cluster, we improved the performance, area efficiency, and energy efficiency of an equivalent state-of-the-art computing cluster.

Chapter 4: This chapter focuses on the computing cluster with shared-L1 memory, which usually only scales to the low tens of cores. We propose **MemPool**, a shared-L1 cluster with 256 cores sharing 1 MiB of L1 SPM under five cycles of latency in the absence of contention. To improve the scalability of this cluster, we propose and evaluate three interconnection networks in terms of latency, throughput, and implementation feasibility. We also analyze the programmability impacts of having this high core count. Namely, we assess the synchronization overhead and propose a lightweight addressing mechanism to keep a core's most often-used addresses in memory banks close to it.

Chapter 5: Due to the high connectivity between all its cores, Mem-Pool is a highly-congested design whose frequency is limited by the wire propagation delay. Furthermore, since MemPool has a simple programming model comprising cores and an L1 SPM of parameterizable size, it presents remarkable flexibility. Both characteristics make **MemPool** an ideal candidate for an exploration of **3DIC** integration. Chapter 5 analyzes the PPA of MemPool instances as 2DIC and monolithic 3DIC implementations partitioned into memory and logic dies. Vertical integration massively reduces MemPool's footprint, allowing for higher operating frequencies and increased energy efficiency.

Chapter 6: We explore vector processing as an option to build PEs of a large-scale shared-L1 cluster. Using **Spatz** as **MemPool**'s PE, we increased the data reuse at each computing element, reducing traffic through our large L1 SPM interconnect. Our hybrid architecture presents characteristics of Multiple Instruction, Multiple Data (MIMD), such as its flexibility, and vector Single Instruction, Multiple Data (SIMD), such as high FU utilization and energy efficiency. Furthermore, for a small area increase, namely Spatz' VRFs, the Spatz-powered MemPool design reaches twice the energy efficiency of a scalar MemPool instance.

Chapter 7: This chapter concludes the thesis with a **summary** of its accomplishments and an **outlook** of future research directions.

Chapter 2

Ara: High-Performance and Energy-Efficient Vector Processing Unit

Vector processors promise to tackle the VNB effectively by exploiting the vector SIMD programming model. This chapter presents Ara [7], a modern VPU based on the RVV ISA.

2.1 Introduction

The end of Dennard scaling caused the race for performance through higher frequencies to halt more than a decade ago when an increasing integration density stopped translating into proportionate increases in performance or energy efficiency [38]. As a result, processor frequencies plateaued, inciting multi-core architectures to become the *de facto* standard to exploit Thread Level Parallelism (TLP). First, however, these architectures need to address the efficiency limitation inherently created by fetching and decoding elementary instructions, which only keep the datapath busy for short periods of time [39], [40].

The strong emergence of massively data-parallel workloads, such as data analytics and machine learning [41], created a major window of opportunity for architectures that effectively exploit data parallelism to achieve energy efficiency. The key challenge in instruction-based programmable architectures is mitigating the VNB [1]. Despite the flexibility of multi-core architectures, they fail to exploit the instruction regularity of data-parallel applications. Each core often executes the same instructions on such architectures, which is wasteful regarding area and energy [42]. The most successful architectures to exploit DLP use GP-GPU [43]. Such architectures leverage data-parallel massively multithreading on GPUs to relax the VNB through the so-called Single Instruction, Multiple Thread (SIMT) approach [44]. As a result, GPUs dominate the energy efficiency race, being present in 90% of the most recent Green500 rank [10]. Furthermore, they are highly successful as data-parallel accelerators in high-performance embedded applications, such as machine learning and self-driving cars [45].

The quest for extreme energy efficiency in data-parallel execution has also revamped interest in vector architectures. This architecture was cutting-edge during another technology scaling crisis—the one related to circuits based on the Emitter-Coupled Logic (ECL) technology [46]. Today, designers and architects are reconsidering vector processing approaches. They promise to address the VNB effectively [47], providing better energy efficiency than a general-purpose processor for applications that fit the vector processing model [42]. A single vector instruction expresses a data-parallel computation on a very long vector, which amortizes the instruction fetching and decoding overhead. The amortizing effect is even more pronounced than on SIMT architectures, where instruction fetches are only amortized over the number of parallel scalar execution units in a "processing block." For the NVIDIA Ampere A100 GPUs, such blocks are only 64 elements long [48]. Therefore, vector processors provide a notably effective model to efficiently execute the data parallelism of scientific and matrix-oriented computations [49], [50], digital signal processing, and machine learning algorithms.

In this chapter, we set out to analyze modern vector processors' scalability and energy efficiency by designing and implementing an RVV-based VPU in an advanced CMOS technology. Ara is a parametric in-order 64-bit vector unit based on the RVV ISA. The vector unit was designed for a peak performance per memory bandwidth ratio of $0.5\,\mathrm{FLOP_{DP}}/\mathrm{B}$ and works in tandem with OpenHW's CVA6 [51], an open-source application-class RV64GC core. Ara supports mixed-precision arithmetic with double, single, and half-precision operands.

2.2 Data-Parallel Programming Models

SIMD architectures share—and, thus, amortize—the instruction fetch among multiple chunks of data. This architectural model can be seen as instructions operating on vectors of operands. Hence, this approach works well as long as the control flow is regular, i.e., it is possible to formulate the problem as vector operations. This section presents an overview of programming models which exploit DLP.

2.2.1 Packed Single Instruction, Multiple Data

Array processors exploit the packed-SIMD programming model. This processor type has several independent and identical PEs, all operating on commands from a shared control unit. Figure 2.1 shows an execution pattern for a dummy instruction sequence of a load (`ld`), a multiplication (`mul`), an addition (`add`), and a store (`st`), each operating on a vector of four elements. The number of PEs unequivocally determines the vector length, and the architecture can be seen as a wide datapath encompassing all subwords [52].

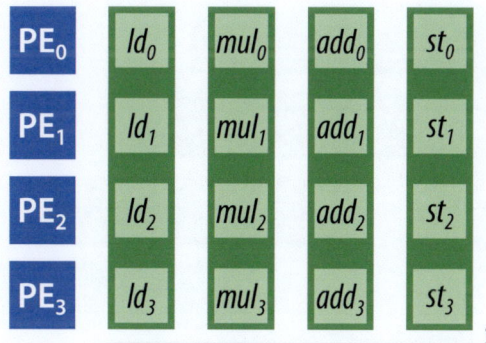

Figure 2.1: Execution pattern on an array processor [53].

A limitation of such an architecture is that the vector length is fixed and encoded in the instruction opcode. Therefore, each expansion of the vector length comes with an ISA extension. For instance, Intel's first Streaming SIMD Extension (SSE) release operates on 128-bit registers, whereas the Advanced Vector Extension (AVX) and AVX-512 subsequent extensions operate on 256 and 512-bit wide registers, respectively [54]. Arm provides packed-SIMD capability via the Neon extension, operating on 128-bit wide registers [55]. RISC-V supports packed-SIMD via Digital Signal Processing (DSP) extensions [56].

2.2.2 Vector Single Instruction, Multiple Data

Vector processors are time-multiplexed versions of array processors, implementing the vector-SIMD programming model. Several specialized functional units stream the elementary micro-operations on consecutive cycles, as shown in Figure 2.2. By doing so, the number of functional units no longer constrains the vector length, which can be dynamically configured. Compared to packed SIMD, long vectors are not subdivided into fixed-size chunks but can be issued using a single vector instruction. Hence, vector processors are potentially more energy-efficient than an equivalent array processor since many control signals can be kept constant throughout the computation. In addition, the instruction fetch cost is amortized among many cycles.

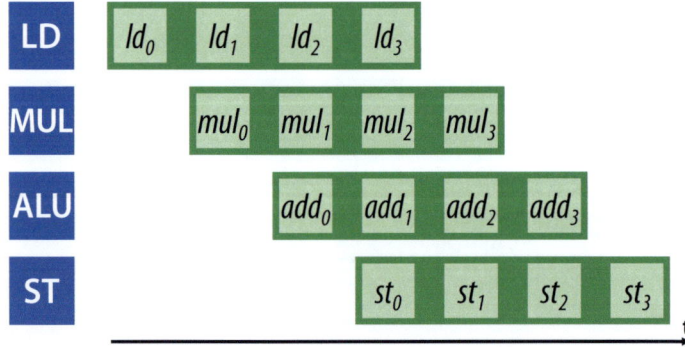

Figure 2.2: Execution pattern on a vector processor [53].

The history of vector processing starts with the traditional vector machines from the sixties and seventies, with the beginnings of the Illiac IV project [49]. The trend continued throughout the next two decades, with work on supercomputers such as the Cray-1 [46]. At the end of the century, however, microprocessor-based systems approached or surpassed the performance of vector supercomputers at much lower costs [57] due to intense work on Very Long Instruction Word (VLIW) and superscalar architectures. Only recently did vector processors get renewed interest from the scientific community, with modern ISAs proposing extensions for vector-SIMD computation.

Arm is moving into high-performance Cray-inspired vector processing with its Scalable Vector Extension (SVE) [58]. The extension is based on the vector register architecture introduced with the Cray-1 and leaves the vector length as an implementation choice (from 128-bit to 2048-bit, in 128-bit increments). The first system to adopt this extension is Fujitsu's A64FX, with a peak performance of $2.7\,\text{TFLOPS}_{\text{DP}}$ in TSMC's $7\,\text{nm}$ process, which is competitive in terms of peak performance to leading-edge GPUs [4]. Arm also started exploring embedded vector machines with its Helium M-Profile Vector Extension (MVE), an optional extension proposed as part of the Armv8.1-M architecture [59]. The Arm Cortex-M55 [60] is the first processor to ship with support to Helium MVE.

The SVE and MVE ISAs are proprietary, leaving their micro-architectural implications opaque and preventing open-source implementations. Over the last few years, RISC-V has become a well-established, modern, and openly available alternative to proprietary ISAs. RISC-V has spurred a wave of publicly available implementations and enabled a public discourse on novel and custom ISA extensions, their micro-architectural implications, and potential standardization. RISC-V leads an effort toward vector processing through its vector ISA extension [6]. This extension is in active development and recently reached its first stable release with version 1.0. When compared with Arm SVE, RISC-V does not put any limits on the vector length. Moreover, RVV makes it possible to trade off the number of architectural vector registers against longer vectors.

2.2.3   Single Instruction, Multiple Thread

SIMT architectures represent an amalgamation of the flexibility of
MIMD and the efficiency of SIMD designs. While SIMD architectures
apply one instruction to multiple data lanes, SIMT designs apply
one instruction to multiple independent threads in parallel [44]. The
NVIDIA Ampere A100 GPU is a state-of-the-art example of this
architecture [48], with 108 "processing blocks," called Streaming
Multiprocessors (SMs) by NVIDIA, each handling 64 threads. Each
SM thread has its state and executes an independent code path [44].

   A SIMD instruction exposes the vector length to the programmer
and requires manual branching control, usually by setting flags that
indicate which lanes are active for a given vector instruction. SIMT
designs, on the other hand, allow the threads to diverge, although they
can achieve higher performance when they remain synchronized [44].
Furthermore, SIMD and SIMT designs handle data access differently.
Since GPUs lack a control processor, hardware must dynamically
coalesce memory accesses into large contiguous chunks [47]. While
this approach simplifies the programming model, it also incurs a
considerable energy overhead [61].

2.2.4   Vector Thread

Another compromise between SIMD and MIMD is the Vector Thread
(VT) programming model [61], which supports loops with cross-iter-
ation dependencies and arbitrary internal control flow [62]. Similar
to SIMT designs—and unlike SIMD architectures—VT architectures
leverage the threading concept instead of the more rigid notion of
lanes, providing a mechanism to handle program divergence. The
main difference between SIMT and VT is that, in the latter, the
vector instructions reside in another thread, and scalar bookkeeping
instructions can potentially run concurrently with the vector ones. This
division alleviates the problem of SIMT threads running redundant
scalar instructions that must be later coalesced in hardware. Hwacha
is a VT architecture based on a custom RISC-V extension, achieving
$64\,\mathrm{GFLOPS_{DP}}$ in STMicroelectronics' 28 nm Fully-Depleted Silicon-
on-Insulator (FD-SOI) technology [63].

2.2.5 Stream Semantic Registers

Stream Semantic Registers (SSRs) intercept access to specific registers at the register file and forward them out of the core and into the memory subsystem [64]. Memory loads and stores can be encoded implicitly in any instruction instead of explicit load/store instructions, which consume issue slots and degrade the utilization of the functional units. In a sense, an SSR machine is a superset of a vector machine [64], using the system's SPM as a VRF. SSRs perform well on sparse-dense computations, with a lightweight address generator fetching the offsets and pushing the address into the memory system without requiring explicit address calculations [65].

2.3 RISC-V Vector Extension

RISC-V proposed RVV, its "V" extension, to explore the vector-SIMD programming model. This extension has been in development since at least as early as 2015 [66]. Ara was one of the first VPUs based on this ISA, with its original version written in 2018 as part of a Master's Thesis [67]. There has since been major development on both Ara and RVV, which led to the release of a stable RVV extension [6] and an open-source Ara release compliant with it [7], [29]. This section discusses the basic concepts of RVV; interested readers are pointed to the official documentation for a complete description of the ISA [6].

Each hart supporting RVV defines two implementation-dependent parameters. Those parameters are ELEN, the maximum size in bits of a vector element that any instruction can produce or consume, and the number of bits in a vector register VLENB $\geq$ ELEN. The vector extension adds 32 vector registers, v0 to v31, each with fixed VLENB bits of state. RVV also adds seven Control and Status Registers (CSRs): vstart, vxsat, vxrm, vcsr, vl, vtype, and vlenb.

The read-only vtype CSR provides the default type to interpret the contents of the VRF. The vector type determines the organization of the elements in each vector register and how multiple vector registers are grouped. Within the vtype CSR,

- The value in `vsew` sets the dynamic Selected Element Width (SEW) value `EW`. By default, a vector register is viewed as being divided into `VLENB/EW` elements;

- Multiple vector registers can be grouped so a single vector instruction can operate on multiple vector registers. This grouping can be used to trade off longer vectors with fewer available vector registers. The Vector Length Multiplier (LMUL) value ℓ, defined with the `vlmul` field, represents the number of vector registers combined to form a vector register group.

The derived value `VLMAX` $= \ell \times$ `VLENB/EW` represents the maximum number of elements a single instruction could operated on given the current SEW and LMUL settings.

Two other important CSRs are `vl` and `vstart`. The read-only `vl` CSR can only be updated with `vsetvl` instructions. It holds an unsigned integer specifying the number of elements to be updated with results from a vector instruction. The `vsetvl` instruction with scalar argument `rs1` updates the `vl` to min(`rs1`, `VLMAX`). Through this instruction, found in all vector-SIMD ISAs, it is possible to write software following a Vector Length Agnostic (VLA) programming model [58]. Through this programming technique, vector software automatically exploits the longest vector length possible of any vector machine without recompiling the software—which is required for a packed-SIMD programming model, where the vector length is encoded into the instruction opcode. Furthermore, the `vstart` read-write CSR specifies the first element to be updated in a vector instruction. A non-zero `vstart` value is required to support restarting the execution of a vector instruction after a resumable trap.

RISC-V's "V" extension is a complex ISA, the largest RISC-V extension to date [68]. The RVV extension include the following:

- Vector load/store instructions: unit-strided (`vle`/`vse`), constant-strided (`vlse`/`vsse`), and scatter-gather (`vlxei`/`vsxei`);

- Vector-vector `vop.vv`, vector-scalar `vop.vx`, and vector-immediate `vop.vi` integer arithmetic instructions;

- Vector-vector `vfop.vv` and vector scalar `vfop.vf` floating-point arithmetic instructions;

- Single-width integer vector reduction (`vredsum`, `vredmax`, `vredmin`, `vredand`, `vredor`, `vredxor`) and widening integer vector reduction instructions (`vwredsum`);

- Single-width floating-point vector reduction (`vfredsum`, `vfredmax`, `vfredmin`) and widening floating-point vector reduction instructions (`vfwredsum`);

- Vector mask register logical instructions (`vmop.mm`);

- Vector permutation instructions (`vmv`, `vslide{1}up`, `vslide{1}down`, `vcompress`, `vrgather`).

The "V" extension was thought for application processors. Hence, it supports all the instructions mentioned above. It also requires that the scalar processor implements the "F" and "D" ISA extensions for single-precision and double-precision floating-point scalar instructions, respectively. Five additional standard extensions, named `Zve*`, are defined to provide varying degrees of vector support and are intended for use with embedded vector processors.

2.4 Architecture

In this section, we introduce the architecture of Ara, a scalable high-performance VPU based on RISC-V's RVV version 1.0. As shown in Figure 2.3, Ara works in tandem with CVA6 [51], an open-source Linux-capable application-class RV64GC core. To this end, CVA6 has been extended to drive the VPU as a tightly-coupled accelerator.

2.4.1 CVA6

OpenHW's CVA6 (previously known as Ariane) is an open-source, in-order, single-issue, 64-bit, application-class processor implementing RV64GC [51]. It supports hardware integer multiply/divide and atomic memory operations and has an IEEE-compliant trans-precision Floating Point Unit (FPU) [69]. The processor has been manufactured in GlobalFoundries' 22FDX 22 nm FD-SOI technology, running at most at 1.7 GHz and achieving energy efficiency of up to 40 GOPS/W on a 32-bit integer matrix multiplication. Furthermore, CVA6 has

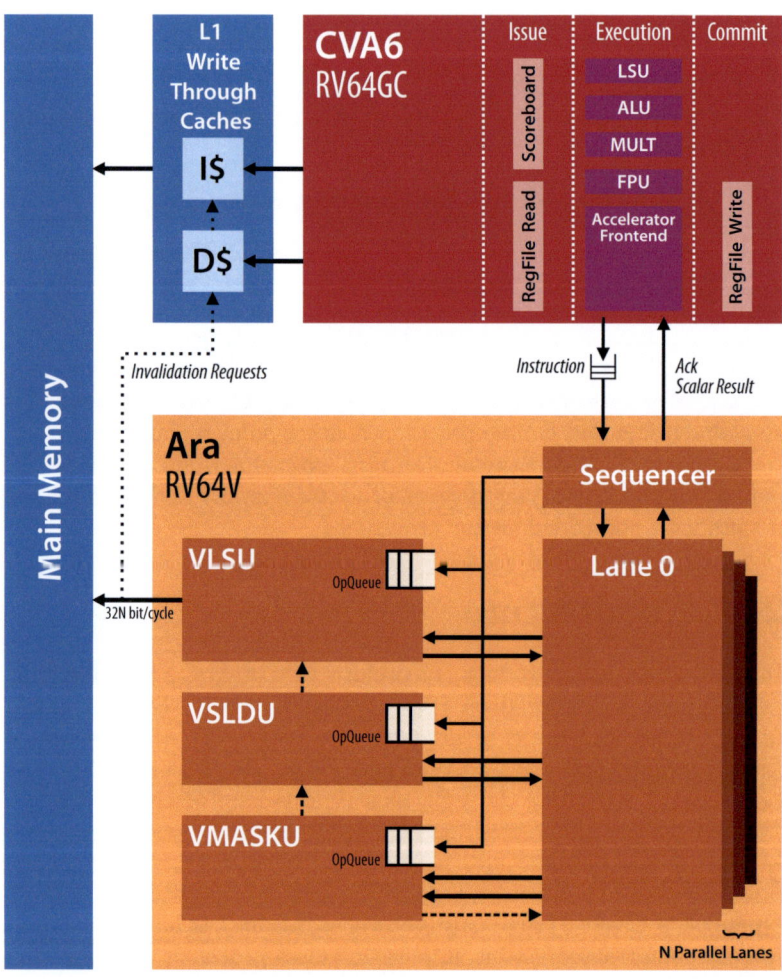

Figure 2.3: Top-level block diagram of an Ara instance with N parallel lanes, highlighting its integration with CVA6.

a six-stage pipeline: Program Counter (PC) generation, instruction fetch, instruction decode, issue, execute, and commit.

CVA6 needs some architectural changes to be able to control our VPU. External accelerator instructions are handled by an accelerator frontend, responsible for dispatching the instructions to the corresponding VPU and acknowledging their eventual completion with CVA6's scoreboard. CVA6 instructions can retire out-of-order from its internal functional units [51], while Ara executes instructions non-speculatively. Therefore, the accelerator frontend waits until a vector instruction reaches the top of CVA6's scoreboard—i.e., it is no longer speculative—to dispatch it to Ara, together with the contents of any scalar registers read by this instruction. The accelerator frontend receives Ara's instruction acknowledgment and propagates any possible scalar results and exceptions to CVA6's scoreboard.

Ara acknowledges instructions as soon as they are deemed safe. This acknowledgment happens early for the execution of most vector instructions, usually as soon as they are decoded. Moreover, since vector instructions can execute for an extended number of cycles, they might be acknowledged many cycles before the end of their execution in the VPU, freeing the scalar cores to continue the execution of the instruction stream. This decoupled execution pattern performs well, except when CVA6 expects a scalar result from the vector unit, e.g., when moving an element from the VRF to CVA6's Register File (RF).

2.4.2 Sequencer

The sequencer is responsible for keeping track of the vector instructions running on Ara, dispatching them to the different vector execution units, and acknowledging them with CVA6. This unit is the single block that has a global view of the vector instruction execution progress across all lanes and execution units. The sequencer can handle up to eight parallel instructions. Those in-flight instructions ensure Ara has instructions enqueued for execution, avoiding starvation due to Ara's frontend's non-speculative instruction dispatch policy.

The sequencer resolves hazards among pending vector instructions. Structural hazards arise due to architectural limitations or if the operation queue of a functional unit is full. The sequencer delays the issue of vector instructions until the structural hazard has been resolved, i.e., the offending instruction finishes its execution.

The sequencer also stores information about which vector instruction is accessing each vector register. This information is used to determine and handle data hazards between instructions. For example, if a vector instruction tries to write to a vector register already being written, the sequencer will flag the existence of a Write After Write (WAW) hazard. Read After Write (RAW) and Write After Read (WAR) hazards are flagged similarly. However, unlike structural hazards, data hazards do not need to stall the sequencer, as they are handled on a per-element basis downstream (Section 2.4.6).

2.4.3   Vector Load/Store Unit

Ara has a single Advanced eXtended Interface (AXI) memory port, whose width is chosen to keep the memory bandwidth per peak performance ratio fixed at $2\,\mathrm{B/FLOP_{DP}}$. Therefore, an Ara instance with N parallel lanes has an AXI memory interface $32N$-bit/cycle wide.

Ara's Vector Load/Store Unit (VLSU) has an address generator responsible for determining which memory addresses will be accessed, depending on the memory instruction in execution. This vector memory instruction can either be:

- unit-stride loads and stores, which access a contiguous chunk of memory;

- constant-stride memory operations, which access memory addresses spaced with a fixed offset; and

- scatters and gathers, which use a vector of offsets to allow general access patterns.

After address generation, the VLSU coalesces unit-stride memory operations into AXI incremental burst requests, avoiding needing to request the individual elements from memory.

CVA6 and Ara each feature separate memory ports, and CVA6 has a private L1 data cache. However, the RISC-V ISA mandates a strictly-coherent memory view between the scalar and vector processors [6]. We add a lightweight hardware mechanism to the Ara system to ensure coherency [29]. We adapted CVA6's L1 data cache to a write-through policy so that the main memory directly accessed by Ara is always up-to-date. Ara invalidates the clashing cache lines in CVA6's data cache when performing a vector store. Moreover, we constrain the issue of scalar and vector memory operations to ensure the coherence between both accelerators. Namely, we only issue:

1. scalar loads only if no vector stores are in-flight;

2. scalar stores only if no vector loads or stores are in-flight; and

3. vector loads or stores only if no scalar stores are pending.

2.4.4 Vector Slide Unit

The Vector Slide Unit (VSLDU) handles instructions that must access all VRF banks simultaneously. It handles, for example, the insertion and extraction of an element into/from a vector, vector permutation instructions such as vector slides ($vd[i] \leftarrow vs[i \pm slideamount]$), and vector reductions (e.g., $vd[0] \leftarrow \sum_i vs[i]$). The VSLDU is also responsible for maintaining the consistency of the vector elements' mapping in the VRF, which requires shuffling and deshuffling elements into their correct lanes depending on the current SEW setting [29]. This operation implies a byte-level crossbar which limits Ara's scalability [7].

2.4.5 Vector Mask Unit

The Vector Mask Unit (VMASKU) handles predicated vector instructions, i.e., instructions executed conditionally depending on the value of an element of the mask vector vmask, in the RVV ISA v0. Since the predication bits of each vector element do not necessarily reside in the same lanes where they are needed, the VMASKU performs a task similar to the VSLDU, in the sense that it shuffles data from all lanes and forwards the masking bits from vmask to the corresponding lanes.

2.4.6 Vector Lane

Vector lanes are Ara's main computational unit, and each Ara instance is configured with some identical and parallel computing lanes. A sequencer keeps track of up to eight parallel vector instructions within each lane. Each lane also has a VRF, an integer Arithmetic and Logic Unit (ALU), a multiplier, and an FPU, as shown in Figure 2.4.

Each lane has part of Ara's whole VRF and execution units. Hence, most of the computation is contained within one lane. Instructions that need to access all the VRF banks simultaneously—e.g., instructions that execute at the VLSU or the VSLDU—use data interfaces between the lanes and the responsible computing units. Each lane also has a command interface attached to the main sequencer, through which the lanes indicate they finished the execution of an instruction.

Lane Sequencer

The sequencer is responsible for issuing vector instructions to the functional units, controlling their execution within a single lane. Unlike the main sequencer, the lane sequencers do not store the state of the running instructions, avoiding data duplication across lanes. The sequencer is also responsible for initiating VRF operand read requests.

Operand fetch and result write-back processes are decoupled from each other. Starvation is avoided via a self-regulated process, thanks to the back pressure caused by unavailable operands. The lane sequencer indirectly limits the rate at which results are produced by throttling the operand request rate. This request throttling handles data hazards by ensuring that dependent instructions run simultaneously. Particularly, if instruction i depends on instruction j, the operands of instruction i are only requested if instruction j committed results to the VRF in the previous cycle. There is no dedicated bypassing logic.

Vector Register File

The VRF is at the core of every vector processor and defines much of its architecture. Because several vector instructions can run in parallel, the register file must provide enough throughput to supply the functional units with operands and absorb their results. In RVV, the predicated floating-point multiply-accumulate instruction `vfmacc.vv` (and its integer equivalent, `vmacc.vv`) has the highest throughput requirement, reading four operands to produce one result.

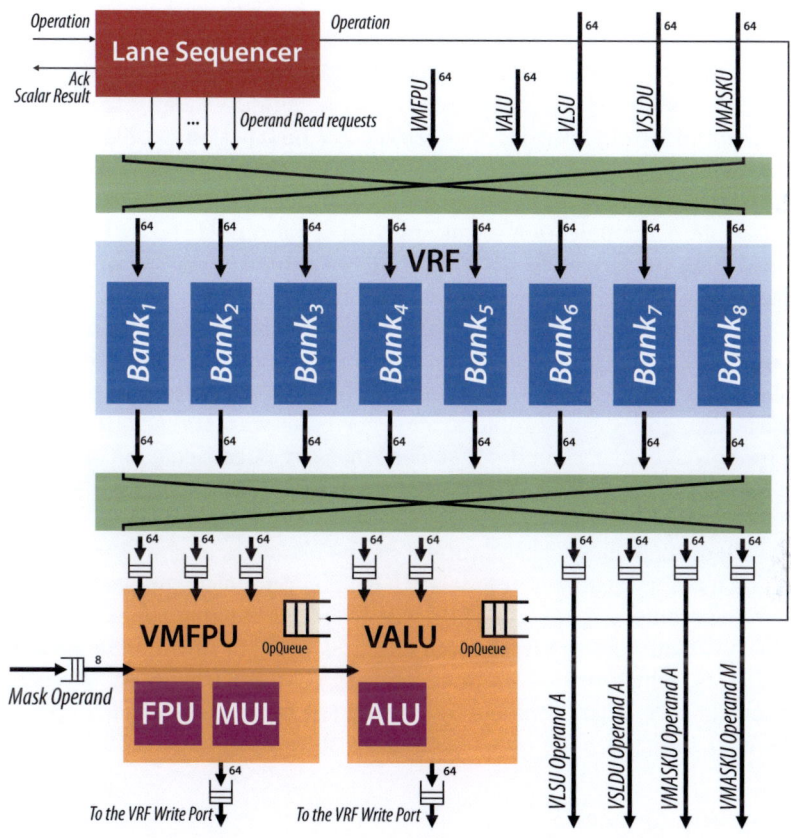

Figure 2.4: Microarchitecture of Ara's lane, highlighting the VRF and the execution units, namely, Vector Arithmetic and Logic Unit (VALU) and Vector Multiplier and Floating Point Unit (VMFPU).

Due to the massive area and power overhead of multi-ported Static
Random-Access Memory (SRAM) banks, which usually require custom
transistor-level design, we opted not to use a monolithic VRF with
several independent ports. Instead, Ara's VRF consists of Single-
Ported Read and Write (1RW) SRAM banks. Each bank stores
elements 64-bit wide, avoiding sub-word selection logic. Therefore,
in steady state regime, five banks are used simultaneously to sustain
maximum throughput for the `vfmacc.vv` instruction. Ara's register
file has eight banks per lane, providing some margin on the throughput
requirement. This VRF structure is replicated at each lane, and all
inter-lane communication is concentrated at the VLSU and VSLDU. We
used high-performance SRAM banks to achieve a target operating
frequency of 1 GHz at worst-case conditions.

A multi-banked VRF organization creates the problem of banking
conflicts, which occur when several functional units need to access
the same bank. In Ara, banking conflicts are resolved dynamically
with a weighted round-robin arbiter per bank with two priority levels.
Low-throughput instructions, such as memory operations, are assigned
a lower priority. Hence, their access pattern does not disturb the
execution of concurrent regular high-throughput instructions.

Figure 2.5 shows the mapping of the elements of a vector on the
eight memory banks of a lane's VRF. The pure element-partitioned
organization of Figure 2.5a [57] leads to initial banking conflicts when
the functional units try to fetch the first element of different vector
registers, which are all mapped onto the same VRF bank. We can
alleviate such initial conflicts by shifting the initial bank of each vector
register in a "barber's pole" fashion, as shown in Figure 2.5b.

Operand Queues

The multi-banked VRF organization can lead to banking conflicts
when several functional units try to access operands in the same bank.
Each lane has a set of operand queues between the VRF and the
functional units to absorb such banking conflicts. There are nine
operand queues: three of them are dedicated to the VMFPU unit, two
of them to the VALU, one to the VLSU, one to the VSLDU, and two to
the VMASKU. Each queue is 64-bit wide. The queue depth depends
on the functional unit's latency and throughput. Low-throughput

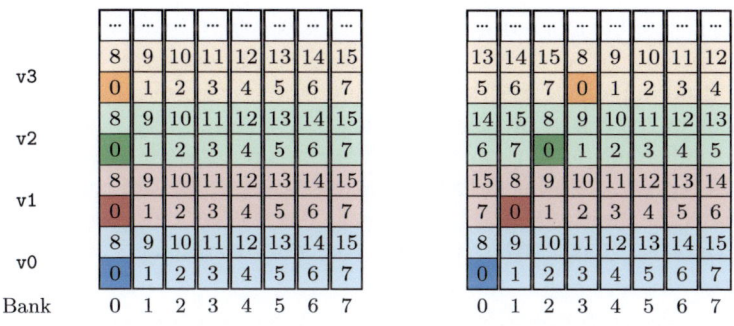

(a) Without "barber's pole" shift.   (b) With "barber's pole" shift.

Figure 2.5: VRF organization inside one lane. Darker colors highlight the initial element of each vector register vi. In a), all vector registers start at the same bank. In b), the vector registers follow a "barber's pole" pattern, the starting bank being shifted for every vector register.

functional units like the VLSU require shallower queues than the VMFPU. Queues between the functional units' output ports and the vector register file absorb banking conflicts on the write-back path to the VRF. Each lane has two queues, one for the VMFPU and one for the VALU. Together with the decoupled operand fetch mechanism and the barber's pole VRF organization, the operand queues allow a pipelined execution of vector instructions. While execution bubbles still occur sporadically due to banking conflicts, it is possible to fill Ara's pipeline even with a succession of short vector instructions.

Vector Execution Units

Each lane has three execution units, an integer ALU, an integer multiplier, and an FPU, all with a 64-bit datapath. The multiplier shares the operand queues with the FPU, and they cannot be used simultaneously. We do not expect the simultaneous use of the integer multiplier and the floating-point unit to be a common execution pattern. Except for this constraint, chaining is allowed between any execution units as long as their instructions have regular access patterns.

It is possible to subdivide the 64-bit datapath, trading off narrower data formats by a corresponding increase in performance. The three execution units have a 64-bit/cycle throughput, regardless of the data format of the computation. We developed our multi-precision SIMD ALU and multiplier, both able to operate on 1×64-bit, 2×32-bit, 4×16-bit, and 8×8-bit signed and unsigned operands. Ara has limited support for multi-precision operations, allowing for data promotions from 8 bit to 16 bit, 16 bit to 32 bit, and 32 bit to 64 bit.

For floating-point operations, we used an open-source, IEEE-compliant, multi-precision FPU developed by Mach et al. [69], [70]. The FPU was configured to support Fused Multiply-Adds (FMAs), additions, multiplications, divisions, square roots, and floating-point comparisons. The FPU has a 64-bit/cycle throughput, i.e., one double precision, two single precision, or four IEEE 754 half-precision floating-point results per cycle. Besides IEEE 754 standard floating-point formats, the FPU also supports custom floating-point formats, 8-bit and 16-bit wide. The narrower formats can be used to achieve significant energy savings compared to a wide floating-point baseline [69].

2.5 Benchmarks

Memory bandwidth is often a limiting factor in processor performance, and many optimizations revolve around scheduling memory and arithmetic operations to hide memory latency. The roofline model can analyze the relationship between processor performance and memory bandwidth [71]. This model shows the achievable peak performance (in FLOP/cycle) as a function of the arithmetic intensity Φ, defined as the algorithm-dependent ratio of operations per memory traffic.

Accordingly to this model, computations can be either memory-bound or compute-bound [72], the peak performance being achievable only if the algorithm's arithmetic intensity, in operations per byte, is higher than the processor's performance per memory bandwidth ratio. Ara enters its compute-bound regime when the algorithm's arithmetic intensity exceeds $0.5\,\mathrm{FLOP_{DP}/B}$. The memory bandwidth determines the slope of the performance boundary in the memory-bound regime. We consider three benchmarks to explore the architecture instances of the vector processor with distinct arithmetic intensities that fully span the two regions of the roofline.

First, we consider the `matmul` algorithm, the multiplication of two $n \times n$ floating-point double-precision matrices, $\mathbf{C} \leftarrow \mathbf{AB} + \mathbf{C}$. The algorithm requires $2n^3$ floating-point operations—one FMA is considered two operations—and at least $32n^2$ bytes of memory transfers. Therefore, `matmul` presents an arithmetic intensity of

$$\Phi_{\texttt{matmul}} = \frac{n}{16} \, \text{FLOP}_{\text{DP}}/\text{B}. \tag{2.1}$$

The matrix multiplication kernel is not inherently embarrassingly memory-bound nor compute-bound since its arithmetic intensity grows with $\mathcal{O}(n)$. Nevertheless, it is interesting how Ara behaves on highly memory-bound and fully compute-bound cases. The `axpy` kernel, $\mathbf{Y} \leftarrow \alpha\mathbf{X} + \mathbf{Y}$, is a common algorithmic building block of more complex Basic Linear Algebra Subprograms (BLAS) routines. Considering vectors of length n, `axpy` requires n FMAs and at least $24n$ bytes of memory transfers. Therefore, `axpy` is a heavily memory-bound algorithm with an arithmetic intensity of $0.083\,\text{FLOP}_{\text{DP}}/\text{B}$.

Finally, we explore the compute-bound spectrum with the tensor convolution `conv`, a routine at the core of Convolutional Neural Networks (CNNs). In terms of size, we took the first layer of GoogLeNet [73], with a $64 \times 3 \times 7 \times 7$ kernel and $3 \times 112 \times 112$ input images. Each point of the input image must be convolved with each element of the kernel matrix, resulting in a total of $64 \times 3 \times 7 \times 7 \times 112 \times 112$ FMAs, or $236\,\text{MFLOP}_{\text{DP}}$. In terms of memory, we will consider that the input matrix (after padding) is loaded exactly once, or $3 \times 118 \times 118$ double precision loads, together with the write-back of the result, or $64 \times 112 \times 112$ double precision stores. The $6.44\,\text{MiB}$ of memory transfers implies an arithmetic intensity of $34.9\,\text{FLOP}_{\text{DP}}/\text{B}$, making this kernel heavily compute-bound on Ara.

2.6 Performance Analysis

This section analyzes Ara's peak performance across several design parameters. Then, we use the matrix multiplication kernel to explore Ara's architectural limitations in depth before analyzing how such limitations translate into the other kernels.

2.6.1   Matrix Multiplication

Figure 2.6 shows the performance of the matrix multiplication kernel $\mathbf{C} \leftarrow \mathbf{AB} + \mathbf{C}$, for several Ara instances and problem sizes $n \times n$. Those results were extracted from a cycle-accurate Register Transfer Level (RTL) simulation of the Ara-based system. For problems "large enough," the performance results meet the peak performance boundary. For example, for a matrix multiplication of size 256×256, an Ara instance with two lanes utilizes its FPUs 98% of the time, while an instance with 16 lanes achieves 97% FPUs utilization. This almost-ideal FPU utilization for large problems is comparable to similar large-scale vector processing units [63], [74]. The performance scalability comes, however, at a price. More lanes require larger problem sizes to exploit the maximum performance fully, even though all problem sizes fall into the compute-bound regime. Smaller problems, however, cannot fully utilize the functional units. It is important to note that this limiting effect can also be observed in other vector processors.

This effect is attributed to two main reasons: first, the initialization of the vector register file before starting computation, and second, the rate at which the vector instructions are issued to Ara. The latter effect, in particular, is related to the rate at which the vector FMA instructions are issued. To understand this, consider that smaller vectors occupy the pipeline for fewer cycles, requiring more vector instructions to utilize the FPUs fully. Assume an Ara computing system with peak performance Π. If every vector FMA instruction occupies the FPUs for τ cycles and they are issued every δ cycles, the measured system performance π is limited by

$$\pi \leq \Pi \frac{\tau}{\delta}. \tag{2.2}$$

For the $n \times n$ matrix multiplication, τ is equal to $2n/\Pi$. With the help of Equation (2.1), we can rewrite this constraint regarding the arithmetic intensity $\Phi_{\texttt{matmul}}$, resulting in

$$\pi \leq \frac{32}{\delta} \Phi_{\texttt{matmul}}. \tag{2.3}$$

This translates to another performance boundary in the roofline plot, which is purely dependent on the instruction issue rate. In our matrix

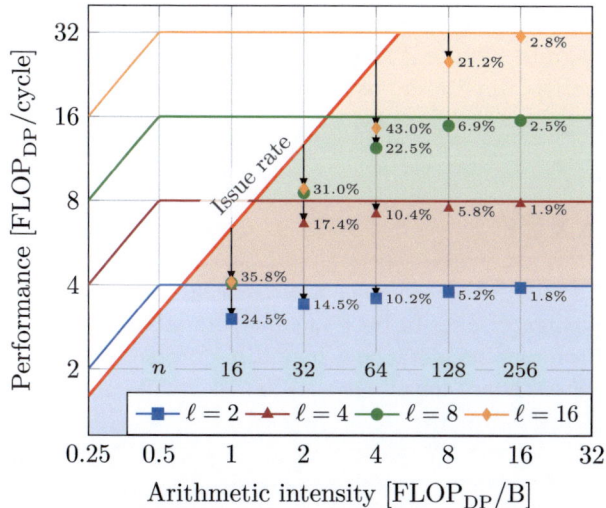

Figure 2.6: Performance results for the matrix multiplication $\mathbf{C} \leftarrow \mathbf{AB} + \mathbf{C}$, with a different number of lanes ℓ, for several $n \times n$ problem sizes. The bold red line depicts a performance boundary due to the instruction issue rate. The small percentages indicate the performance loss concerning the theoretically achievable peak performance.

multiplication kernel, the vector FMA instructions are issued every five cycles, i.e., $\delta = 5$. This shifts the roofline of the architecture, as illustrated by the bold line in Figure 2.6. Note that, for 16 lanes, even the performance of a 64×64 matrix multiplication is limited by the vector instruction issue rate.

The performance degradation with shorter vectors could be mitigated with a more complex instruction issue mechanism, either going superscalar or introducing a VLIW ISA to increase the instruction issue rate. However, shorter vectors bring vector processors to an execution paradigm closer to an array processor, where the vector instructions execute for a single cycle. This pressures the issue logic, demanding more than a simple single-issue in-order core. For example, all Arm Cortex-A cores with Neon capability are also superscalar [75]. Another alternative would be using a MIMD approach where the lanes would be decoupled, running instructions issued by different scalar cores [76]. While fine-grain temporal sharing of the vector units increases the FPU utilization, duplication of the instruction issue logic degrades the design's peak energy efficiency.

2.6.2   AXPY

Figure 2.7 shows the performance results for all considered benchmarks and Ara configurations. In both memory-bound and compute-bound regions of the roofline plot, the achieved performance tends to achieve the roofline boundary for all the considered architecture instances.

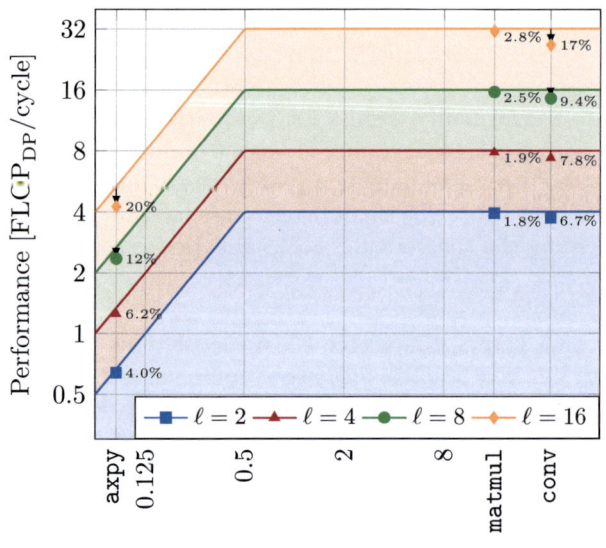

Figure 2.7: Performance results for all considered benchmarks, with a different number of lanes ℓ. The axpy kernel uses vectors of length 256, matmul operates on 256×256 matrices, and the conv kernel uses GoogLeNet's [73] sizes. The small percentages indicate the performance loss concerning the theoretically achievable peak performance.

As discussed in Section 2.5, axpy is a heavily memory-bound kernel with an arithmetic intensity of $0.083\,\mathrm{FLOP_{DP}/B}$. Therefore, its performance on Ara is much less than the system's peak performance in the compute-bound region. For example, for an axpy kernel between vectors with 256 elements, an Ara instance with two lanes achieves a $0.65\,\mathrm{FLOP_{DP}}$/cycle performance, which is 98% of the theoretical performance limit. Furthermore, for 16 lanes, the achieved $4.27\,\mathrm{FLOP_{DP}}$/cycle is still 80% of the theoretical limit. In this case, the configuration of the vector unit is responsible for increasing the runtime from the ideal 96 cycles to 120 cycles.

2.6.3 Convolution

The conv kernel is heavily compute-bound, with an arithmetic intensity of up to $34.9\,\mathrm{FLOP_{DP}/B}$. On an Ara instance with two lanes, it performs up to $3.73\,\mathrm{FLOP_{DP}}$/cycle. However, we notice some performance degradation for sixteen lanes, where the kernel achieves $26.7\,\mathrm{FLOP_{DP}}$/cycle, i.e., an FPU utilization of 83.2%. The reason for this performance drop lies in the problem size. In this case, each lane holds only seven elements of the vectors with 112 elements, i.e., the vectors do not even occupy the eight banks of a lane. With such short instructions, the system needs more time to achieve a steady state banking access pattern and incur banking conflicts that would otherwise be amortized across longer vectors.

2.6.4 Comparison with Hwacha

We compared Ara's performance against Hwacha, a state-of-the-art publicly available vector processor. Unfortunately, we could not reproduce the 32×32 double-precision matrix multiplication performance claimed by [42]. This is because Hwacha relies on a closed-source L2 cache, whereas its public version has a limited memory system with no banked cache and a broadcast hub to ensure coherence. This limits Hwacha's memory bandwidth to 128 bit/cycle, starving the FMA units and capping the achievable performance.

Table 2.1 compares Ara's and Hwacha's performance [42] for a matrix multiplication between matrices of size $n \times n$. The roofline boundaries are identical between the compared architectures for a fair comparison. For small problems for which a direct comparison is possible, Ara's FPU utilization is much higher than that of equivalent Hwacha instances. For example, Ara utilizes its FPUs 66% more than the equivalent Hwacha instance for a relatively small 32×32 matrix multiplication on instances with two lanes. Since Hwacha is also coupled to a single-issue in-order core, it performs poorly on the same small matrices and vector lengths seen on Ara. For what concerns large problems, another more recent reference on Hwacha [63] claims a 95% FPU utilization for a 128×128 `matmul` kernel, close to Ara's performance level. However, we could not reproduced those results on the current open-source version of Hwacha due to the memory system limitation outlined above.

Table 2.1: Normalized performance of equivalent Ara and Hwacha instances for a matrix multiplication between matrices of size $n \times n$.

Π	$8\,\mathrm{FLOP_{DP}/cycle}$		$16\,\mathrm{FLOP_{DP}/cycle}$		$32\,\mathrm{FLOP_{DP}/cycle}$	
n	Ara	Hwacha[a]	Ara	Hwacha	Ara	Hwacha
16	49.5%	—	25.4%	—	12.8%	—
32	82.6%	49.9%	53.4%	35.6%	27.6%	22.4%
64	89.6%	—	77.5%	—	45.6%	—
128	94.3%	—	93.1%	—	78.8%	—

[a]Performance results extracted from [42].

2.7   Implementation and Execution of a Matrix Multiplication

Here we analyze in depth the implementation and execution of the $n \times n$ matrix multiplication. We assume the matrices are stored in row-major order. Our implementation uses a tiled approach working on t rows of matrix $\mathbf{C}$ at a time. Figure 2.8 presents the matrix multiplication algorithm, working on tiles of size $t \times n$. The algorithm showcases how the ISA handles scalability via strip-mined loops [57]. Line 3 uses the `vsetvl` instruction, which sets the vector length for the following vector instructions, and enables the same code to be used for vector processors with different maximum vector length `VLMAX`.

```
 1:  c ← 0;
 2:  while c < n do {Strip-mining loop}
 3:      vl ← min(n − c, VLMAX);
 4:      r ← 0;
 5:      while r < n do
 6:          for j ← 0 to min(r, t) − 1 do {Phase I}
 7:              Load row C[r + j, c] into vector register vCj;
 8:          end for
 9:          for i ← 0 to n − 1 do {Phase II}
10:              Load row B[i, c] into vector register vB;
11:              for j ← 0 to min(r, b) − 1 do
12:                  Load element A[j, i] into register fA;
13:                  vCj ← fA · vB + vCj;
14:              end for
15:          end for
16:          for j ← 0 to min(r, t) − 1 do {Phase III}
17:              Store vector register vCj into C[r + j, c];
18:          end for
19:          r ← r + t;
20:      end while
21:      c ← c + vl;
22: end while
```

Figure 2.8: Algorithm for the matrix multiplication $\mathbf{C} \leftarrow \mathbf{AB} + \mathbf{C}$.

Once inside the strip-mined loop, there are three distinct computation phases: I) read a block of matrix $\mathbf{C}$; II) the actual computation of the matrix multiplication, and; III) write the result to memory. Phases I and III take $\mathcal{O}(n)$ cycles, whereas the phase II takes $\mathcal{O}(n^2)$ cycles. The core part of Figure 2.8 is the `for` loop of Line 11, where most of the time is spent and where the FPUs are used. After loading one row of matrix $\mathbf{B}$, the kernel consists of three repeating instructions, responsible for, respectively:

1. load the element $\mathbf{A}[j, i]$ into a general-purpose register `fA`;

2. bump address $A[j, i]$ preparing for next iteration;

3. multiply-accumulate instruction vCj ← fA · vB + vCj.

As CVA6 is a single-issue core, this kernel runs in at least three cycles. In steady state, however, we measure that each loop iteration runs in five cycles. The reason for this is one bubble due to the data dependence between the scalar load, which takes two cycles.

We used loop unrolling and software pipelining to code the algorithm of Figure 2.8 as our C implementation. For example, we unrolled the for loop of line 11. This avoids any branching at the end of the loop. Moreover, two vectors hold rows of matrix **B**. This double buffering allows for the simultaneous loading of one row in vector vB1, while vB0 is used for the FMAs, and vice-versa. The three phases of the computation can be distinguished clearly in Figure 2.9, which shows the utilization of the VLSU and FPU for a 32×32 matrix multiplication on a four-lane Ara instance. Note how the FPUs are almost fully utilized during phase II while being almost idle otherwise.

2.8   Physical Implementation

In this section, we analyze the implementation of several Ara instances in terms of area, power, and energy efficiency. First, Ara was synthesized for GlobalFoundries' 22FDX 22 nm FD-SOI technology using Synopsys Design Compiler 2017.09. We then used Cadence Innovus 18.11.00 to place and route the design. For this technology, one gate equivalent (GE) equals $0.199\,\mu\text{m}^2$. Next, Ara's figures of merit are measured by running the kernels on a cycle-accurate RTL simulation. Finally, we used Synopsys PrimeTime 2016.12 to extract the power figures with activities obtained with timing information from the implemented design at nominal operating conditions (TT, 0.80 V, 25 °C) and 1 GHz. Table 2.2 summarizes Ara's design parameters.

Because the maximum frequencies achieved after synthesis are usually higher than the ones achieved after the back-end flow, the system was synthesized for a clock period constraint 250 ps tighter than the target clock period of 1 ns. In addition, the system can be tuned for even higher frequencies by deploying Forward Body Biasing (FBB) techniques at the expense of increased leakage power. On average, the

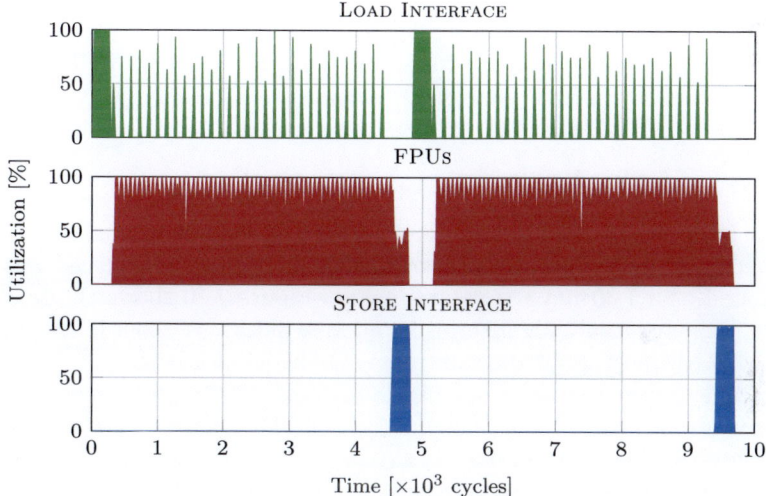

Figure 2.9: Utilization of Ara's functional units for a 32×32 matrix multiplication on an Ara instance with four lanes.

Table 2.2: Design parameters.

	# Lanes	$\ell \in [2, 4, 8, 16]$
	AXI data width	32ℓ bit
	Target frequency	1 GHz
VRF	Size	16 KiB/lane
	# Banks	8 bank/lane
	Bank width	64 bit

final designs have a mix of 72.9% Low Voltage Threshold (LVT) cells and 27.1% Super-Low Voltage Threshold (SLVT) cells.

2.8.1   Area Analysis

We implemented four Ara instances, with two, four, eight, and sixteen lanes. In particular, the instance with four lanes was placed and routed as a 1.40 mm × 0.80 mm macro. Figure 2.10 shows the final implemented result, highlighting its internal blocks. Without its caches, CVA6 occupies about the same area (524 kGE) as a lane.

Our vector processor is scalable because CVA6 can be reused to drive a wide range of Ara configurations without changes. Furthermore, each vector lane touches only its section of the VRF. Hence it does not introduce any scalability bottlenecks. However, scalability is limited by the units that must interface with all lanes simultaneously, namely the main sequencer, the VLSU, and the VSLDU. Therefore, similar vector processors [63], [74] have a dedicated memory port per lane instead, which solves the scalability issue locally by controlling the growth of the memory interface. However, this pushes the memory interconnect scaling issue further upstream: the upper levels of the memory hierarchy must aggregate multiple parallel requests from all these ports to achieve their maximum memory throughput.

Due to their significant area and timing impact, we decided not to deploy lane-level Power Gating (PG) or Body Biasing (BB) techniques. Regarding area, both techniques would require an isolation ring 10-µm-wide around each PG/BB domain or at least an 8% increase in the area of each lane. Regarding timing, isolation cells between power

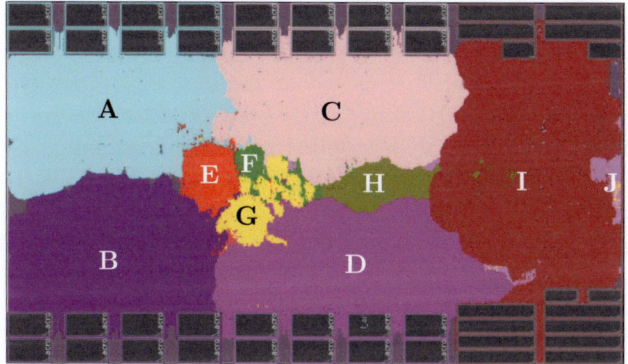

(a) Place-and-route results of an Ara instance with four lanes, highlighting its blocks: A-D) Lanes; E) VSLDU; F) sequencer; G) VLSU; H) Ara front end; I) CVA6; J) memory interconnect.

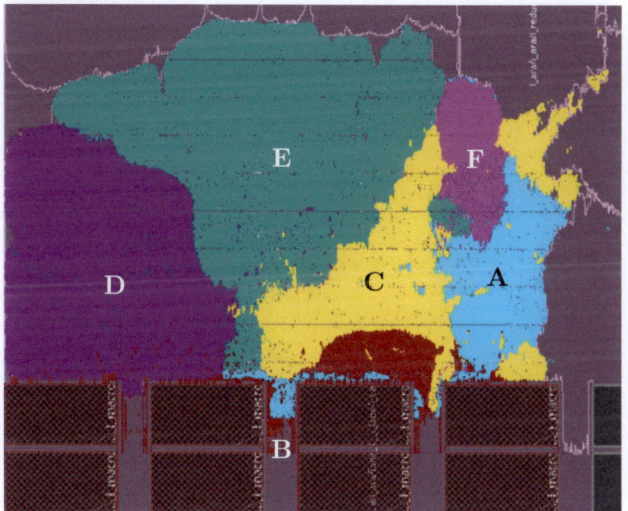

(b) Detail of one of Ara's lanes, highlighting its blocks: A) lane sequencer; B) VRF; C) operand queues; D) multiplier; E) FPU; F) ALU.

Figure 2.10: Place-and-route results of an Ara instance with four lanes in GlobalFoundries' 22 nm technology on a 1.40 mm × 0.80 mm macro.

domains and separated clock trees would impact Ara's operating frequency. Assuming these cells would be in the critical path between the lanes and the VLSU, this would incur a 10% clock frequency penalty. Reverse Body Biasing (RBB) lowers the leakage and impacts frequency since it cannot be applied to high-performance LVT and SLVT cells. Furthermore, PG (and, to a lesser degree, BB) would introduce significant turn-on transition times, which are only tolerable if coupled with a scheduling policy for power managing the lanes. Therefore, these techniques are out of the scope of the current work.

2.8.2 Performance, Power, and Area Results

Tables 2.3 and 2.4 summarize the post-implementation PPA results of several Ara instances. Overall, the instances achieve nominal operating frequencies around 1.2 GHz at nominal operating conditions.

Table 2.3: Post-implementation PPA comparison between several Ara instances implemented with GlobalFoundries' 22FDX 22 nm FD-SOI technology.

Figure of merit	Instance					
	$\ell = 2$			$\ell = 4$		
Clock (nominal) [GHz]	1.25			1.25		
Clock (worst-case) [GHz]	0.92			0.93		
Area [kGE]	2228			3434		
Area per lane [kGE]	1114			858		
Kernel	matmul[a]	conv[b]	axpy[c]	matmul	conv	axpy
Performance [GFLOPS$_{\text{DP}}$]	4.91	4.66	0.82	9.80	9.22	1.56
Core power [mW]	138	130	68.2	259	239	113
CVA6/Ara [mW]	22/116	22/108	20/48	27/232	29/210	25/88
Core power per lane [mW]	69	65	34	65	60	28
Efficiency [GFLOPS$_{\text{DP}}$/W]	35.6	35.8	12.0	37.8	38.6	13.8

[a]Double-precision floating-point 256×256 matrix multiplication. [b]Double-precision floating-point tensor convolution with sizes from the first layer of GoogLeNet. Input size is $3 \times 112 \times 112$ and kernel size is $64 \times 3 \times 7 \times 7$. [c]Double precision axpy of vectors with length 256.

Table 2.4: Post-implementation PPA comparison between several Ara instances implemented with GlobalFoundries' 22FDX 22 nm FD-SOI technology (continuation).

Figure of merit	Instance					
	$\ell = 8$			$\ell = 16$		
Clock (nominal) [GHz]	1.17			1.04		
Clock (worst-case) [GHz]	0.87			0.78		
Area [kGE]	5902			10735		
Area per lane [kGE]	738			671		
Kernel	matmul[a]	conv[b]	axpy[c]	matmul	conv	axpy
Performance [GFLOPS$_{DP}$]	18.2	16.9	2.80	32.4	27.7	4.44
Core power [mW]	456	420	183	794	676	280
CVA6/Ara [mW]	28/428	29/391	24/159	31/763	31/646	25/255
Core power per lane [mW]	57	54	23	50	42	15
Efficiency [GFLOPS$_{DP}$/W]	39.9	40.2	15.3	40.8	41.0	15.9

[a] Double-precision floating-point 256 × 256 matrix multiplication. [b] Double-precision floating-point tensor convolution with sizes from the first layer of GoogLeNet. Input size is 3 × 112 × 112 and kernel size is 64 × 3 × 7 × 7. [c] Double precision axpy of vectors with length 256.

The two-lane Ara instance has its critical path inside the double precision FMA. The FPUs rely on the register retiming feature from Synopsys Design Compiler. This placement could be further improved by hand-tuning or increasing the number of pipeline stages [70]. Another critical path is the combinational handshake between the VLSU and its operand queues. Both paths are about 40 Fan-Out Four (FO4) gate delays long. Timing of the larger Ara instances becomes increasingly critical due to the widening of Ara's memory interface since the VLSU must collect 64-bit words from all the lanes to realign and pack them into a wide word to be sent to memory. The instance with sixteen lanes incurs a 17% frequency penalty compared to the two-lane equivalent instance.

CVA6's footprint and power consumption are amortized among the lanes. Figure 2.11 shows the area breakdown of an Ara instance with four lanes. Ara's total area (excluding the scalar core) is 2.46 MGE, of which each lane amounts to 575 kGE. The area of the vector unit is dominated by the lanes, while the other blocks amount to only 7% of the total area. The area of the lanes is dominated by the VRF (35%), the FPU (27%), and the multiplier (18%).

Regarding the post-synthesis logic area, a Hwacha instance with four lanes is $0.354\,\mathrm{mm}^2$ large [42], or 1.1 MGE. When comparing post-synthesis results, Hwacha is 9% smaller than the equivalent Ara instance. The trend is also valid for equivalent instances with eight and sixteen lanes. The main reason for this area difference is that Hwacha has only half as many multipliers as Ara [77]. These multipliers make up for a 9% area difference. Moreover, these Hwacha instances do not support mixed-precision arithmetic [42], whose support would incur a 4% area overhead [78]. However, Ara has a simpler execution mechanism than Hwacha [77], contributing to the area difference.

We used the implemented designs to analyze Ara's performance and energy efficiency when running the considered benchmarks. Due to the asymmetry between the code that runs in CVA6 and Ara, we extracted switching activities by running the benchmarks with netlists back annotated with timing information. As expected, the energy efficiency of Ara coupled to a CVA6 core is considerably higher than that of a CVA6 core alone. For instance, a 256×256 integer matrix multiplication achieves up to 43.6 GOPS/W on an Ara with four lanes, whereas a comparable benchmark runs at 17 GOPS/W on CVA6 [51].

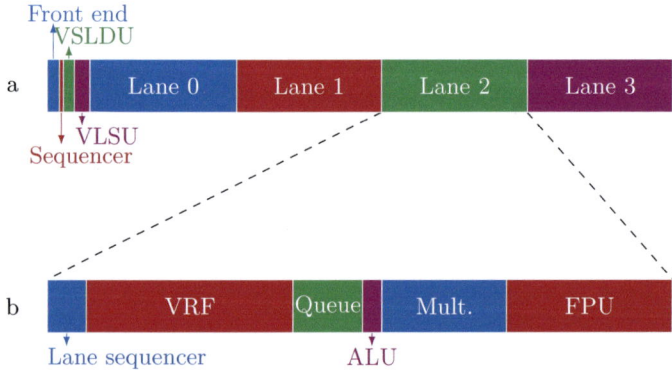

Figure 2.11: Area breakdown of a) an Ara instance with four lanes with detail on b) one of its lanes. Ara's total area, excluding the scalar processor, is 2.46 MGE. Each lane has about 575 kGE.

In that case, the instruction and data caches alone are responsible for 46% of CVA6's power dissipation. In Ara's case, most memory accesses go directly into the VRF. Furthermore, energy spent for cache accesses can be amortized over many vector lanes and cycles, increasing the system's energy efficiency with increasing lanes.

A Hwacha implementation in STMicroelectronics' 28 nm FD-SOI technology achieves a peak energy efficiency of 40 GFLOPS$_{DP}$/W [63]. Adjusting for technology scaling gains [38], Hwacha's energy efficiency of 41 GFLOPS$_{DP}$/W is comparable to that of the larger Ara instances.

2.9   Conclusions

In this chapter, we presented Ara, a parametric, high-performance, energy-efficient 64-bit vector unit based on RISC-V's RVV ISA version 1.0. Ara is a coprocessor that is tightly coupled to OpenHW's CVA6, an open-source application-class RV64GC core. Ara's microarchitecture was designed with scalability in mind. To this end, it comprises a set of identical lanes, each hosting part of the system's vector register file and functional units. The lanes communicate via the VLSU and the VSLDU, responsible for executing instructions that touch all the VRF banks simultaneously. These units arguably represent the weak points regarding scalability because they get wider with an increasing number of lanes. Other architectures take an alternative approach, with several narrow memory ports instead of a single wide one. However, this approach does not solve the scalability problem but deflects it further to the memory interconnect and cache subsystem.

We measured the performance of Ara using matrix multiplication, tensor convolution, and AXPY double-precision floating-point kernels. For *large enough* problems, the compute-bound kernels saturate the FPUs, with the performance of a 256×256 matrix multiplication only 3% below the theoretically achievable peak performance. We decided not to restrain the performance analysis to very large problems and observed a performance degradation for problems whose size is comparable to the number of vector lanes. This is not a limitation of Ara per se but rather of vector processors in general when coupled to a single-issue in-order core. The main reason for the low FPU utilization for small problems is the rate at which the scalar core issues vector instructions. With our `matmul` implementation, CVA6 issues a vector FMA instruction every five cycles, and the shorter the vector length is, the more vector instructions are required to fill the pipeline. By decoupling operand fetch and result write-back, Ara tries eliminating bubbles that would significantly impact short-lived vector instructions. While the achieved performance, in this case, is far from the peak, it is nonetheless close to the performance boundary defined by instruction issue rate.

In terms of PPA, we presented post-implementation results for Ara configurations with two up to sixteen lanes in GlobalFoundries' 22FDX FD-SOI node. We showed that Ara achieves a clock frequency higher than 1 GHz in typical operating conditions. When running equivalent integer matrix multiplication benchmarks, our design is $2.5\times$ more energy efficient than CVA6 alone. An instance of our design with sixteen lanes achieves up to about 41 GFLOPS$_{\text{DP}}$/W running computationally intensive benchmarks, comparable to the energy efficiency of state-of-the-art vector processor implementations.

To this end, it would be interesting to investigate whether and to what extent this performance limit could be mitigated by leveraging a superscalar or VLIW-capable core to drive the vector coprocessor. While using multiple small cores to drive the vector lanes increases their utilization, maintaining an optimal energy efficiency might mean the usage of fewer lanes than physically available, i.e., lower overall utilization of the functional units. Another topic is a multi-core Ara system, i.e., a hybrid between a vector-SIMD and a MIMD architecture. In any case, care must be taken to find an equilibrium between the high-performance and energy-efficiency requirements of the design.

Chapter 3

The Case for Short Vectors: Building High-Performance Computing Systems out of Compact Vector Units

The pervasiveness of AI and ML applications triggered an explosion of computational requirements across many application domains. For example, the required computing of the largest ML model doubles every 3.4 months, while its parameter count doubles every 2.3 months [79], [80]. As a result, large-scale computing systems struggle to keep up with the increasing complexity of such ML models. In fact, the performance of the fastest supercomputers only doubles every 1.2 years [80], while their power budget is capped around 20 MW by infrastructure and operating cost constraints. Furthermore, smart devices running AI applications at the Internet-of-Things (IoT) edge [81] are also tightly constrained in their power budget due to battery lifetime and passive cooling requirements. Therefore, small and large modern computing architectures must optimize their data movement energy and delay [82].

Another major issue for present computer architectures stems from the drastic slowdown of technology scaling, particularly SRAM area scaling. For example, the SRAM bit cell area on TSMC's cutting-edge N3E technology node did not scale compared to its previous N5 node, still coming at $0.021\,\mu m^2$, while logic area scaled down by 70% [83]. The flattening of SRAM scaling challenges almost every hardware design. However, it is particularly disastrous for AI hardware, which exploits SRAMs to implement high-bandwidth, low-latency on-chip storage. As a result, modern AI accelerators resort to large swaths of Standard Cell Memorys (SCMs)[84], which dominate their total area. Furthermore, interconnects have trouble keeping up with transistor scaling [85]. As transistors become more densely packed on a chip, the metal wires that connect them become an important performance bottleneck. The increasing memory and bandwidth requirements of modern computing applications demand large interconnect networks, leading to a considerable area overhead due to the interconnect between PEs and memories.

The extreme domain specialization of hardware architectures can boost their energy efficiency and performance at the price of loss of flexibility. This is often not acceptable given the rapidly evolving nature of applications. This paper focuses on fully programmable architectures based on instruction processors. Particularly, we tackle the interconnect and memory scaling issue on the shared-L1 cluster of Figure 3.1, a generic template and building block for programmable computing architectures. Each shared-L1 cluster contains a set of PEs sharing tightly-coupled L1 memory through a low-latency interconnect [30]. The cluster's L1 memory is typically implemented as a multi-banked SRAM data cache or SPM. In addition, each PE has some private high-bandwidth L0 SCM.

Simple SoCs for edge-AI, such as GreenWaves' GAP-8 [81], comprise a small shared-L1 cluster coupled with ML accelerators. Replicated and interconnected through some latency-tolerant Network-on-Chip (NoC), the cluster also serves as a template for building high-performance computing systems, such as MemPool [14] and Manticore [86]. Furthermore, GPUs, which dominate the Top500 supercomputer list [5], follow the shared-L1 cluster architectural model. For example, NVIDIA Hopper GPUs are composed of several SMs with four tensor cores

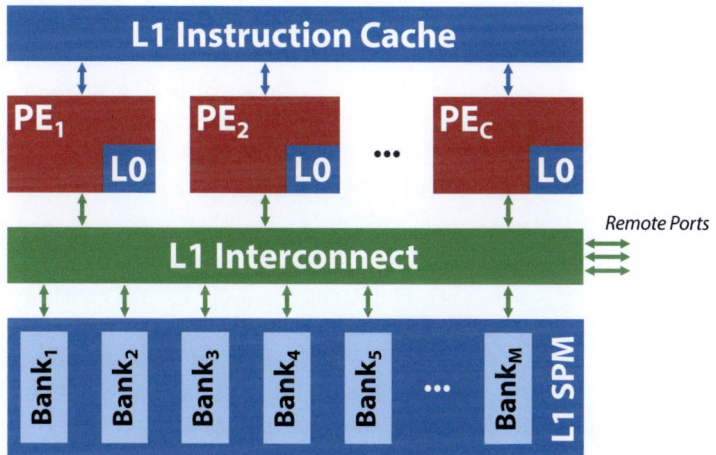

Figure 3.1: A simple shared-L1 cluster with C PEs and a multi-banked L1 SPM implementation with M SRAM banks.

and an L1 data cache with 256 KiB. Each tensor core controls several FMA units, with each SM capable of up to 1024 FMAs per cycle [87].

The slow SRAM and interconnect scaling make the design of the cluster's L1 interconnect and SPM increasingly challenging as they struggle to provide the PEs with high-bandwidth, low-latency L1 access. To alleviate this issue, Kung's architectural "balance" suggests that we can trade bandwidth at upper levels of the memory hierarchy against memory capacity at lower levels [88]. Therefore, an architecture can increase the capacity of each PE's SCM-based L0 memory to relax the bandwidth requirements of the multi-banked SRAM-based L1 memory. In a typical shared-L1 cluster, where the PEs are cores, the L0 memory is the PE's General-Purpose Register File (GPR). Unfortunately, the GPR's register width and count are hardcoded in the ISA and are unavailable as architectural knobs. For example, on RISC-V's RV64I ISA, the GPR comprises 32 64-bit registers, 256 B [68].

In his seminal Turing award lecture, Backus discussed the issues stemming from the word-at-a-time style of programming inherited from the von Neumann computer [1]. The SIMD abstraction amortizes the VNB associated with fetching and dispatching instructions that only operate on a single word. It also provides architectures with a knob on their GPR capacity through wider datapaths and registers. Unfortunately, typical packed-SIMD ISAs, such as Arm's Neon [55] and Intel's AVX family [54], encode the register width in the opcode. Therefore, a change in the GPR capacity requires an ISA extension, and vectorized software cannot easily exploit wider datapaths.

On the other hand, vector-SIMD architectures have long been touted as one of the most efficient approaches to amortize the VNB. Unlike packed SIMD, vector-SIMD designs decouple the datapath width and vector register width (or *vector length*). As a result, the vector SIMD approach promises high performance and energy efficiency without requiring the ultra-wide datapaths of packed-SIMD-based architectures [89]. In addition, the vector length is typically much longer than the datapath width. Therefore, each vector instruction executes its micro-operations in a time-multiplexed fashion, further amortizing the VNB by reducing the instruction issue count. Moreover, the VLA programming technique is a lightweight syntax that allows vectorized software to adapt automatically to the current vector length at runtime [90].

This chapter analyzes streamlined vector processors as the PE of shared-L1 clusters, exploiting the reconfigurability of the L0 VRF to alleviate the bandwidth requirements of the L1 SPM. However, the long history of vector processing limits the application of a vector processor as the PE of a shared-L1 cluster. From its inception with the Cray-1 [46] machine to the modern Fujitsu A64FX [4], vector processing has always been associated with supercomputers. Vector processors usually include all microarchitectural tricks to increase ILP, e.g., renaming, out-of-order execution, speculation, and branch prediction, which increase the area and energy overhead of classical high-performance vector processors. As a result, typical vector processors are implemented with long vectors to minimize the VNB-related overhead of such complex instruction issue mechanisms [29], [91]. However, the defining characteristic of a vector processor is not ILP but DLP. This key observation has led to the design of more streamlined vector cores where most hardware resources are dedicated to DLP support, i.e., a wide VRF with parallel execution lanes [7]. In this vein, the idea of an embedded vector machine is gaining traction with modern vector

ISAs. Arm's MVE [59] and the Zve* subset of RVV [6] target small vector machines for edge data-parallel processing.

We present Spatz, an open-source compact VPU based on the RVV specification [6], and use it as the building block of a large-scale, high-performance computing system. We amortize the VNB by coupling Spatz with a lightweight scalar core [92]. Therefore, we can forgo the long vectors of typical VPUs and can exploit a small latch-based SCM VRF as the L0 memory of the computing cluster.

3.1 Vector Register File

The VRF is at the core of any vector processor. It must provide enough bandwidth for the functional units to achieve high utilization. In the RISC-V ISA, the vector instruction with the highest bandwidth requirements is the floating-point multiply-accumulate between two vectors, vfmacc.vv (and its integer equivalent, vmacc.vv) [6]. The VRF must handle reading three operands and writing one result per cycle to sustain one FMA per cycle. Furthermore, more VRF bandwidth is required to execute memory operations concurrently with high-bandwidth multiply-accumulate operations.

Large vector processors are typically coupled with equally complex scalar processors. For example, CVA6, an application-class RV64GC scalar core, consumes 317 pJ per operation of a simple dot product kernel, with only 28 pJ spent on the actual computation [51]. Therefore, long vectors are needed to amortize the large energy overhead associated with fetching and dispatching individual instructions. Typical large vector units achieve long vectors and high bandwidth through a large multi-banked VRF, with five [91] to eight [7] 1RW SRAM banks per FPU. However, this approach requires inflexible fine-grained scheduling of the VRF bank accesses [91] or an architecture that can handle banking conflicts when multiple operands reside at the same bank [7]. Therefore, VRFs are coupled with operand "queues" which store the operands until they are all simultaneously available.

Instead of achieving high functional unit utilization through hardware complexity, the RISC-V-based Snitch core tries to tackle the VNB by maximizing the cores' compute/control ratio, mitigating the efficiency loss due to deep pipelines and dynamic scheduling [92].

The Snitch-based shared-L1 cluster couples Snitch cores, typically RV32I or RV32E, with large double-precision FPUs. It achieves an energy efficiency of $79\,\mathrm{GFLOPS_{DP}}/\mathrm{W}$ on a double-precision matrix multiplication kernel [92], almost double that of state-of-the-art vector machines [91]. This cluster's high performance is linked to SSRs [64], which stream L1 data into and from the FPUs without explicit load/store instructions. As a result, SSRs incur high L1 traffic. For example, each core must read two L1 SPM words per cycle to sustain the execution of a matrix multiplication kernel without incurring systematic structural hazards. This traffic is particularly taxing on the cluster's physical implementation, as the L1 SPM interconnect is the critical factor for its scalability [30]. Furthermore, the breakdown of SRAM and interconnect scaling makes achieving the L1 bandwidth required by SSRs challenging.

The vector-SIMD abstraction provides a clean abstraction for software to adapt automatically to the microarchitecture's current vector length [90]. Therefore, we elect a streamlined VPU with a small VRF to act as the PE of our proposed shared-L1 cluster. The VRF is used as an architectural knob to balance the bandwidth and energy cost of an L1 SRAM with the size and energy cost of the L0 SCM [88]. If the VPU achieves a high compute/control ratio, we can explore the capacity/bandwidth trade-off without needing large VRFs.

The VPU is based on the RVV extension version 1.0 of the open-source RISC-V ISA [6]. The extension adds 32 architectural vector registers, v0 to v32, each with VLEN bytes. We assume that the VPU operates on vector elements 8-B wide. Therefore, each vector register has $\mathtt{vl} = {}^{\mathtt{VLEN}}/_8$ vector elements. Furthermore, the RVV extension adds the concept of a *vector register group* so that a single vector instruction can operate on multiple vector registers. The LMUL ℓ, with $\ell \in \{1, 2, 4, 8\}$, represents how many vector registers are combined to form a vector register group. As a result, LMUL trades available vector registers against longer vectors at runtime. Taking it into account, RVV provides ${}^{32}/_\ell$ vector registers, each with ${}^{\ell \times \mathtt{VLEN}}/_8$ elements.

We implement the VRF as a multi-banked, multi-ported, latch-based SCM. The 32 VLEN bytes of the VRF are divided into two SCM banks with Three Read Ports and one Write Port (3R1W) and 16 VLEN bytes each. A single 3R1W SCM cut can provide enough bandwidth for executing the vfmacc.vv instruction and multiple SCM banks ensure that other instructions can execute concurrently with the high-bandwidth vector multiply-accumulate instructions. Furthermore, since all operands of a vector instruction can be read simultaneously, we can forgo any "operand buffers" to time-multiplex the VRF operand fetching.

Figure 3.2 shows the architecture of a 3R1W latch-based SCM with R rows, each W-bytes wide. This SCM architecture is similar to that of [93], [94], with manually-inserted Integrated Clock Gating (ICG) cells gating the many clocks reaching the latch array. Besides the clock (CLK), write enable (WE), write address (WADDR), and write data (WDATA) ports, the SCM also has a write byte strobe (WBE) port to select which bytes are written at each write transaction. The write data is stored in registers before being stored in the latch array. The three read address (RADDR[i]) ports directly control muxes that select a row to forward to the corresponding read data (RDATA[i]) port. Each cell of the storage array comprises eight data latches and an AND2 standard cell, 28 GE in total. For comparison, an equivalent storage array cell based on multi-bit flip-flop standard cells would occupy 49 GE.

We implemented the SCM of Figure 3.2 with Synopsys' Fusion Compiler 2022.03, for many combinations of W and R, at 950 MHz in worst-case conditions (SS, 0.72 V, 125 °C) using GlobalFoundries' 12LPP advanced 12 nm Fin Field-Effect Transistor (FinFET) node. Then, we used Synopsys' PrimePower 2022.03 to measure its read and write energy consumption, initialized with random numbers, at 1 GHz and nominal operating conditions (TT, 0.80 V, 25 °C). Such results are summarized in Figure 3.3.

We interpolate the read and write energy consumption of the SCM as a polynomial function on the SCM width W and capacity K. Using the least-squares algorithm to fit parameterized functions to the points of Figure 3.3, it costs

$$\hat{\varepsilon}_{\text{L0}}^{\text{read}}(W, K) = 47.759W + 0.018WK + 0.275K \text{ fJ} \qquad (3.1)$$

to read W bytes out of the SCM, and

$$\hat{\varepsilon}_{\text{L0}}^{\text{write}}(W, K) = 72.077W + 0.006WK + 3.111K \text{ fJ} \qquad (3.2)$$

to write W bytes into the SCM. For comparison, it costs $\hat{\varepsilon}_{\text{L1}}^{\text{read}} = 4.63 \text{ pJ}$ to read and $\hat{\varepsilon}_{\text{L1}}^{\text{write}} = 5.77 \text{ pJ}$ to write 8 bytes into a 1RW SRAM of capacity 8 KiB in the same technology.

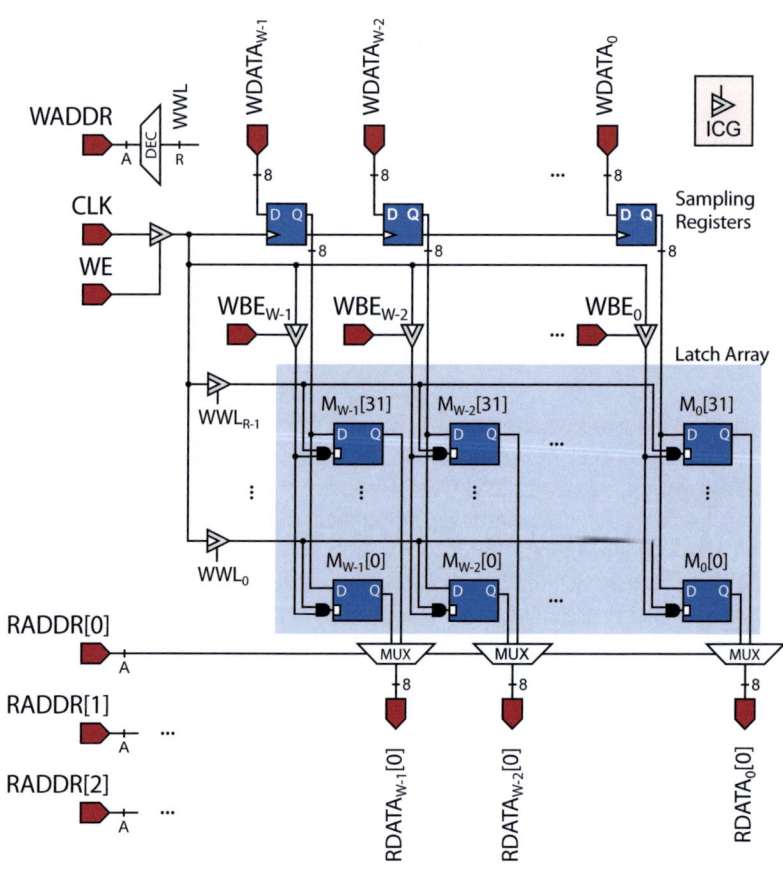

Figure 3.2: Architecture of a 3R1W latch-based SCM with R W-byte-wide rows, for a total capacity $K = WR$ bytes.

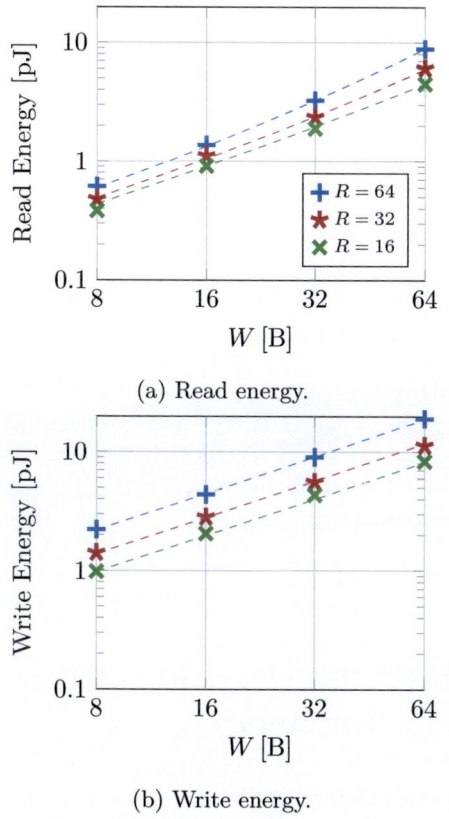

(a) Read energy.

(b) Write energy.

Figure 3.3: Energy consumption of a 3R1W latch-based SCM with R rows of width W and capacity $K = WR$ bytes.

We can gather further insight into the L0 and L1 energy consumption by normalizing the cost per byte accessed. For example, it takes 0.58 pJ/B to read data from an 1RW SRAM of width 8 B and capacity 8 KiB. According to our model, it takes 35% less energy, only 0.38 pJ/B, to read data from an L0 SCM with the same capacity and width. This comparison is not favorable towards the SRAMs since our model does not scale to this capacity (the largest 8-B-wide SCM we considered has a capacity of only 512 B). However, our results back our conclusion that latch-based SCMs are an energy-efficient approach for building small-capacity storage buffers. Unfortunately, this SCM with a capacity of 8 KiB would be at least 25× larger than its equivalent SRAM, which constitutes a major drawback of latch-based SCMs with large capacity.

In the following section, we will tune the L0 SCM capacity to minimize the overall energy consumption of a shared-L1 computing cluster. In particular, we consider the L1 SPM to have a fixed configuration. An extension of this work would be the multi-variate optimization of the cluster's energy consumption as a function of both the L0 SCM and L1 SPM configurations. This multi-variate analysis requires a model of the SRAM energy consumption, which can be inferred from either commercial or open-source memory macro generators.

3.2   Optimizing the Shared-L1 Cluster's Energy Efficiency

Equipped with the efficient L0 SCM architecture of Section 3.1, we focus on the shared-L1 cluster. This section will analyze the trade-off between the L0 SCM capacity and the L1 SRAM bandwidth to minimize the cluster's energy consumption by generalizing the model of Choi et al. [95] by applying their analysis to our hybrid SRAM and SCM-based memory hierarchy. We will focus on the matrix multiplication between two double-precision floating-point matrices, $C \leftarrow A \cdot B$, as the foundational example of an embarrassingly-parallel workload.

Figure 3.4 shows the architecture of a shared-L1 cluster equipped with compact vector PEs. The C PEs control F double-precision FPUs each. Each PE has a VRF divided into two 3R1W SCM banks, each $8F$-bytes wide. Since the F double-precision FPUs of each PE produce $8F$ bytes per cycle, a single 3R1W SCM bank provides enough bandwidth to sustain F FMAs per cycle. Furthermore, the L1 SPM is implemented as 16 SRAM banks of 8 KiB each, 128 KiB. All matrices are $n \times n$ and are preallocated in the cluster's SPM.

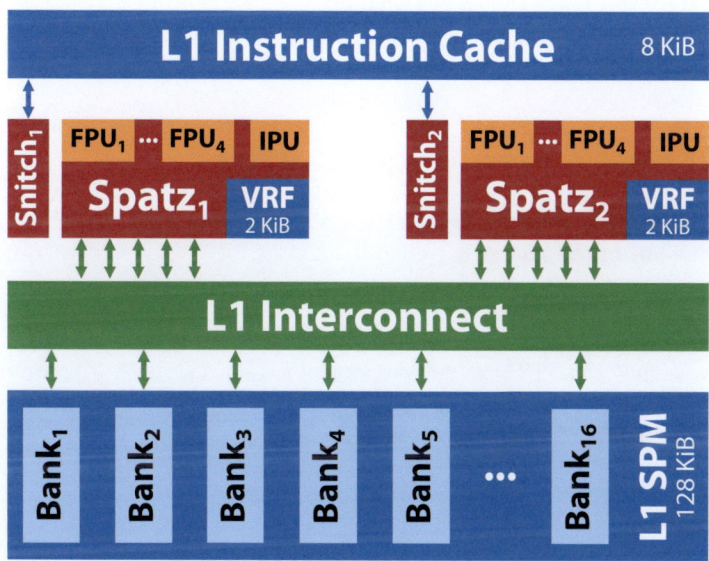

Figure 3.4: A shared-L1 cluster design with C vector PEs, each controlling F FPUs, and a multi-banked L1 SPM with 16 SRAM banks of 8 KiB each.

Kung's balance principle states that the machine's inherent balance point should be no greater than the algorithm's arithmetic intensity [88]. The architectural balance relationship is generalized by [96], considering the machine's degree of memory parallelism and the algorithm's degree of compute parallelism. Applying the relationship to the matrix multiplication kernel on our shared-L1 cluster, we find that

$$\frac{CF}{\beta} \leq \sqrt{Z}, \tag{3.3}$$

where β is the PE's bandwidth into the L1 SPM, and Z is the total capacity of a PE's VRF. Therefore, if we increase the VRF capacity by a factor α, i.e., $Z' = \alpha Z$, we can decrease the L1 bandwidth by a factor $\beta' = \beta/\sqrt{\alpha}$ without changing the machine's balance. In other words, we can trade L0 capacity against L1 bandwidth for relaxing the physical scalability issue of the PE-to-L1 interconnect. Furthermore, we can exploit the L0 capacity knob to optimize the cluster's energy efficiency.

3.2.1 Energy Consumption Model

In the following, we will analyze the energy consumption of each major component of the shared-L1 cluster.

FPUs

Assume that the FPUs achieve peak utilization, i.e., each execute one FMA per cycle. If it costs $\hat{\varepsilon}_{\text{FPU}}$ pJ for an FPU to execute an FMA instruction, the CF FPUs consume

$$\varepsilon_{\text{FPU}} = CF\hat{\varepsilon}_{\text{FPU}} \text{ pJ/cycle}. \tag{3.4}$$

PEs

It costs $\hat{\varepsilon}'_{\text{PE}}$ pJ for a PE to fetch, decode, and dispatch the i instructions of the kernel's hot loop. This loop is four instructions long in a typical vectorized matrix multiplication kernel [29]. Therefore, on average, each PE would consume $\hat{\varepsilon}_{\text{PE}} \overset{\Delta}{=} \hat{\varepsilon}'_{\text{PE}}/i$ pJ every cycle to fetch, issue, and dispatch the instructions of the hot loop, as long as the PE sustains an Instructions per Cycle (IPC) rate of 1.

The vector-SIMD abstraction amortizes this von-Neumann-related bottleneck in two ways. First, the instruction issue cost of each PE is amortized by its F FPUs running in parallel. Furthermore, since each

vector instruction potentially encodes enough micro-operations to keep
the FPU datapath busy for many cycles, the PE can keep the FPUs
completely utilized at a lower IPC. As discussed in Section 3.1, each of
the $32/\ell$ vector registers has $\ell \times \text{VLENB}/8$ elements. Since the FPUs produce
F elements per cycle, a vector instruction takes $\ell \times \text{VLENB}/8F$ cycles to
execute. In particular, our matrix multiplication implementation uses
$\ell = 4$. Therefore, the C PEs consume

$$\varepsilon_{\text{PE}} = \hat{\varepsilon}_{\text{PE}} \frac{2CF}{\text{VLENB}} \text{ pJ/cycle.} \tag{3.5}$$

L0 SCM

The F FPUs of each PE must each be able to fetch three double-
precision operands out of the VRF to achieve a peak collective result
throughput of F double-precision results per cycle without any hazards.
Since each SCM bank is $16\,\text{VLENB}$ B large, we can apply Equations (3.1)
and (3.2) to estimate that the L0 of the C PEs consume, on average,

$$\varepsilon_{\text{L0}} = C[3\hat{\varepsilon}_{\text{L0}}^{\text{read}}(8F, 16\,\text{VLENB}) + \hat{\varepsilon}_{\text{L0}}^{\text{write}}(8F, 16\,\text{VLENB})] \text{ pJ/cycle.} \tag{3.6}$$

L1 SPM

Since the FPUs operate on operands stored in the L0 SCM, we must
account for the data movement cost between the two memory hierarchy
levels in the shared-L1 cluster. We will split the analysis into transfers
from L0 to L1 and vice-versa. First, regardless of the L0 capacity,
we must move n^2 elements from the L0 to the L1, corresponding
to the n^2 elements of matrix $\mathbf{C}$. Assuming that the $n \times n$ matrix
multiplication kernel takes n^3/CF cycles to execute, i.e., we achieve
peak FPU utilization, it costs

$$\begin{aligned} \varepsilon_{\text{L0}\to\text{L1}} &= \frac{1}{n^3/CF} \left[\frac{n^2\hat{\varepsilon}_{\text{L0}}^{\text{read}}(8F, 16\,\text{VLENB})}{F} + n^2\hat{\varepsilon}_{\text{L1}}^{\text{write}} \right] \\ &= \frac{C\hat{\varepsilon}_{\text{L0}}^{\text{read}}(8F, 16\,\text{VLENB}) + CF\hat{\varepsilon}_{\text{L1}}^{\text{write}}}{n} \text{ pJ/cycle} \end{aligned} \tag{3.7}$$

to transfer the matrix multiplication results from the L0 to the L1.
Furthermore, we can use Equation (3.3) to estimate the cost of L1

to L0 transfers as a function of the L0 SCM capacity. We assume that a an FPU needs at least eight 8-B wide registers to achieve full utilization, a total capacity of 64 bytes. This accounts for four registers to store intermediate accumulations (since our FMA pipeline has four cycles of latency), and four registers to hold matrix operands. In this case, each FPU requires 2 words per cycle out of the L1 SPM, at a cost $\varepsilon_{\mathrm{L1}}^{\mathrm{read}} = 2\hat{\varepsilon}_{\mathrm{L1}}^{\mathrm{read}}$ pJ/cycle. Therefore, considering that each VRF has a capacity of $32\,\mathtt{VLENB}$ bytes, the C PEs spend

$$\varepsilon_{\mathrm{L1}\rightarrow\mathrm{L0}} = C\left[\frac{2F\hat{\varepsilon}_{\mathrm{L1}}^{\mathrm{read}} + 2\hat{\varepsilon}_{\mathrm{L0}}^{\mathrm{write}}(8F, 16\,\mathtt{VLENB})}{\sqrt{32\,\mathtt{VLENB}/64}}\right] \text{ pJ/cycle} \qquad (3.8)$$

copying elements from the L1 memory into the L0 VRF. Therefore, data transfers between the L0 and the L1 memories consume $\varepsilon_{\mathrm{L1}} = \varepsilon_{\mathrm{L0}\rightarrow\mathrm{L1}} + \varepsilon_{\mathrm{L1}\rightarrow\mathrm{L0}}$ pJ/cycle.

3.2.2   Energy Efficiency Optimization

Assume a shared-L1 cluster implementation with $C = 2$ PEs, each controlling $F = 4$ FPUs. The eight FPUs per cluster are similar to equivalent Snitch-based clusters [30]. Based on [92], we estimate that it costs $\hat{\varepsilon}_{\mathrm{PE}} = 3.1\,\mathrm{pJ}$ for Snitch to fetch, decode, and dispatch an instruction of the matrix multiplication and $\hat{\varepsilon}_{\mathrm{FPU}} = 13.3\,\mathrm{pJ}$ for an FPU to execute a double-precision FMA. We can use Equations (3.4) to (3.8) to estimate the energy consumption of the shared-L1 cluster as a function of the vector length $\mathtt{VLENB}$, as seen in Figure 3.5.

The energy breakdown highlights the benefit of a lightweight PE. The FPUs dominate the cluster's energy consumption, altogether responsible for about 60% of its energy consumption. On the other hand, Snitch is responsible for less than 1% of the cluster's energy consumption per cycle. Therefore, longer vectors do little to amortize the cluster's VNB since the instruction dispatch overhead is negligible. Furthermore, the breakdown also highlights the data movement overhead and the balance between L0 and L1 energy consumption, which together amount to 30% of the cluster's energy consumption.

We can exploit the L0/L1 energy consumption balance to optimize the energy efficiency of the cluster while running the matrix multiplication kernel. As seen in Figure 3.6, the cluster reaches a peak

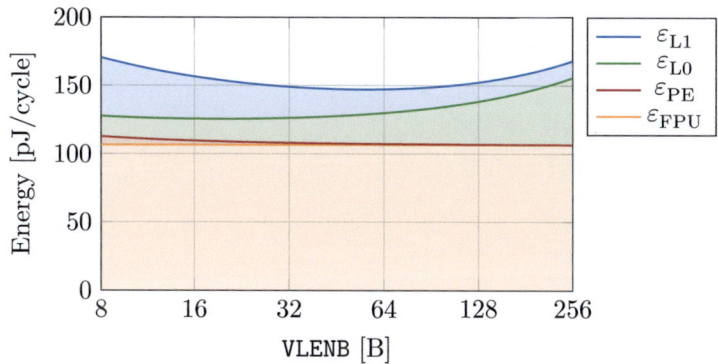

Figure 3.5: Breakdown of the energy consumption per cycle of the shared-L1 cluster, as a function of its vector length VLENB.

energy efficiency of $108.8\,\mathrm{GFLOPS_{DP}/W}$ for a vector length of 58 B. Rounding the vector length to a power-of-two, the cluster reaches an energy efficiency of $108.7\,\mathrm{GFLOPS_{DP}/W}$ for a vector length of 64 B.

Assuming VLENB $= 64$ B, each VRF is 2 KiB large, divided into two SCM banks with 32 rows of 32 B, 1 KiB large. Therefore, the $C = 2$ VRFs account for 4 KiB of L0 storage, compared to the 128 KiB of L1 SPM storage divided into 16 SRAM banks. In this scenario, the FPUs consume $\varepsilon_{\mathrm{FPU}} = 106.5\,\mathrm{pJ/cycle}$, the VRFs consume $\varepsilon_{\mathrm{L0}} = 22.7\,\mathrm{pJ/cycle}$, and the L1 SRAM banks consume $\varepsilon_{\mathrm{L1}} = 17.2\,\mathrm{pJ/cycle}$. Furthermore, each vector instruction takes 8 cycles to execute.

Applying Equation (3.3), we expect the PEs to fetch about 3 L1 words per cycle. Since the cluster has $M = 16$ SRAM banks, we have enough bandwidth for a Direct Memory Access (DMA) engine to concurrently load data from an external L2 memory into the L1 SPM while the PEs execute their computations.

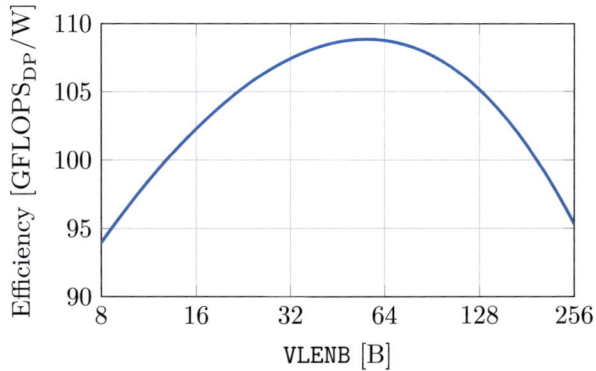

Figure 3.6: Energy efficiency of the cluster executing a 256 × 256 matrix multiplication kernel, as a function of the vector length VLENB.

3.3   Spatz: A Compact Vector Processing Unit

Spatz is a compact parametric VPU based on RVV version 1.0. Figure 3.7 shows the microarchitecture of $Spatz_F$, a Spatz instance with F FPUs, and its integration with a shared-L1 cluster. Snitch and Spatz form a Core Complex (CC) integrated within a shared-L1 cluster with 16 SRAM banks of 8 KiB each. This section describes Spatz' architecture, highlighting its main components.

3.3.1   Instruction Dispatch

Spatz implements the RVV ISA, version 1.0 [6]. We target the Zve64d subset, designed for embedded vector machines with 8, 16, 32, and 64-bit integer and floating-point support. Spatz is processor-agnostic and communicates with the scalar core through CORE-V's X-Interface accelerator interface [97]. Therefore, Spatz can be used with any core compatible with the X-Interface. Snitch's small footprint is particularly adapted for an execution paradigm where most of the computation happens in the vector unit.

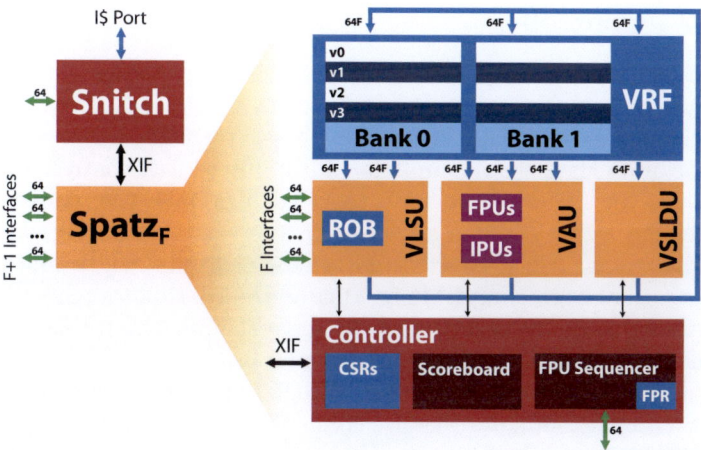

Figure 3.7: Microarchitecture of the Spatz-based CC, containing a Spatz instance with F FPUs, G Integer Processing Units (IPUs), and a Snitch scalar core. Snitch and Spatz communicate through CORE-V's X-Interface (XIF). Each Spatz has $F + 1$ 64-bit memory interfaces.

Since the accelerator interface specification is still in its infancy, it needs to be better adapted to the memory bandwidth requirements of a vector machine. We extended the X-Interface to consider cases where the accelerator makes its memory accesses through a memory interface wider than the scalar cores' one. Furthermore, we guarantee the ordering between Spatz' and Snitch's memory requests by stalling the scalar core's Load/Store Unit (LSU) while Spatz' VLSU executes a memory operation and vice-versa.

3.3.2 Controller

Snitch only pre-decodes vector instructions, dispatching the vector instruction and any scalar operands to the vector unit. Spatz' controller decodes the vector instructions, keeps track of their execution, and acknowledges their completion with Snitch. The controller also manages the CSRs of the RVV ISA. For example, the `vlen` CSR defines the vector length of all vector instructions. Another important CSR is `vtype`, which controls the vector elements' width and the vector register grouping LMUL. Finally, the controller orchestrates the execution of the vector instructions in the functional units. The scoreboard keeps track of the element-wise progression of each vector instruction. Hazards are handled through operand backpressure. In addition, Spatz supports vector chaining on an element basis.

Within the controller, the FPU Sequencer manages the scalar Floating-Point Register File (FPR). It implements a simple scoreboard to manage access to instructions that access the FPR, e.g., vector instruction with scalar floating-point operands and scalar floating-point instructions. Furthermore, the sequencer also manages scalar floating-point memory operations, hence its dedicated 64-bit memory interface. The FPU sequencer is only instantiated when Spatz is configured with FPU support.

3.3.3 Vector Register File

The VRF is the core of any vector machine. We implemented Spatz' VRF as a multi-banked multi-ported register file with two 3R1W banks. Each bank is implemented as a latch-based SCM. The VRF is centralized and serves all functional units. Its ports match the throughput requirements of the `vfmacc` instruction, which reads three double-precision operands to produce one double-precision result. Each bank is VLEN/2 bits wide, and each of the 32 VLEN-bit vector registers occupies one row in each of the two VRF banks. Each VRF port is $64F$-bit wide. We studied Spatz' VRF in Section 3.1.

The centralized VRF helps the implementation of vector instructions with irregular access patterns, e.g., vector slides ($\mathtt{vd}[i] \leftarrow \mathtt{vs}[i \pm \mathtt{shamt}]$) and reductions ($\mathtt{vd}[0] \leftarrow \Sigma_i \mathtt{vs}[i]$). Namely, a lane-based vector architecture, where the vector registers of the VRF are divided into lanes based on their index i, would need extra logic to shuffle the elements and store them in the correct lane, with important scalability implications [7].

3.3.4 Functional Units

Spatz has three functional units: the VLSU, the Vector Arithmetic Unit (VAU), and the VSLDU.

Vector Arithmetic Unit

The VAU is Spatz' main functional unit, hosting F transprecision FPUs [69] and G IPUs. Each FPU supports fp8, fp16, fp32, and fp64 computation. Each IPU supports 8, 16, 32, and 64-bit computation. All functional units maintain a throughput of 64 bit/cycle, regardless of the element width. Spatz completely decouples the number of integer G and floating-point F functional units. Therefore, we can tune Spatz to focus on integer or floating-point workloads. In this chapter, we will analyze the case where $G = 1$. Therefore, Spatz mainly focuses on floating-point workloads, with the integer datapath mainly used for address computations. Furthermore, we also reuse Spatz' datapath to execute some scalar instructions by reinterpreting scalar multiplications, integer divisions, and floating-point operations as vector instructions of unit length that commit into the GPR.

The analysis of this chapter is a "worst-case scenario" concerning the benefits of vector processing since the cluster's power consumption is completely dominated by the FPUs, as seen in Figure 3.5. Since integer computations are energetically cheaper than floating-point computations, data movement is responsible for a larger fraction of the cluster's energy consumption. Therefore, Spatz' impact on energy efficiency would be even higher in an integer computational system.

Vector Load/Store Unit

The VLSU handles the memory interfaces of Spatz, with support for unit-strided, constant-strided, and indexed memory accesses. The VLSU supports a parametric number of 64-bit wide memory interfaces. By default, the number of memory interfaces F matches the number of FUs in the design. This implies a peak operation per memory bandwidth ratio of $0.25\,\text{FLOP}_{\text{DP}}/\text{B}$.

Spatz' independent and narrow memory interfaces allow the reuse of the same 64-bit wide L1 SPM interconnect used by the scalar cores. The independent interfaces also allow fast execution of constant-strided and scatter-gather memory operations, as the VLSU does not need to coalesce requests into wide memory transfers. However, since the L1 SPM interconnect does not guarantee the ordering between the responses of the individual memory requests, a Reorder Buffer (ROB) sits between the memory interfaces and the VRF. The ROB ensures that the memory responses are written in order to the VRF, simplifying Spatz' vector chaining mechanism.

Vector Slide Unit

The VSLDU executes vector permutation instructions. Examples of such instructions include vector slide up/down and vector moves. The unit operates on two private $64F$-bit wide register banks. Between those two register banks, an all-to-all interconnect allows the implementation of any permutation scheme. Common operations, e.g., slides, produce results at $64F$ bits per cycle ratio, which matches Spatz' other functional units' peak throughput. The register banks also play a role similar to the ROB of Spatz' VLSU. The VSLDU does double-buffering on those registers and ensures that the unit commits to the VRF in $64F$-bit-wide words, simplifying the chaining calculation.

3.4 Performance Analysis

We implemented a shared-L1 cluster with two Spatz-based CCs, each controlling four FPUs and an IPU. The cluster has eight double-precision FPUs, 4 KiB of L0 VRF, 8 KiB of L1 Instruction Cache (I\$), and 128 KiB of SPM divided into 16 banks. The cluster's architecture can be seen in Figure 3.8.

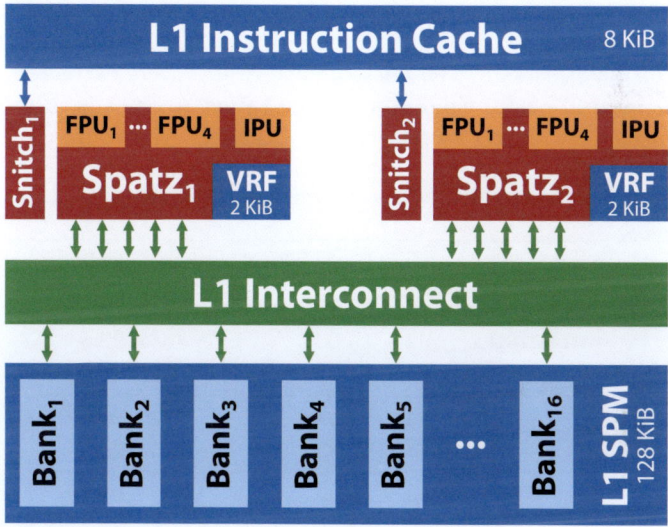

Figure 3.8: A shared-L1 cluster with two Spatz PEs, each controlling four multi-precision FPUs and one IPU, and a multi-banked L1 SPM with 128 KiB.

The Spatz-based cluster's performance metrics were then evaluated using a set of common data-parallel workloads,

matmul: Matrix multiplication between two $n \times n$ double-precision floating point matrices;

wid-matmul$_w$: Widening matrix multiplication of two $n \times n$ matrices of element width w into a matrix of width $2w$;

conv2d: 2D convolution of a double-precision floating point matrix of size $n \times n$ with a kernel of size 7×7.

dotp: Scalar product between two double-precision, floating-point vectors of length n;

fft: Implementation of Cooley-Tukey's Fast Fourier Transform (FFT) algorithm on a vector with n complex double-precision floating point samples.

All kernels operate on data residing in the cluster's L1 memory. Furthermore, all workloads operate on double-precision floating-point elements, except wid-matmul$_w$, which targets low-precision floating-point formats instead. The performance results were extracted with a cycle-accurate RTL simulation of the target workloads. Table 3.1 summarizes the cluster's performance and FPU utilization.

Table 3.1: Spatz cluster's multi-core performance and FPU utilization.

Benchmark	n	Perf. [FLOP/cycle]	Util. [%]
matmul	16	11.57	72.3
	32	15.00	93.8
	64	15.67	97.9
wid-matmul$_{16}$	64	57.53	89.9
	128	61.52	96.1
wid-matmul$_8$	64	112.9	88.2
	128	121.8	95.2
conv2d	32	14.91	93.2
	64	15.20	95.0
dotp	256	1.67	10.4
	4096	5.45	34.0
fft	128	7.03	43.9
	256	8.42	52.6

We will assess the PPA of the Spatz-based cluster against a baseline scalar cluster using eight Snitch cores as PEs. Snitch is a single-issue core, and its instruction issue rate limits the performance of the scalar shared-L1 cluster. Therefore, we will compare all cluster metrics against a specialized Snitch-based cluster implementing SSRs, a stream-based ISA extension. In particular, RISC-V floating point instructions access the FPR, while most bookkeeping instructions access the GPR instead [68]. SSRs exploit this to implement an energy efficient pseudo-double-issue execution between floating-point and integer instructions [92]. With hardware loops to remove branches and the elision of explicit memory load and store instructions, the Snitch-based SSR cluster is highly competitive with the Spatz cluster.

Figure 3.9 shows the speed-up of the Spatz-based and SSR-based clusters versus the Snitch-based baseline cluster, on a set of data-parallel workloads. For example, Spatz achieves $15.46\,\text{FLOP}_{\text{DP}}/\text{cycle}$ (96.6% of the theoretical peak performance) running a 64×64 matrix multiplication. This is $5.2\times$ higher than the baseline performance, $2.99\,\text{FLOP}_{\text{DP}}/\text{cycle}$. Meanwhile, the SSR-based cluster achieves up to $14.67\,\text{FLOP}_{\text{DP}}/\text{cycle}$, a $4.9\times$ speed-up versus the baseline. A similar trend is also seen for the *conv2d* kernel, with the Spatz-based and SSR-based achieving $6.8\times$ and $6.5\times$ speed-ups versus the baseline Snitch-based cluster, respectively. We also achieve high performance with the *wid-matmul*$_{16}$, a widening matrix multiplication that operates on 16-bit floating point operands and accumulates in a 32-bit register. In this scenario, the 64-bit ExSdotp [98] datapath of each FPU can execute four half-precision FMAs per cycle. For a large 128×128 matrix multiplication, Spatz reaches $61.5\,\text{FLOPS}_{\text{HP}}/\text{cycle}$, an FMA utilization of 96.1%. In comparison, the SSR-based cluster achieves $52.0\,\text{FLOPS}_{\text{HP}}/\text{cycle}$ on the same kernel, an FPU utilization 15.5% lower than that of the Spatz cluster. Similar trends are seen for lower precision, e.g., *wid-matmul*$_8$.

In general, SSR's performance drop on the *matmul* and *conv2d* kernels is explained due to banking conflicts in the L1 SPM, which degrade the performance of SSR-based solutions due to their high L1 SPM bandwidth requirements. However, the SSR-based cluster reaches much higher performance on the *dotp* kernel. The Spatz-based cluster reaches a $1.42\times$ speed-up versus the baseline, while the SSR-based cluster reaches a $3.00\times$ speed-up versus the baseline. This is due to *dotp*'s very low data reuse, since we must fetch two 64-bit elements from the L1 SPM for each FMA operation. The SSR-based cluster's large L1 SPM interconnect can supply this throughput to the cores. On the other hand, the smaller L1 interconnect of the Spatz cluster

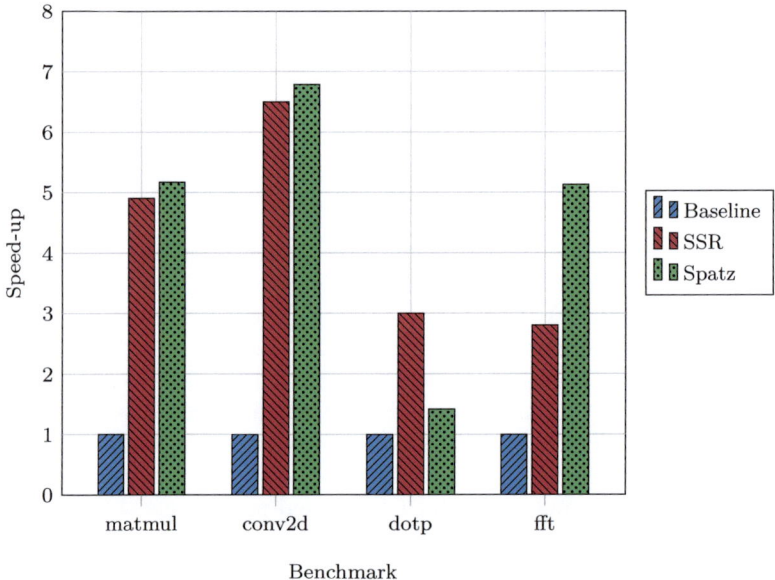

Figure 3.9: Spatz and SSR-based cluster's speed-ups versus the Snitch baseline cluster on a set of data-parallel workloads. All clusters have the same number of FPUs and, therefore, the same peak achievable performance.

can provide a single 64-bit element per cycle to each FPU, throttling the execution of the *dotp* kernel.

The *fft* kernel highlights the cluster's performance on less linear workloads. The SSR-based cluster achieves up to $3.84\,\mathrm{FLOPS_{DP}}/\mathrm{cycle}$ on an FFT with 128 double-precision complex samples, $2.8\times$ faster than the baseline cluster. The low speed-up is due to the frequent synchronization between the FFT stages [92]. On the other hand, the Spatz-based cluster achieves $7.03\,\mathrm{FLOPS_{DP}}/\mathrm{cycle}$ on the same problem, $5.13\times$ faster than the baseline. Spatz benefits from a fast scatter-gather execution mechanism (Section 3.3.4). Furthermore, since many FFT butterflies execute within a Spatz core, there is much less need for intra-Spatz atomic synchronization.

3.5 Implementation Results

In this section, we analyze the figures of merit of a Spatz-based shared-L1 cluster with key data-parallel workloads.

3.5.1 Methodology

We used Synopsys Fusion Compiler 2022.03 to synthesize, place, and route the cluster with GlobalFoundries' 12LPP 12 nm advanced FinFET node. We target a minimum operating frequency of 950 MHz under worst-case conditions (SS, 0.72 V, 125 °C). Furthermore, we used Synopsys PrimeTime 2022.02 for sign-off Static Timing Analysis (STA) and power estimation under nominal conditions (TT, 0.80 V, 25 °C) at 1 GHz using switching activities extracted from gate-level simulations.

3.5.2 Area Analysis and Breakdown

Each Spatz-based CC is about 1.01 MGE large. Figure 3.10 shows a post-implementation area breakdown of this CC, highlighting its main blocks. The VAU is the largest block, with its 694 kGE occupying 69% of the CC's area. Within the VAU, each FPU is 142 kGE large, with the remaining 126 kGE being occupied by the IPU—particularly by its 64-bit multiplier—and by the vector reduction logic. The VRF occupies 169 kGE, 17% of the CC's area. The remaining blocks have small contributions to the CC's area, with Snitch's 25 kGE, in particular, occupying only 2.5% of the CC's overall footprint.

The cluster was implemented as a block of dimensions 737 μm × 1003 μm, 0.74 μm^2 in total. Figure 3.11 shows the placed-and-routed Spatz-based shared-L1 cluster, highlighting its main hierarchical blocks. The cluster was implemented with an overall standard cell density of 52%. The L1 SPM interconnect and the VRF are routing-intensive blocks and therefore achieve a lower utilization of the standard cell area. For example, while highly-computational blocks such as the

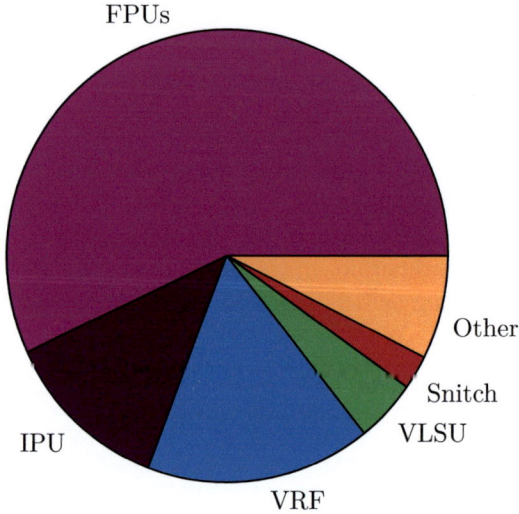

Figure 3.10: Post-implementation area distribution of the Spatz-based CC, 1.01-MGE-large. The slices correspond to (A) FPUs, 586 kGE; (B) IPU, 126 kGE; (C) VRF, 169 kGE; (D) VLSU, 46 kGE; (E) Snitch, 25 kGE; (O) other smaller blocks, e.g., VSLDU, FPU sequencer, and controller, 76 kGE.

FPUs achieve a standard cell utilization of 60%, the VRFs are placed and routed at a standard cell utilization of 49%.

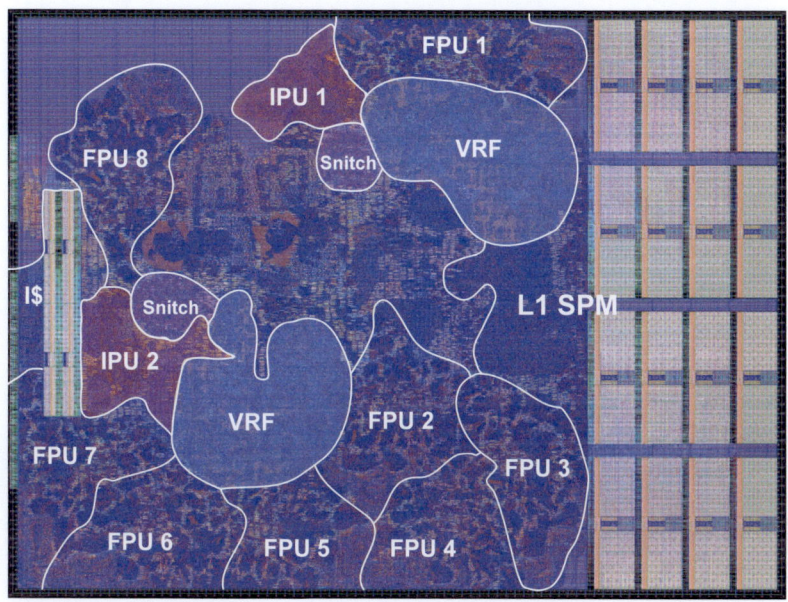

Figure 3.11: Placed-and-routed Spatz-based shared-L1 cluster, implemented as a 737 μm × 1003 μm block. The cluster's main blocks are highlighted: namely the Snitch cores, VRFs, IPUs, FPUs, L1 SPM, and I$.

The critical path of the Spatz cluster starts at Snitch's L0 I$, through the Snitch core, and Spatz' instruction decoder. This critical path is about 45-gates long. Furthermore, another long path starting at the L0 I$ and through Snitch (without leaving the core) is about the same length. Therefore, Spatz' inclusion does not limit the cluster operating frequency, which is the same as that of the scalar Snitch-based cluster [30].

3.5.3   Energy Breakdown

We measured the energy consumption per elementary operation of the Spatz-based cluster in nominal operating conditions at 1 GHz, using switching activities extracted from a gate-level simulation. Figure 3.12 shows Spatz' energy breakdown when running the `vload` (load), `vfadd` (floating-point addition), `vfmul` (multiplication), and `vfmacc` (multiply-accumulate) double-precision instructions.

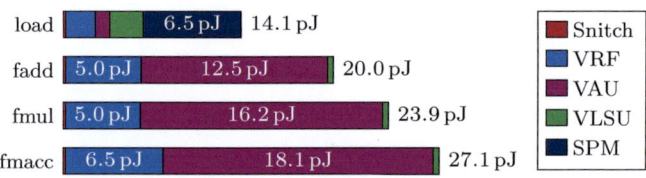

Figure 3.12: Breakdown of the Spatz-based cluster's energy consumption per elementary operation of several vector instructions.

Snitch consumes only 0.19 pJ per elementary operation while issuing instructions to the vector unit. The low energy requirement is because Snitch only needs to issue an instruction every 32 cycles to keep Spatz' FPUs fully utilized. For the computational operations, the FPUs are responsible for most of Spatz' energy consumption, up to 67% of the cluster's overall energy consumption when running the `vfmacc` instruction, followed by the VRF, which is responsible for 24%. Also of note is the reduction in VRF energy consumption between the `vfadd` and `vfmul` instructions, which read two operands and write one result to the VRF per cycle, and the `vfmacc` instruction, which reads an additional third operand.

Each FPU of the Spatz cluster consumes 18.1 pJ to execute an FMA operation while executing the `vfmacc` instruction. This ε_{FPU} value is 38% higher than what we estimated from [92]'s results, lowering our cluster's expected energy efficiency. It is unclear what lowered the energy efficiency of the FPUs. However, adding packed-SIMD support and including low-precision floating-point formats help justify the efficiency drop. The FPU implementation of [69], which has packed-SIMD vector support, consumes 26.1 pJ to execute a double-precision FMA operation, in line with what we measure in Spatz.

3.5.4 Power Consumption and Energy Efficiency

The Spatz cluster consumes 164 mW to execute the 64×64 *matmul* kernel. Therefore, the Spatz cluster achieves $15.7\,\text{GFLOPS}_{\text{DP}}$ running the 64×64 *matmul*, for an energy efficiency of $95.7\,\text{GFLOPS}_{\text{DP}}/\text{W}$. Figure 3.13 shows a breakdown of the power consumption of the cluster's hierarchical blocks.

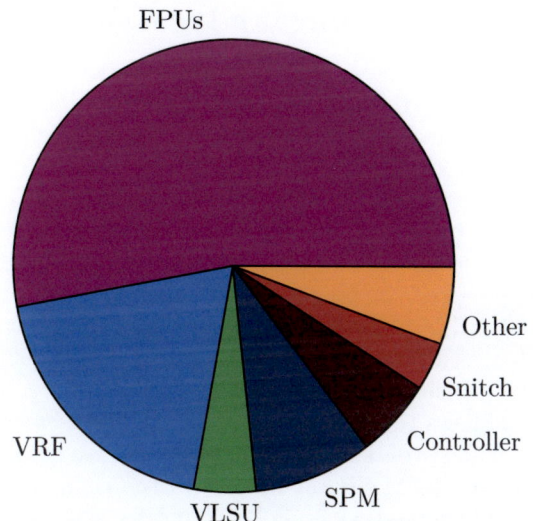

Figure 3.13: Average power consumption breakdown of the Spatz-based cluster running a 64×64 double-precision floating-point matrix multiplication. At 1 GHz, the cluster achieves $15.7\,\text{GFLOPS}_{\text{DP}}$ and consumes, on average, 164 mW to execute the workload at nominal operating conditions (TT, 0.80 V, 25 °C). The slices correspond to (A) FPUs, 87 mW; (B) VRF, 34 mW; (C) VLSU, 7.5 mW; (D) L1 SPM memories and interconnect, 15.4 mW; (E) Spatz' controller, 10.3 mW; (F) Snitch, 5.6 mW; (O) other smaller blocks, 9.1 mW.

The eight FPUs consume 87 mW, 54% of the cluster's overall power consumption. In comparison, the FPUs consumed only 41% of the power consumption of the equivalent Snitch-based cluster [92]. Furthermore, the VRF consumes 32 mW (19%). This power consumption ratio

mirrors the analysis from Section 3.2.2. However, we underestimated
the VRF energy consumption by 30%, probably due to timing pressure
in the VRF interface with the FUs. Spatz' VLSU consumes 7.0 mW
(4.2%), and the L1 SPM SRAMs and interconnect consume 15.4 mW
(8.0%). Finally, Spatz' controller consumes 9.3 mW (5.8%) and the
Snitch cores and I$ consume 5.6 mW (3.4%).

3.5.5   PPA comparison with the SSR-based cluster

We can use other Snitch-based cluster implementations in the literature
as proxies to evaluate the area of the Spatz-based cluster. First, the
Snitch-based cluster of [92] was implemented with GlobalFoundries'
22FDX FD-SOI node, containing 128 KiB of L1 SPM divided into
32 SRAM banks and eight double-precision FPUs. The cluster was
implemented as a block of dimensions 858 μm × 1046 μm, 0.90 mm^2 in
total. However, the cluster's FPUs did not have packed-SIMD support
when running low-precision operations, i.e., each FPU can only execute
one fp64, fp32, fp16, or fp8 operation per cycle. Therefore, an area
comparison between our design and the Snitch cluster [92] would be
biased towards the smaller footprint of the latter.

Figure 3.14 shows the area efficiency of the Spatz-based and SSR
based clusters on a set of data-parallel workloads. We did not consider
the area of the L1 SPM SRAM macros in the computation. Both
clusters are implemented with GlobalFoundries' 12LPP node, on a
similar target frequency. The SSR-based cluster [30] is 0.90-mm^2 large,
with 0.17 mm^2 occupied by 128 KiB of L1 SPM. The Spatz-based
cluster is 0.72 mm^2 large, with 0.14 mm^2 occupied by also 128 KiB
of L1 SPM. On the *matmul* kernel, the Spatz-based cluster reaches
up to 26.7 GFLOPS$_{DP}$/mm^2, 32% higher than the efficiency of the
SSR-based cluster. More strikingly, the Spatz-based cluster reaches an
area efficiency of 12.1 GFLOPS$_{DP}$/mm^2 on *fft* kernel, which is 2.3×
larger than the 5.3 GFLOPS$_{DP}$/mm^2 area efficiency of the SSR-based
cluster on the same kernel.

In terms of energy efficiency, Figure 3.15, the Spatz cluster reaches
up to 99.3 GFLOPS$_{DP}$/W. In general, Spatz achieves higher energy
efficiency than the SSR-based cluster for highly compute-intensive
workloads such as *matmul* and *conv2d*. For data-intensive workloads
such as *dotp*, Spatz reaches 47.4 GFLOPS$_{DP}$/W, 36% lower than the

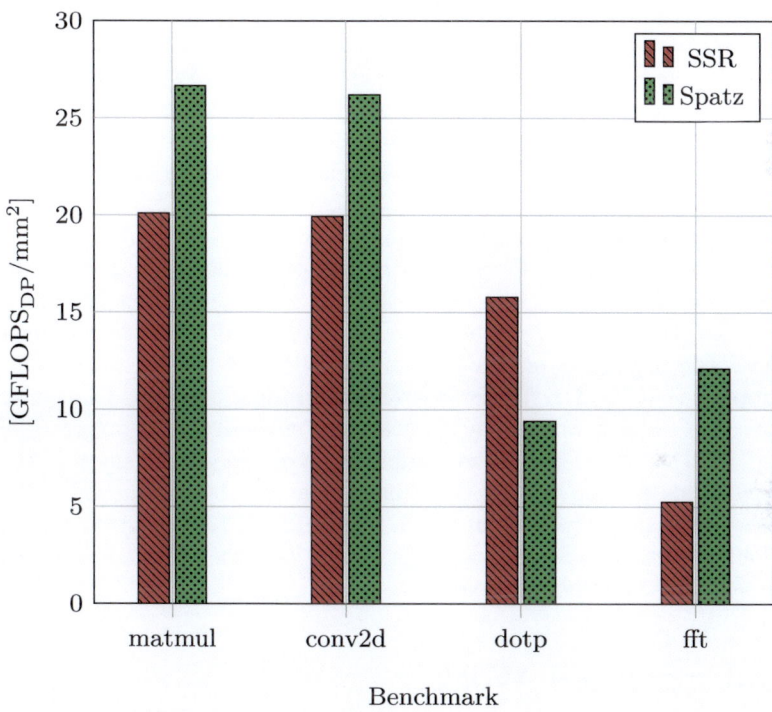

Figure 3.14: Area efficiency metric of the Spatz-based and SSR-based clusters on a set of data-parallel workloads. The considered cluster area does not include the area of the L1 SPM SRAM macros.

energy efficiency of the SSR-based cluster on the same workload. The dot product workload in particular has very little data reuse. Therefore, transferring data from the L1 SPM to the L0 VRF does not improve data locality, explaining the energy efficiency drop. Finally, for the *fft* kernel, Spatz reaches $72\,\text{GFLOPS}_{DP}/\text{W}$, 45% larger than the energy efficiency of the SSR-based cluster.

Spatz efficiency scales well for lower-precision formats. For example, the Spatz cluster achieves $358\,\text{GFLOPS}_{HP}/\text{W}$ on a 128×128 *wid-matmul*$_{16}$ matrix multiplication between fp16 elements. This is $3.74\times$ higher than the peak efficiency achieved by the *matmul* double-precision kernel, with further energy efficiency gains possible with the ExSdotp [98] extension.

Finally, we analyze the cluster's combined area and energy efficiency in Figure 3.16. Thanks to the small footprint and highly-competitive energy efficiency of the Spatz cluster, it reaches up to $171\,\text{GFLOPS}_{DP}/\text{mm}^2/\text{W}$ on the *conv2d* workload. This is 30% larger than the peak area/energy efficiency of the SSR-based cluster. This implies that, under the same area constraints, a shared-L1 cluster based on Spatz would reach an energy efficiency 30% larger than an SSR-based cluster. The combined area/energy efficiency of the Spatz cluster is 20% lower than that of the SSR-based cluster for the *dotp* workload. However, for an *fft*, Spatz' $125\,\text{GFLOPS}_{DP}/\text{mm}^2/\text{W}$ is double the achieved combined area/energy efficiency of the SSR-based cluster on the same workload.

3.6   Related Work

The long history of vector processing limits the application of a vector processor as the PE of a shared-L1 cluster. From its inception with the Cray-1 [46] machine to the modern Fujitsu A64FX [4], vector processing has always been associated with supercomputers. Vector processors usually include all microarchitectural tricks to increase ILP, e.g., renaming, out-of-order execution, speculation, and branch prediction, which increase the area and energy overhead of classical high-performance vector processors. As a result, typical vector processors are implemented with long vectors to minimize the VNB-related overhead of such complex instruction issue mechanisms [29], [91].

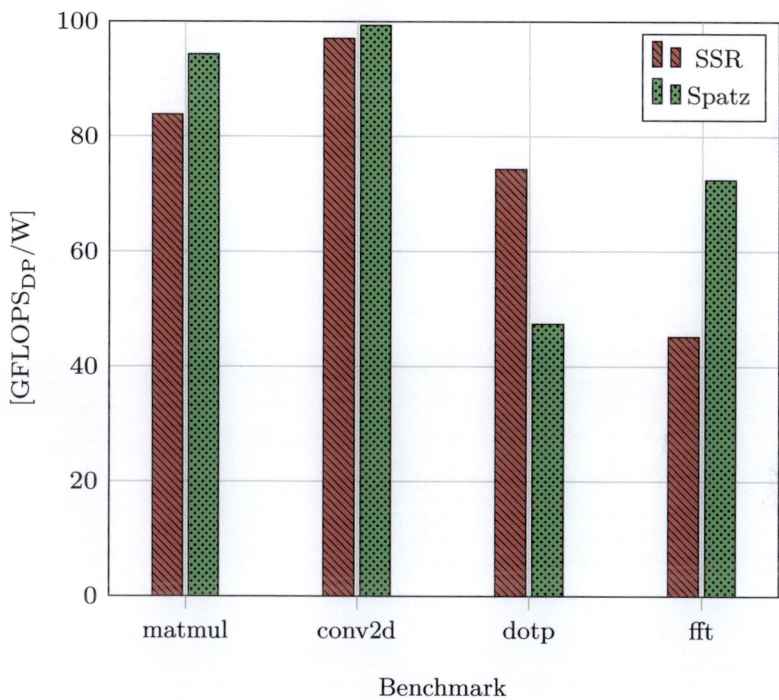

Figure 3.15: Energy efficiency metric of the Spatz-based and SSR-based clusters on a set of data-parallel workloads.

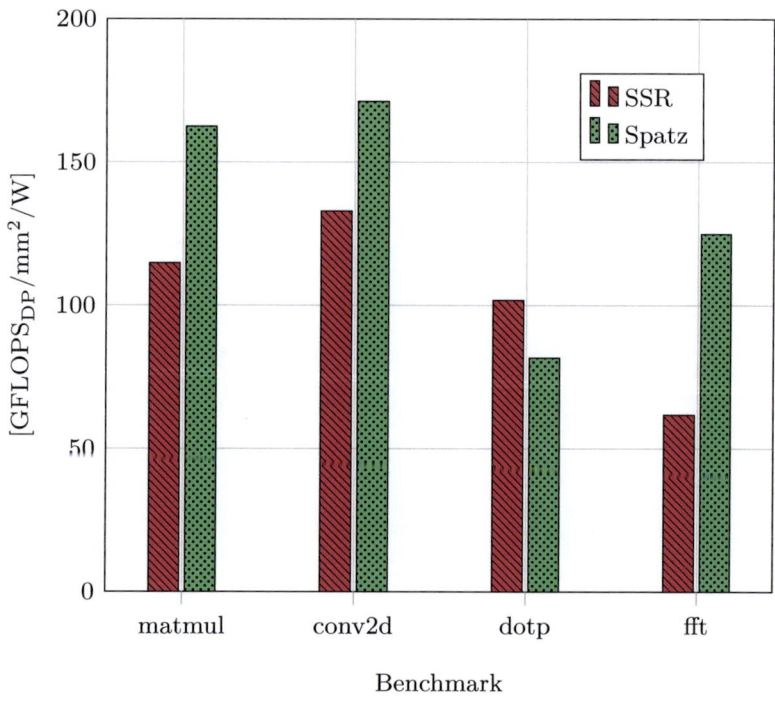

Figure 3.16: Combined area/energy efficiency metric of the Spatz-based and SSR-based clusters on a set of data-parallel workloads. The considered cluster area does not include the area of the L1 SPM SRAM macros.

However, the defining characteristic of a vector processor is not ILP but DLP. This key observation has led to the design of streamlined vector cores where most hardware resources are dedicated to DLP support [7]. In this vein, the idea of an embedded vector machine is gaining traction with modern vector ISAs. Arm's MVE [59] and the Zve* subset of RISC-V's RVV ISA [6] target small vector machines for edge data-parallel processing.

Arm's Helium MVE is an optional extension proposed as part of the Armv8.1-M architecture [59]. The Arm Cortex-M55 [60] is the first processor to ship with support to MVE. However, no quantitative assessment of the performance and efficiency of a Cortex-M55 silicon implementation has been reported in the open literature; hence, a quantitative comparison with Spatz is impossible. For what concerns a qualitative comparison, we observe that the Helium MVE defines eight 128-bit wide vector registers as aliases to the floating-point register file. On the M55 processor, the 64-bit datapath means Helium operates on a "dual-beat regime," i.e., vector instructions execute in two cycles. This is enough to overlap the execution of successive vector instructions in different processing units without a superscalar core. However, the scalar core must frequently issue instructions to the Helium-capable processing unit to keep its pipeline busy. In contrast, Spatz' longer vector registers and RVV's LMUL register grouping allow for a maximum vector length of 4096 bits, keeping Spatz busy for 32 cycles. This long execution, as shown by our results, massively amortizes the energy overhead of the scalar core, which is a considerable part of the overall energy consumption even on extremely data-parallel kernels such as the matrix multiplication.

In general, architectures based on a tightly-coupled cluster of small vector processors have not been explored in past literature, possibly due to the novelty of small vector machines. Many vector processing units have been proposed in recent years, thanks to new vector ISAs such as Arm's SVE [59] and RISC-V's RVV [6]. Examples of such large-scale vector architectures based on the RVV ISA include BSC's Vitruvius [91], PULP Platform's Ara [7], and SiFive's P270 [99] and X280 [100] cores. However, most of those units are large 64-bit vector processors supporting double-precision floating-point operations, attached to high-performance application-class scalar processors; hence they achieve comparatively low efficiency due to the complex micro-architecture of their supporting scalar cores [51].

Small-scale vector units have been proposed for Field-Programma-ble Gate Arrays (FPGAs), where the leanness of the vector processor is a constraint due to limited FPGA resources. Vicuna [101] is a timing-predictable RVV-compliant vector processor, synthesized on a Xilinx Series 7 FPGA. Its VRF was implemented as a multi-ported Random Access Memory (RAM) due to concerns with timing anomalies with a multi-banked VRF. Vicuna's largest configuration achieves up to 117 OP/cycle on an 8-bit 1024 × 1024 matrix multiplication kernel. Vicuna's multi-ported VRF is similar to Spatz' VRF. There is no study about Vicuna's scaling nor an ASIC implementation of this architecture, making a power or energy efficiency comparison with Spatz difficult. The same can be said about other small-scale RVV vector units demonstrated on FPGAs [102], [103].

3.7   Conclusions

The computing cluster comprising a set of PEs sharing tightly-coupled L1 memory through a low-latency interconnect is a common albeit ubiquitous architectural template. This cluster can be replicated and interconnected through a latency-tolerant NoC to build large-scale com-puting systems. Therefore, optimizing the cluster's energy efficiency is the key challenge to improving the overall system's efficiency.

We used Kung's architectural balance [88] concept to amortize the energy cost of accessing the L1 SPM by tuning the capacity of the L0 memory private to each PE. We developed a mathematical model to analyze the energy consumption of the cluster running a double-precision floating-point matrix multiplication kernel as a function of the L0 size. We concluded that a very small L0 memory is needed to balance the L0 and L1 data access costs. Based on this result, we explored compact vector processing units as an option to build the PEs of shared-L1 clusters. This differs from typical vector processors, whose VRFs is much larger to amortize the overhead of typically-used ILP techniques (e.g., renaming and out-of-order execution).

We present Spatz, an open-source compact VPU based on the RVV specification [6], and use it as the building block of a high-performance computing system. We amortize the VNB by coupling Spatz with the lightweight Snitch core [92]. We focus on a cluster containing eight multi-precision FPUs and 128 KiB of L1 SPM. We implemented this cluster as a 0.74-mm^2-large macro with GlobalFoundries' Fin-FET 12 nm node at an operating frequency of 950 MHz in worst-case operating conditions (SS, 0.72 V, 125 °C).

Spatz improves both the area and energy efficiency of compute-intensive workloads on programmable architectures. Spatz reaches up to 99.3 GFLOPS$_{\mathrm{DP}}$/W on a 2D convolution, and 95.7 GFLOPS$_{\mathrm{DP}}$/W on a 64×64 double-precision floating-point matrix multiplication. Furthermore, Spatz' peak area/energy efficiency, 171 GFLOPS$_{\mathrm{DP}}$/mm^2/W, is 30% larger than that of a specialized, state-of-the-art stream-based programmable cluster. In other words, under the same area constraint, a Spatz-based cluster would reach a peak energy efficiency 30% larger than a cluster based on streamer PEs. Spatz' high area/energy efficiency trend is also valid when running an FFT. For this workload, Spatz reaches 125 GFLOPS$_{\mathrm{DP}}$/mm^2/W, highlighting the resilience of this architecture to compute-intensive workloads with a non-linear data access pattern.

This chapter shows that vector processors are a sound approach for building PE for shared-L1 clusters. The addition of a VRF acting as L0 memory allows for a reduction in the bandwidth requirement in the L1 interconnect. Given the slowdown of wiring and SRAM technology scaling, this bandwidth reduction simplifies the cluster's low-latency interconnect, the typical factor limiting the physical implementation of this cluster.

Chapter 4

MemPool: A Scaled-Up, Low-Latency Shared-L1 Manycore System

Despite its ubiquity, the cluster of tightly-coupled cores sharing low-latency L1 memory usually only scales up to low tens of cores. In this Chapter, we defy this constraint with MemPool [14], a scaled-up manycore cluster with 256 cores sharing 1 MiB of SPM within at most five cycles of latency in the absence of contention.

4.1 Introduction

Modern workloads have remarkably diverse computational requirements. Besides being highly compute-intensive, today's algorithms are typically embarrassingly parallel—e.g., image processing and machine learning applications—and have many independent dataflow threads—e.g., ray tracing and micro-kernels on servers. Furthermore, the failure of Dennard scaling [3] has implied a power wall for computing, limiting processor frequencies [104]. Core count scaling has been used instead to achieve high performance under a limited power budget. Multi-core architectures have been the *de facto* standard for exploiting TLP [105] on irregular workloads since the last decade.

Traditional multi-core architectures are usually built by replicating shared-L1 clusters with a fairly low core count. Such traditional Central Processing Units (CPUs) have a simple programming model. The task of extracting ILP from the instruction flow is shifted toward the compiler, the hardware, or the programmer. Compilers can extract ILP from the instruction flow and translate it to VLIW instructions [106], but control flow limits the performance of this approach [107]. Large-scale CPUs like Intel's Sapphire Rapids exploit ILP through complex superscalar processors with support for four threads per core and deep out-of-order buffers [108]. However, such complex tiles and cores have a significant overall power overhead. Finally, the SIMD abstraction is another option to improve the parallelism of the instruction flow. SIMD instructions operate on multiple data with a single instruction. While SIMD is an efficient option to exploit parallelism, it targets the restrictive DLP algorithms and has limited capability to handle data dependencies [57].

Computer architects must devise creative ways to push performance past the scaling limitations of the computing cluster. For example, SMs implement a SIMT scheme [44], replicating functional units that work in lock-step and sacrificing control over individual cores, introducing problems such as thread divergence, leading to underutilized functional units on applications with irregular data access patterns. A different approach to scaling beyond tens of cores is replicating the simple compute cluster. This approach is found in GPUs and in high-performance accelerators such as Manticore [86] or Esperanto's ET-SoC-1 [109]. However, multiple clusters with isolated L1 memories expand the memory hierarchy and introduce communication overhead between clusters. Furthermore, the additional hierarchy significantly complicates the parallelization and the programming model.

This chapter tackles the challenge of building a general-purpose manycore system with a large, low-latency shared L1 memory. It avoids the problems related to SIMT or multi-cluster designs while maintaining the benefits of the compute cluster architecture. MemPool is an open-source, parametric, and flexible manycore architecture scalable to hundreds of independently-programmable 32-bit RISC-V cores sharing a large amount of L1 memory. Specifically, we focus on a MemPool implementation with 256 cores and 1 MiB of L1 SPM accessible within, at most, five cycles of zero-load latency.

MemPool runs at 700 MHz in typical conditions. The critical path of the design is dominated by wire propagation delay (37%), with 27 out of its 36 gates being either buffers or inverter pairs. Its PE-to-L1 interconnect has an average latency of fewer than six cycles, even for a heavy injected load of 0.33 request/core/cycle. Our addressing scheme helps to keep the memory requests in local banks accessible within one cycle, which leads to performance gains of up to 20% in real-world benchmarks. This scheme is also highly effective in energy consumption since local memory requests consume only half of the energy required for remote memory accesses. In a nutshell, we demonstrate in this chapter that we can scale the core count of an L1-shared cluster to ten times more cores than previously considered achievable, with cycle counts on various benchmarks that are comparable with an ideal, non-implementable full-crossbar baseline.

4.2 Architecture

MemPool is a flexible and parametric manycore architecture with 256 individually-programmable cores sharing 1 MiB of low-latency L1 SPM. The next sections detail its architecture in a bottom-up fashion.

4.2.1 Processing Element

The PEs of MemPool are compact RISC-V-based cores. To scale the architecture, they must have a small footprint, tolerate and hide the L1 interconnect latency and be extensible to support custom instructions. Snitch, a single-stage 32-bit RISC-V core supporting the RV32I instruction set, meets these requirements [92]. While Snitch is a single-issue core, it features a scoreboard supporting multiple outstanding instructions, which is crucial for two reasons. First, it allows issuing multiple outstanding load or store requests without blocking the pipeline if there are no RAW dependencies. Second, Snitch features an accelerator port to add complex, pipelined functional units such as a multiplier. Snitch can offload suitable instructions to those functional units and continue its operation.

We extend Snitch for MemPool by adding the capability to reorder load responses and retire them out-of-order, which is required due to MemPool's NUMA interconnect not giving ordering guarantees for responses. By supporting up to eight outstanding transactions, Snitch can completely hide the L1 interconnect's five cycles of latency through instruction scheduling with headroom for further load-induced latency.

We configure Snitch to support RV32IMAXpulpimg. The `Xpulpimg` ISA [110] is supported by a pipelined IPU connected to Snitch's accelerator port. Instructions like Multiply-Accumulate (MAC) and load-post-increment drastically reduce the instruction count for data-parallel kernels, resulting in a significant speedup. To fit the new changes, we extend Snitch's register file to have three read ports to supply all the operands necessary for a MAC and two write ports to reduce contention when retiring instructions with different latencies.

4.2.2   L1 Interconnect Topologies

MemPool's fundamental implementation question is connecting 256 cores and 1 MiB of L1 SPM while maintaining flexibility, high throughput, and low latency. We tackle the throughput constraint by implementing the L1 as 1024 SRAM banks of 1 KiB each. Therefore, we can rephrase MemPool's fundamental implementation question as connecting 256 cores with 1024 SRAM banks.

The straightforward implementation of the L1 memory interconnect is a fully-connected 256×1024 logarithmic crossbar. This topology has no internal routing conflicts, thanks to dedicated paths between each master-slave pair providing the highest possible throughput. Unfortunately, crossbars have quadratic area cost [111], which is prohibitively expensive at MemPool's scale. So instead, we opted to implement this interconnect hierarchically, with highly-connected islands of cores and SRAM banks, the *tiles*, connected at an upper hierarchy. Figure 4.1 shows one tile architecture with its interconnects in more detail. The tiles contain four cores and 16 SRAM banks—i.e., 16 KiB of total capacity—accessible within the tile in a single cycle.

The cores share K master ports to access remote tiles. An address decoder at the output of the cores statically decides where to send the cores' requests. Furthermore, each tile has K slave request ports, receiving memory requests from remote tiles. There is a register

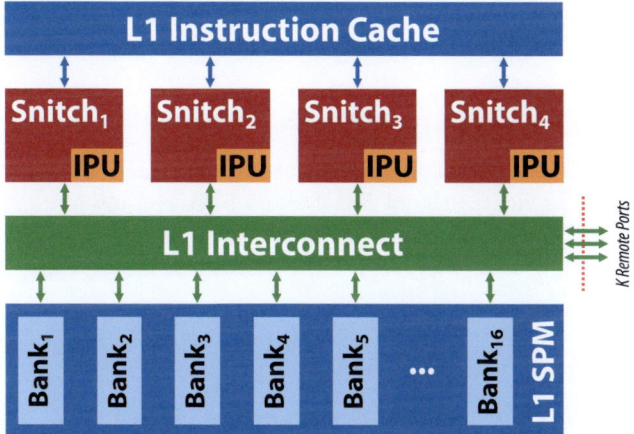

Figure 4.1: Tile architecture. Each Snitch-based CC has an IPU implementing the `Xpulpimg` ISA. Dashed lines indicate a register.

boundary at the master request and response ports, which breaks timing paths between tiles. Both request and response interconnects are realized as fully-connected crossbars. Requests hold metadata to route them back to the correct core and ensure their proper ordering by the ROB. Finally, inside each tile, we have a 4-way L1 I$. The cache has a 32-bit AXI refill port. These ports can be connected to a low-overhead refill network (e.g., a ring), which is noncritical, and hence it is not further discussed in this work.

We evaluated three network topologies for MemPool's global L1 SPM interconnection network between tiles.

Top_1: Single 64×64 Radix-4 Butterfly

Each tile in this configuration has a single remote port for communication with remote tiles, i.e., $K = 1$. A single 64×64 radix-4 butterfly network, with a single pipeline stage midway through its $\log_4(64) = 3$ layers, connects the tiles. Therefore, data in any remote memory bank can be accessed within five cycles. Inside the tile, two 4×1 crossbars arbitrate the core requests and the memory responses. This design creates a bottleneck at the tile boundary, since the traffic of four cores is concentrated through a single remote memory port.

Top$_4$: Four Parallel 64×64 Radix-4 Butterflies

To reduce the traffic bottleneck at the tile boundary, we evaluated a system that replicates the global 64×64 butterfly interconnect four times. That is, each tile has four master request and response ports, each associated with their own 64×64 interconnect. Each master request port is dedicated to a core.

Top$_H$: Hierarchical Approach

Both Top$_1$ and Top$_4$ have a uniform access pattern, with a 5-cycle access latency between any two tiles. Hence, requests between two tiles must cross the whole interconnect, regardless of how physically close they are. This leads to decreased efficiency and increased routing congestion due to longer paths toward the center of the design. We introduce a new hierarchy level to maintain the bandwidth of Top$_4$ while avoiding long detours between neighboring tiles. Figure 4.2a shows a *group* of 16 tiles. Cores access remote memory banks in the same local group within three cycles thanks to the local interconnect, a 16×16 fully-connected crossbar.

MemPool comprises four groups, as shown in Figure 4.2b. Inside each group, the *north* (N), *northeast* (NE), and *east* (E) 16×16 fully-connected crossbars are responsible for communication between groups. Each tile has corresponding N, NE, and E ports, and a *local* (L) port to access tiles within the same local group. A 4×4 crossbar inside each tile routes the requests to the correct port. A register boundary at the groups' initiator interfaces increases the zero-load access latency of a memory bank in a remote local group to 5 cycles.

4.3   Hybrid Addressing Scheme

MemPool has a sequentially interleaved memory mapping across all memory banks in order to minimize banking conflicts. However, this also implies that most memory requests target remote tiles. Optimally, all cores' requests would remain in the local tile, which would lower the

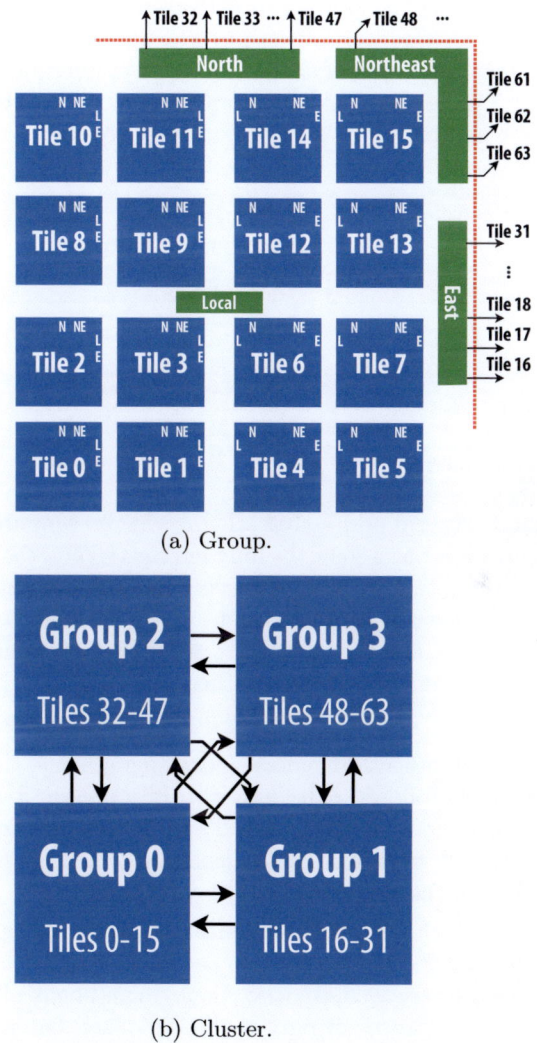

(a) Group.

(b) Cluster.

Figure 4.2: Top$_H$ architecture. Dashed lines indicate a register.

latency and power consumption. With the scrambling logic, visualized
in Figure 4.3, we transform an interleaved memory map into a *hybrid*
one, by adding *sequential regions* in which contiguous addresses target
a single tile. The top half shows the classical fully interleaved memory
scheme. The address and memory map at the bottom is a hybrid
memory map created by swapping the address bits.

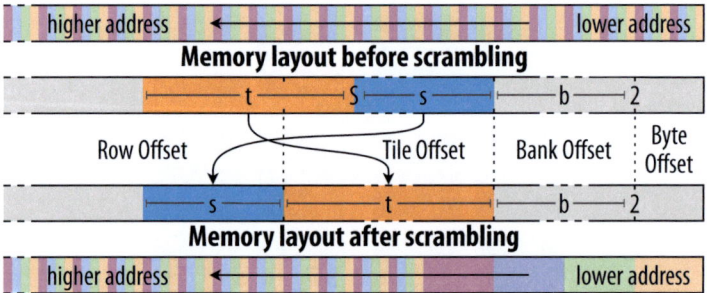

Figure 4.3: Hybrid addressing scheme via the scrambling logic. The
upper and lower parts show the fully interleaved and the hybrid memory
map, respectively. The outer bars visualize the memory map, with the
shades representing different tiles to which the addresses are mapped.
The inner bars are the addresses, with the scrambling in between
leading from one scheme to the other.

With an interleaved memory addressing scheme, the addresses are
interpreted as follows. The first two bits are the byte offset, after
which b bits identify one of the 2^b banks of each tile. The next t
bits distinguish between the 2^t tiles. The remaining address bits are
interpreted as the row offset within each bank.

Consider each tile with a sequential memory region of 2^S bytes, or
2^s rows in the tile's banks. Since the banks inside the same tile are
still accessed interleaved, we leave the byte and bank offsets untouched.
The next s bits represent part of the tile offset, but we need them to
represent the banks' next row within the same tile. Therefore, we shift
them t bits to the left—where the row offset starts—and fill them with
the t bits we replaced. This creates 2^t sequential regions, one for each
tile. In total, we dedicate the first 2^{S+t} bytes to sequential regions.

We leave the subsequent bytes interleaved by conditionally applying the scrambling to addresses inside the sequential memory region.

The hybrid addressing scheme's key benefit is giving the programmer the additional capability to store private data, such as a core's stack, in the same tile. It reduces the number of transactions between tiles, making better use of the tiles' fully-connected, high-throughput crossbar. Sequential memory regions are prone to banking conflicts. However, by only mapping private data to the sequential region, the cores' accesses remain distributed across all banks. In contrast to aliasing or completely private memories, we do not complicate programmability but, by applying the same address transformation for all cores, give all cores the same memory view and keep the L1 memory region contiguous and shared. The beneficiary of the sequential region are programs that make heavy use of the stack or work on local data.

4.4 L1 Interconnect Analysis

In this section, we analyze the three proposed network topologies in terms of average latency and throughput, as a function of the injected load λ, measured in requests per core per cycle. The results were extracted using an extensive cycle-accurate RTL simulation. Each core is replaced by a synthetic traffic generator, which generates new requests following a Poisson process of rate λ. The requests have a random uniformly distributed destination memory bank.

4.4.1 Latency/Throughput

Figure 4.4a shows the different topologies' throughput, with an increasing load. For a load of 0.10 request/core/cycle, Top_1 becomes congested, while Top_4 and Top_H support almost four times that load, about 0.38 request/core/cycle. Top_H's throughput is slightly higher than Top_4's throughput, thanks to its smaller diameter.

As a counterpart to Figure 4.4a, Figure 4.4b shows the average round-trip latency of the requests for an increasing load. It elevates the point where the topologies become congested by showing the explosion of the average latency. The average latency of Top_H only reaches 6 cycles at a network load of 0.33 request/core/cycle. Thanks to Top_H's

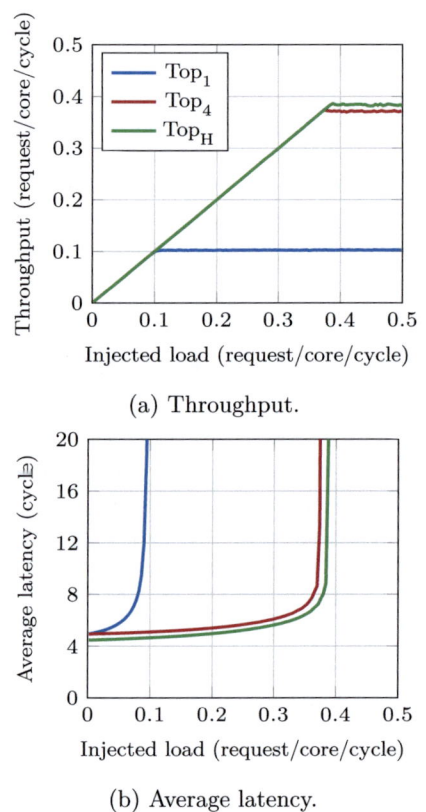

(a) Throughput.

(b) Average latency.

Figure 4.4: Analysis of the proposed network topologies, in terms of throughput and average latency, as a function of the injected load.

three-cycle latency to a group, it achieves a smaller average latency than Top_4. Both results imply that the Top_1's traffic concentration at the tiles' ports leads to unacceptable performance degradation.

4.4.2 Hybrid Addressing Scheme Analysis

To evaluate the performance impact of the hybrid addressing scheme, we analyze Top_H taking the hybrid addressing scheme into account. The traffic generator creates requests to the local tile's sequential region with probability ρ, and outside with probability $1 - \rho$.

Figure 4.5a shows the throughput of Top_H for different ρ. It shows a clear trend of an increased throughput for a larger ρ. The scrambling logic, or using local memory in general, can vastly improve the system's throughput by preventing the congestion in the global interconnect, besides lowering the overall average access latency as seen in Figure 4.5b. An application making 25% of its accesses to the stack, mapped at the sequential region, can gain up to 50% in performance by using the scrambling logic, without changing the code.

4.5 Physical implementation

In this section, we analyze the feasibility of MemPool using the Top_1, Top_4, and Top_H topologies. We also analyze them in terms of power, performance, and area results.

4.5.1 Methodology

MemPool was synthesized, placed, and routed for GlobalFoundries 22FDX 22 nm FD-SOI technology using Synopsys Fusion Compiler 2022.03. Each tile has 2 KiB of instruction cache, and 16 KiB of SPM—i.e., the MemPool cluster has 1 MiB of L1 SPM. We target an operating frequency of 500 MHz at worst-case conditions (SS, 0.72 V, 125 °C). MemPool's power results were extracted with switching activities obtained by simulating the benchmarks on a netlist back-annotated with post-implementation delay information. We used Synopsys PrimeTime 2022.03 to carry out sign-off STA and power analysis at typical conditions (TT, 0.80 V, 25 °C).

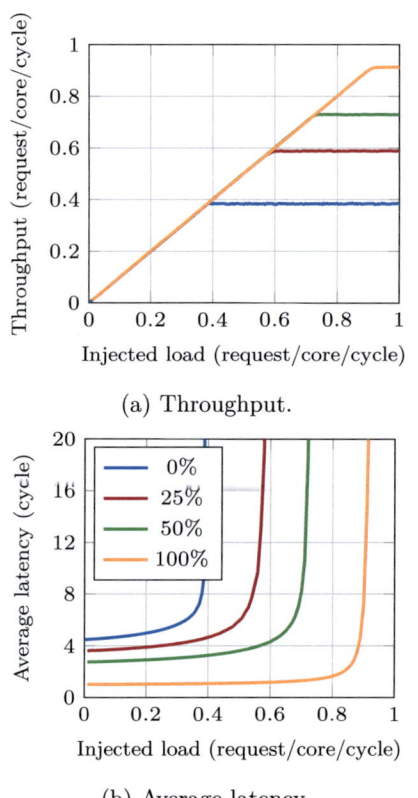

(a) Throughput.

(b) Average latency.

Figure 4.5: Network analysis of Top_H with our hybrid addressing scheme, as a function of the injected load, for different probabilities of requesting data in the local tile's sequential region ρ.

4.5.2   Feasibility Analysis

Due to the size and the regularity of MemPool's design, we evaluated MemPool's feasibility with a hierarchical implementation flow. The tile was implemented as a square $425\,\mu m \times 425\,\mu m$ macro ($908\,kGE$). The most complex tile—i.e., Top_H's tile—is shown in Figure 4.6. The tile's critical path (53 FO4 gates long) starts at a register after the instruction cache, passing through a Snitch core and the request interconnect, before arriving at a SPM bank. The tile achieves a utilization of 72.8%, the area is dominated by the I\$ (23.6%) and by the L1 SPM (40.2%).

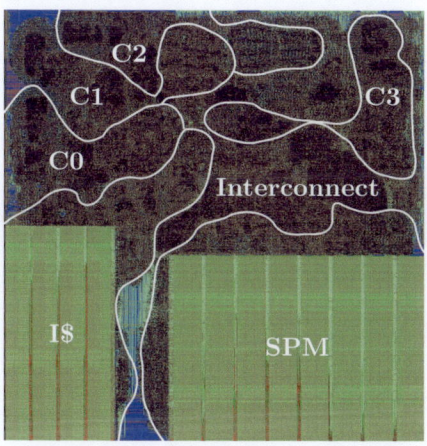

Figure 4.6: Placed and routed Top_H tile, as a $425\,\mu m \times 425\,\mu m$ macro.

We evaluated MemPool's feasibility by implementing this design as a $4.6\,mm \times 4.6\,mm$ macro, i.e., 55% of the design area is covered by the tiles. The area overhead was driven by congestion, which is the main constraint of the design, particularly at the center of the design.

Figure 4.7a shows the placed-and-routed Top_1 macro. With its 64×64 radix-4 butterfly topology, the connection between any two remote tiles needs to cross the whole network, regardless of the physical distance between the tiles. Therefore, all wiring and cells are drawn towards the center of the design, which is heavily congested. Top_4 is four times more congested than Top_1, which is enough to make it physically infeasible with reasonable clock rates. The placed-and-routed Top_H macro can be see in Figure 4.7b. Similarly to Top_1, there is a high cell and wiring density at the center of the design, due to the connection between the two diagonally placed groups (Figure 4.2b). However, unlike $Top_{1/4}$, Top_H distributes the cells and the wiring through the use of the directional group interconnects.

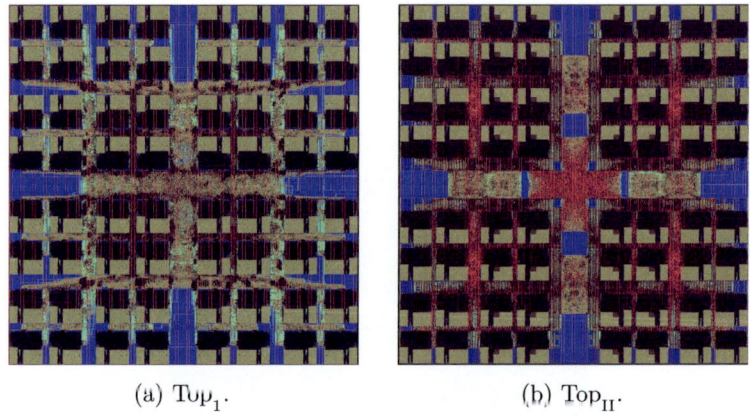

(a) Top_1.   (b) Top_H.

Figure 4.7: Placed and routed Top_1 and Top_H MemPool clusters, implemented as 4.6 mm × 4.6 mm macros. The dark blue regions are devoid of standard cells.

Top_4 and Top_H achieve much better performance results (in terms of latency and throughput) than Top_1. However, out of these two high-performance topologies, only Top_H is physically feasible. Therefore, we elect to build the MemPool cluster following the Top_H organization.

4.5.3 Implementation Flow

As we saw in the feasibility analysis of Section 4.5.2, the routing of MemPool is one of the fundamental challenges for its physical implementation. The problem is amplified by MemPool's large size, which demands a hierarchical implementation flow. A key advantage of the chosen Top_H interconnect is the introduction of the additional group hierarchy. It allows us to skip the tile hierarchy, implement a flat group as the first hierarchy level, and later construct the cluster out of group macros. Moving to a larger first hierarchy block allows the tools to implement all interconnects flat and seamlessly route through the tiles, which would otherwise be black boxes. This gain in freedom significantly improves resource utilization and allows us to implement MemPool on a smaller footprint than Figure 4.7b.

The annotated die shot of the fully placed and routed MemPool group can be seen in Figure 4.8, as a 1.66 mm × 1.66 mm macro. We place the tiles' memory macros in a 4 × 4 grid, flipping the upper half of the grid to create an open area in the middle of the group, where the tool has space to place the interconnects. The annotations show how all the tiles are clustered around their memory macros but drawn to the center to minimize wiring delay towards the interconnect. The remote SPM interconnects fit between the tiles. An AXI interconnect and read-only I$ cache are placed on the left boundary. The MemPool cluster instantiates four identical groups and is 11.78 mm^2 large.

Figure 4.9 shows the hierarchical area distribution of MemPool's group. It shows that we succeeded in adding an AXI interconnect with minimal area overhead, despite including a full level of cache hierarchy and a specialized DMA. Within a tile, most of the area is occupied by SPM banks, followed by the four cores and their instruction cache. The cores area is split between the Snitch core itself and its IPU.

4.6 Evaluation

4.6.1 Microarchitecture Benchmarking

We evaluate MemPool's performance, power, and energy efficiency with various DSP kernels from a wide range of domains. All kernels operate on 32-bit integers as input and outputs and are parallelized across all of MemPool's cores. The measurements include a final synchronization barrier in the end. Specifically, we select the following kernels:

matmul: A matrix-matrix multiplication of size $m \times n$ is parallelized across all cores. Each core operates on a 4 × 4 output tile, fully utilizing Snitch's register file to maximize computational intensity. This leads to eight load instructions per 16 MAC operations.

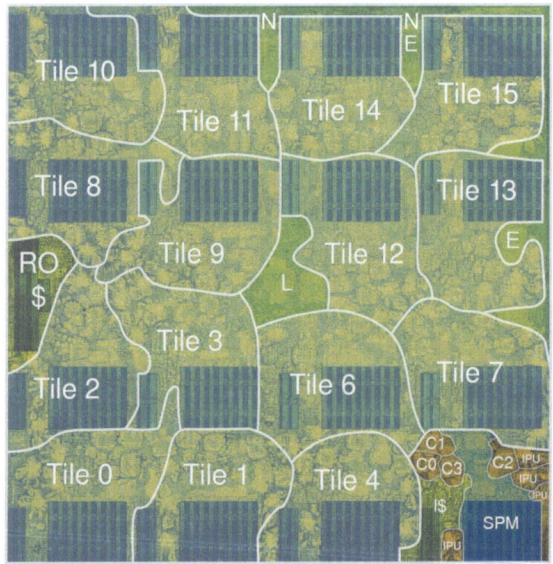

Figure 4.8: Annotated dieshot of placed and routed MemPool group with 16 tiles, the read-only I$, and the interconnects between tiles of the same group (L) as well as to other groups (N, NE, E). Tile 5 is annotated in more detail showing its four cores, their IPUs, the instruction cache, and the SPM memory with its interconnect.

conv2d: A 2D convolution on an $m \times n$ image with a 3×3 kernel. Each core computes the output pixels mapped to its tile, which leads to mostly local accesses except for some pixels at the edge of a tile. To maximize data reuse, the kernel operates on a 4×3 output tile.

dct: This kernel computes the 2D Discrete Cosine Transform (DCT) of 8×8 blocks in an $m \times n$ image. The cores use their stack to store intermediate results, and blocks are assigned such that each core only makes local accesses.

Table 4.1 shows the performance metrics of the selected kernels. All results were extracted with the methodology described in Section 4.5.1.

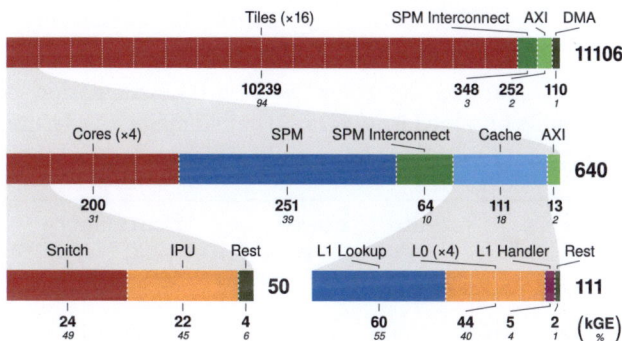

Figure 4.9: Hierarchical area breakdown of a MemPool group in kGE with annotations showing the *percentage* of the immediate parent component. The whole group occupies 11 MGE, most of which is occupied by tiles, while the interconnects and DMAs only make up a small percentage. The cores and SPM banks occupy most of the area.

The full MemPool cluster consumes roughly 1 W and consistently achieves a high IPC, especially for compute-intensive kernels, where we can reach up to 336 OP/cycle thanks to the MAC ISA extension. In terms of energy-efficiency, MemPool reaches 170 GOPS/W.

A comparison with a single-core system, which represents an idealized, conflict-free system, evaluates how well MemPool scales, using weak scaling, which means the problem size scales with the system size. Figure 4.10 shows the speedup of MemPool with and without a full synchronization barrier after the execution. It allows analyzing whether the inherent final synchronization step or conflicts between cores prevent ideal scaling. For compute-intensive kernels such as `matmul`, `conv`, and `dct`, the speedup is very close to ideal even considering the final barrier. While `conv` and `dct`'s performance, excluding the synchronization, is on par with the single-core system, the `matmul`'s speedup indicates that conflicts lead to performance losses. For kernels with low compute intensity, the final synchronization step becomes noticeable. However, they still achieve 75% of the ideal speedup. Overall, MemPool achieves speedups very close to the ideal, only losing 10% due to synchronization in compute intensive workloads.

Table 4.1: Benchmark results extracted from RTL simulation, coupled
with power results obtained from post-layout simulations. An operation
corresponds to a 32-bit addition or multiplication.

Kernel	Size	Util. IPC	Power (W)	Performance (OP/cycle)	(GOPS/W)
matmul	256×256	0.88	1.25	285	136
conv	96×1024	0.87	1.19	336	170
dct	192×1024	0.93	1.02	168	99

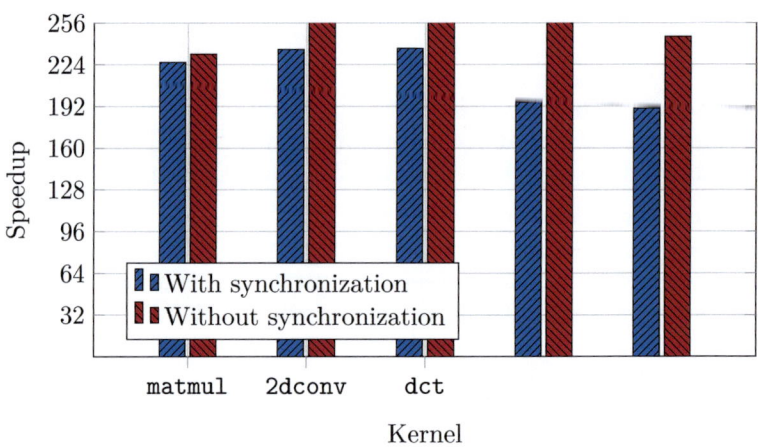

Figure 4.10: Speedup of MemPool over single-core execution using
weak scaling, i.e., the problem scales with the core count. We show the
speedup with and without a final synchronization barrier to analyze
the main cause of performance losses.

4.6.2 Energy of Individual Instructions

The energy consumed by different instructions quantifies the benefits of our ISA extensions and hybrid addressing scheme. Figure 4.11 shows the energy breakdown, including dynamic and static power, while all cores execute the instruction with randomized data. We report the energy per core per cycle since all instructions are fully pipelined, and we execute one instruction per cycle per core.

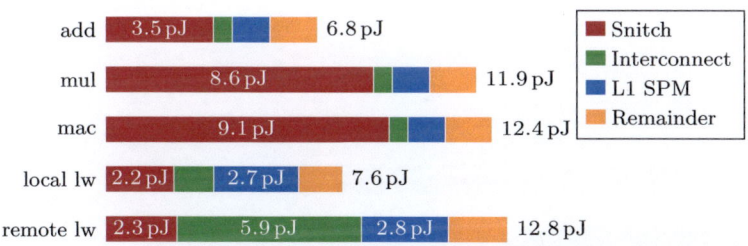

Figure 4.11: Energy breakdown of individual instructions extracted from post-layout simulations. We measure the energy of three different arithmetic instructions and the load word instruction when loading from banks in the same (*local*) tile or *remote* ones, thereby passing through the groups. The *Remainder* category includes all components with very small contributions, like the caches, DMA, AXI, etc.

The arithmetic instructions' energy consumption motivates our ISA supporting instructions like the MAC. Fusing the addition and multiplication increases the energy consumption by only 0.5 pJ, but eliminates the need for the **add** instruction, thereby saving 33%.

Similarly, the energy of local and remote memory transactions emphasizes the benefit of our hybrid addressing scheme. A remote transaction consumes 1.7× the energy of a local one. Therefore, the hybrid addressing scheme improves energy efficiency by reducing the number of remote accesses. Comparing remote loads to arithmetic instructions also shows how efficient MemPool's interconnect design is. Crossing the whole MemPool macro takes roughly the same energy as a MAC operation, thanks to the pipelined interconnect.

4.6.3   Power Breakdown

To gain deeper insights into MemPool's power consumption, Figure 4.12 breaks the power consumption down into individual components. Despite scaling the cluster to 256 cores with low-latency access to L1, most of the power is still spent on computation. Specifically, 43% of the power is consumed by the cores, while the contribution of the SPM interconnect is kept at 21% despite its size, and the memory banks themselves account for another 21%.

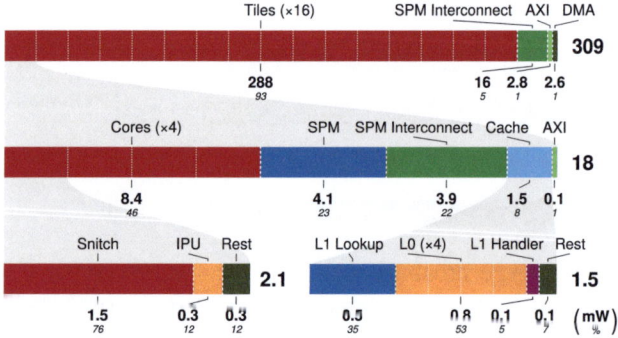

Figure 4.12: Hierarchical power breakdown of MemPool group when executing a `matmul` kernel. The results are shown in mW and % and are extracted using Synopsys PrimeTime with annotations from a post-layout simulation.

4.7   Related Work

Energy-efficient manycore systems have been studied extensively, and various architectural approaches exist to tackle scaling parallel systems [112]. In the following, we focus on systems based on clusters of PEs. A cluster of PEs sharing a low-latency L1 memory is a typical architecture for efficiently tackling today's parallel workloads [113]. For example, GreenWaves' GAP8 processor's [114] compute power comes from eight independent RISC-V cores coupled to a shared L1 SPM. Its primary architectural idea is very similar to MemPool, although we presents a way to scale this idea to 256 cores.

Ramon Chip's RC64 [115] targets task parallelism and implements a similar architecture to MemPool, coupling 64 DSP cores to a shared SPM accessible in a small number of cycles. Each core is equipped with a private instruction and data cache, as well as a private SPM to reduce bandwidth requirements to the shared SPM. MemPool scales the single-cluster design even further without relying on costly data caches to reduce bandwidth requirements.

Other architectures rely on replicating the small compute cluster to scale to hundreds of cores. Manticore [86] is built out of a similar compute cluster as GAP8, coupling eight small 32-bit RISC-V cores to a low-latency shared L1 memory. This cluster is replicated and connected to a shared L2 memory via an AXI interconnect to build a system of 1024 PEs per chiplet. Kalray's MPPS3-80 [116] follows a similar approach with larger cores. Sixteen 64-bit processors with private L1 data caches form a cluster with 4 MiB of L2 SPM memory. The chip features five clusters, resulting in 80 cores. Esperanto's ET-SoC-1 [109] has a similar hierarchy and has 1088 64-bit RISC-V cores organized in 34 *shires* of 32 cores and 4 MiB of SPM each. While this approach allows scaling into the manycore regime, it creates many small clusters with private memories, complicating the programming model and incurring communication overhead between clusters.

Modern GPUs resemble multi-cluster designs, with SMs corresponding to shared-memory clusters that act as basic building blocks. NVIDIA's leading-edge H100 [87] features 144 SPMs, each featuring 128 fp32 units. However, GPUs operate in the SIMT regime, meaning that a single instruction stream controls multiple compute units. Each SM has four scheduler and dispatch units controlling 32 fp32 units each, resulting in four independent instruction streams per SM or 576 per GPU. GPUs feature thousands of compute units, but their utilization is limited by the SIMT regime. Especially for irregular and non-data-oblivious algorithms, thread divergence and synchronization restrict the GPU's performance. In contrast, MemPool gives each PE its instruction stream, making it much more flexible and efficient.

An alternative way to scale to hundreds of PEs is to sacrifice the low-latency interconnect between memory banks and processors and directly connect neighboring cores through a 2D mesh (or similar topology) interconnect. Many multicore SoCs have been designed following this pattern [117]–[119]. As examples, Celerity [118] and KiloCore [119] are architectures with small cores with private instruction and data memories and neighbor-to-neighbor communication scaled to 496 or 1000 cores. Replication enables high core counts, but communication latency between distant cores quickly increases to 45 or 64 cycles, respectively, requiring careful dataflow management.

TILE64 [117] and Epiphany-V [120] connect similar cores, caches, and DMAs in a 2D mesh but scale the architecture to up to 1024 cores. While all PEs still have access to other PE's memory, the NoC limits the inter-core bandwidth and imposes a high latency. Programming distributed cores requires distributing workloads in a spatially-aware fashion and carefully fitting local data within local memories to reach acceptable performance. Consequently, efficiently programming this class of architectures is challenging, especially for algorithms requiring PEs to access a shared pool of data. MemPool's low-latency interconnect greatly simplifies workload distribution and access to shared data, even when they present irregular access patterns.

MemPool is the first architecture to scale the shared-memory cluster with a low-latency interconnect to hundreds of individually programmable PEs. In contrast to smaller cluster-based architectures, MemPool allows for more parallelism and processing power while also providing a larger L1 memory to reduce communication overhead and facilitate latency hiding from/to higher-level memories. There is a physical limit to scaling a single cluster, and for extremely large core counts (thousands), moving to multiple clusters is inevitable. The MemPool architecture remains attractive even in a multi-cluster regime, as it reduces the need to finely partition shared data and greatly eases inter-cluster communication latency hiding with large block transfers.

4.8   Conclusions

MemPool presents a scalable, shared-L1-memory manycore RISC-V system. Even when scaling to 256 cores, all cores can access inter-tile or intra-cluster memory banks within at most five cycles of latency thanks to a sophisticated hierarchical SPM interconnect. Thanks to the capability to program each core independently, the presented cache hierarchy, and the refill interconnect, all cores can be highly utilized, i.e., up to 96% in common kernels for signal and image processing.

MemPool is implemented and evaluated in GlobalFoundries' 22FDX 22 nm FD-SOI technology. It runs at 600 MHz (60 FO4 gate delays) in typical operating conditions (TT, 0.80 V, 25 °C) and occupies an area of 12.9 mm^2. By tailoring the Snitch cores to MemPool, and through enhancements like our DSP extension and hybrid addressing scheme, MemPool achieves very highf performance and comes close to that of an ideally-scaled shared-L1 computing cluster.

Finally, MemPool's performance is limited mainly by the inherent load-store architecture and synchronization associated with parallel programming. Architectural stalls contribute only a few percent of speedup loss over a comprehensive set of data-parallel kernels. A Nevertheless, the MemPool cluster achieves a performance up to 229 GOPS and an energy efficiency up to 192 GOPS/W. On average, each of MemPool's 256 cores achieves an IPC of 0.96.

Chapter 5

MemPool-3D: Boosting Performance and Efficiency of Manycore Clusters with 3D Integration

5.1 Introduction

Vertical integration promises to address the scaling problems of the traditional 2D integration foreseen by Moore's Law [22]. 3DICs promise better PPA than 2DIC counterparts, thanks to a drastic reduction of the interconnect lengths, particularly of long global wires, while enabling a smaller form factor by adding the third dimension [23], [24].

Advances in flip-chip interconnection technology allow for the miniaturization of the inter-die connections. While Controlled Collapse Chip Connection (C4) solder bumps have a pitch of around $100\,\mu m$ [121], Face-to-Face (F2F) wafer-to-wafer HB enables interconnect pitches in the micrometer range while maintaining reasonable yield rates [122].

Such a fine pitch can be leveraged to implement 3DIC designs with a very high interconnect density. For the implementation of F2F-bonded 3DICs, the Macro-3D flow [26] provides state-of-the-art PPA optimization capabilities for memory-on-logic partitioning schemes. Since the flow is aware of all metal layers in the die stack, the Back End of the Line (BEOL) routing resources of both dies can be shared [26]. It is, therefore, possible to use one chip's BEOL to avoid congestion bottlenecks in the other chip. This resource sharing allows for a more efficient routing utilization, which is extremely useful for the implementation of highly congested designs.

Manycore systems achieve better PPA through vertical integration thanks to the shorter interconnect lengths. Although some manycore systems explore 3DIC implementations [24], [123], [124], they use a 2D-mesh network to connect their processing elements, failing to exploit the interconnection capabilities of a denser pitch. In this chapter, we use MemPool [14] as our target design, an open-source manycore system with 256 cores and a configurable amount of shared L1 SPM connected with a low-latency interconnect. Routing congestion severely limits MemPool's implementation, with its operating frequency bounded by the wire propagation delay. This makes MemPool an ideal candidate for 3D design. With the holistic view over all metal layers in the Macro-3D flow, the BEOL resources in both dies are combined, alleviating MemPool's congestion and achieving a higher operating frequency thanks to reductions in the wire length. In this chapter, we explore the architectural and the technology parameter spaces by analyzing the PPA impact of MemPool's L1 SPM capacity scaling, from 1 MiB to 8 MiB, on 2D and 3D implementations. The contributions we propose here are the following:

- A flexible partitioning scheme of MemPool into logic and memory dies, capable of achieving high utilization of the memory die for large memory capacities;

- The complete 2D and Macro-3D implementations of MemPool in a commercial 28 nm technology node, for all considered SPM capacities, and an analysis of the instances in terms of power, performance, area, footprint, and energy efficiency;

- An exploration of MemPool's SPM capacity and its impact on the runtime of a common matrix multiplication kernel, including an analysis of the off-chip memory bandwidth's influence.

5.2 Architecture

As discussed in Chapter 4, MemPool is an open-source shared-L1 manycore cluster with 256 very-small cores sharing a multi-banked shared-L1 SPM through a low-latency interconnect [14], [125]. Its maximum operating frequency shows a high sensibility to the available routing resources and footprint size. MemPool is built hierarchically through the replication of tiles, whose architecture can be seen in Figure 5.1. Each tile contains four very-small Snitch RV32IMAX-pulpimg cores [92], 2 KiB of L1 I\$, and 16 SRAM banks of SPM locally accessible within one cycle. The cores can execute instructions of the Xpulpimg extension, e.g., multiply-accumulate and load/store post-increment instructions. A logarithmic crossbar connects local cores and banks. In addition, four remote ports per tile allow remote tiles to access local SPM banks.

In our physical implementations with Macro-3D, the tile is partitioned into a logic and a memory die. A possible partitioning would assign all the memory banks of a tile to the memory die, namely 2 KiB of instruction cache and a multi-banked SPM of parameterizable capacity, as shown in Figure 5.1. The area requirement of 60 kGE per Snitch core and the tile interconnect's logic define the footprint required for the logic die. With the default SPM capacity of 1 MiB utilizing only 51% of the memory die area, an increase of the SPM capacity can be used to balance the area requirement of both dies. As we will analyze in Section 5.3.2, the 8 MiB 3D design uses an adjusted partitioning scheme due to the increased SRAM size.

The MemPool cluster is built hierarchically using the tile as the starting point. Sixteen tiles form a *group*, whose architecture is shown in Figure 4.2a. Each core can access SPM banks in the same group within three cycles. Four 16×16 radix-4 butterfly networks are used in each group to connect tiles within the same group (*local* interconnect) or in different groups (*north*, *northeast*, and *east* interconnects).

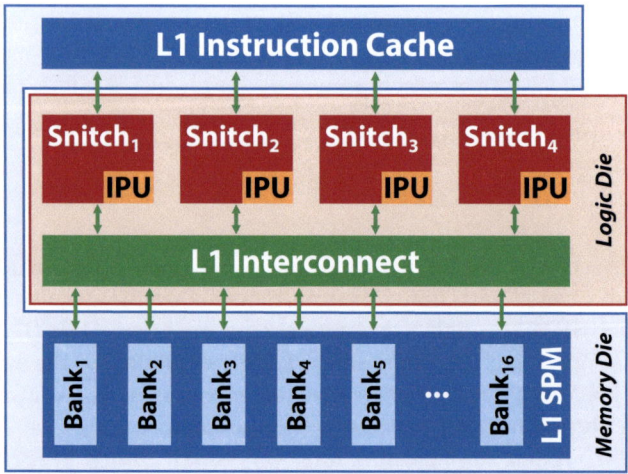

Figure 5.1: Tile architecture, highlighting a partitioning into the logic and the memory dies, used for the 1 MiB, 2 MiB, and 4 MiB 3D designs.

At the top level of the architecture, the cluster has four identical groups, as shown in Figure 4.2b. Each core can access SPM banks in other groups with five cycles of latency. At this hierarchical level, there are only point-to-point connections between groups. This chapter focuses on implementing the groups since only a few cells (about five thousand) need to be placed between them at the cluster level.

The dissimilarity between the tile and group makes MemPool a highly suitable architecture for 3D integration. While the tile has a high logic density, the group is highly congested due to its global interconnects. The 2D MemPool's critical path goes from one tile to the other diagonally opposed to it. Approximately 37% of its timing is wire propagation delay, and 75% of its cells are buffers [14].

5.3 Physical Implementation

5.3.1 Methodology

MemPool is synthesized and implemented in a commercial 28 nm high-κ technology node. In the 3D implementations, we use a fine F2F via pitch of 1.0 μm. The F2F via size, resistance, and capacitance is 0.5 μm × 0.5 μm, 0.5 Ω, and 1 fF respectively [122]. The 3D BEOL comprises six metal layers in both tiers (M6M6), separated by the F2F via layer, similarly to the setup proposed by Bamberg et al. [26].

Tiles are first synthesized using Synopsys Design Compiler 2021.06 and then implemented with the corresponding flow in Cadence Innovus 20.13. We use a uniform 1 GHz frequency target on the typical corner to implement all the designs. The 2D tiles use a six-layer BEOL (M6), while the 3D tiles use the mirrored M6M6 stack mentioned above. The implemented tiles—abstracted into black boxes with full blockages on all utilized routing layers—are used for the groups' syntheses and physical implementations, similarly to the reference flow in [14].

The 3D groups use the same BEOL as the tiles, i.e., M6M6, while the 2D groups have two extra layers (M8) to allow over-the-tile routing. When abstracting a tile implementation, the physical representation by default creates obstructions on all metal layers that are available for routing. In the 2D case, this affects M1 to M6. As the Macro-3D tile utilizes the BEOL of the logic and the memory die simultaneously, the tile abstraction blocks not only M1 to M6 of the logic die, but also M1 to M6 of the memory die. The 3D tile abstractions, therefore, prevent any inter-tile routing on the group level where tiles are placed.

Here, we analyze a total of eight MemPool configurations. Each configuration is named MemPool$_{Capacity}^{Flow}$, where *Capacity* is the total capacity of the shared-L1 SPM at the MemPool cluster, i.e., one of 1 MiB, 2 MiB, 4 MiB, and 8 MiB, and *Flow* is either 2D or 3D.

5.3.2 Tile Implementation

The tiles are implemented to target a standard cell density of 90% in the logic die. Figure 5.2 shows the memory die floorplanning used to implement some of the considered MemPool-3D configurations. We use the partitioning of Figure 5.1 to implement the tiles of the MemPool-3D configurations with 1 MiB to 4 MiB of SPM. The memory die of the MemPool$_{1\,\text{MiB}}^{\text{3D}}$ configuration, shown in Figure 5.2a, only utilizes 51% of the area of the memory die. On the other hand, the instance with 4 MiB of SPM, shown in Figure 5.2b, achieves a much higher 89% utilization, with a tile footprint only 13% higher than the MemPool$_{1\,\text{MiB}}^{\text{3D}}$ tile.

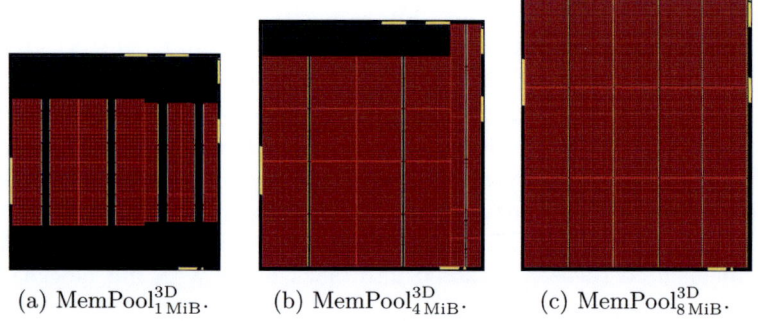

(a) MemPool$_{1\,\text{MiB}}^{\text{3D}}$.   (b) MemPool$_{4\,\text{MiB}}^{\text{3D}}$.   (c) MemPool$_{8\,\text{MiB}}^{\text{3D}}$.

Figure 5.2: Floorplan of the tile's memory die used to implement the MemPool$_{1\,\text{MiB}}^{\text{3D}}$, MemPool$_{4\,\text{MiD}}^{\text{3D}}$, and MemPool$_{8\,\text{MiB}}^{\text{3D}}$. Images to scale.

The MemPool$_{8\,\text{MiB}}^{\text{3D}}$ configuration uses a partitioning different from the one shown in Figure 5.1 due to the increased area of the memory macros. In this configuration, 15 out of the 16 SPM macros are arranged in a 5×3 array in the memory die. This memory die achieves near 100% utilization, as shown in Figure 5.2c, while its footprint is 40% larger than the MemPool$_{1\,\text{MiB}}^{\text{3D}}$ design. As we can see in Table 5.1, both dies still keep a balanced area ratio with this partitioning. The core utilization of the logic die is 84%, only 6% below the target utilization. The extra area of the logic die is used by one SPM bank and all the tile's instruction cache banks.

There is a negligible PPA difference across all tile instances. The fastest tile, MemPool$_{4\,\text{MiB}}^{\text{3D}}$, achieves a frequency only 6% higher than the slowest tile, MemPool$_{2\,\text{MiB}}^{\text{3D}}$. The tile is primarily constrained by external delays that model the group rather than internal register-to-register paths. While 3D integration can reduce the wire length of these paths, the primary effect is reducing the tile's footprint, leading to shorter interconnects and, thus, group level PPA improvements.

Table 5.1: Tile implementation results, normalized by the results of the baseline $\text{MemPool}^{\text{2D}}_{\text{1 MiB}}$ configuration.

Flow	SPM Capacity	Footprint	Core utilization	
			Logic die	*Memory die*
2D	1 MiB	1.000	90%	—
	2 MiB	1.104	90%	—
	4 MiB	1.420	84%	—
	8 MiB	1.817	86%	—
3D	1 MiB	0.667	90%	51%
	2 MiB	0.667	90%	65%
	4 MiB	0.767	85%	89%
	8 MiB	0.933	84%	100%

5.3.3   Group Implementation

Area and Footprint

The group is at the critical level in the implementation of MemPool. When deriving the channel widths between tiles, we need to consider that the group is densely connected at the design's center, where most of the logic of the local interconnect is placed. This causes heavy congestion, creating Design Rule Violations (DRVs) and degrades timing if the tiles are not sufficiently spaced in the center of the design. Figure 5.3 exemplifies this by showing the routing and cell density map of the $\text{MemPool}^{\text{3D}}_{\text{4 MiB}}$ instance. The four group interconnects can be seen as pockets of very high cell density in Figure 5.3b.

Figure 5.4 shows the groups with 8 MiB of SPM. The width of the channels between tiles is kept constant for all trials of each flow. The rationale is that the group interconnects' size is largely independent of the SPM capacity, except for the additional address bits.

The channels between the 3D tiles are 18% narrower than the 2D counterparts since the 3D designs have the twelve layers of the mirrored M6M6 BEOL to route the group interconnects. In contrast, the 2D trials can only use the eight layers of the M8 BEOL. This

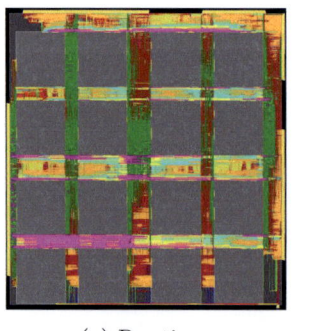

(a) Routing.

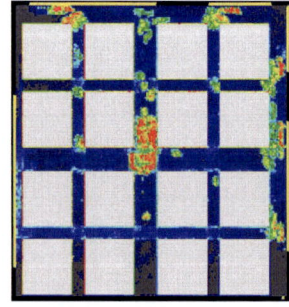

(b) Cell density map.

Figure 5.3: Routing and cell density map of the MemPool$^{3D}_{4\,MiB}$ group. Yellow and red colors indicate regions with a very high cell density. Dark blue and gray regions have a cell density close to zero.

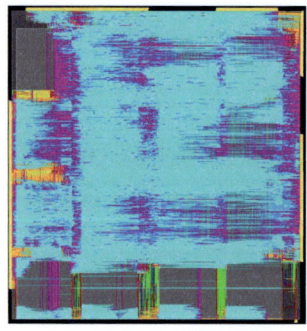

(a) MemPool$^{2D}_{8\,MiB}$.

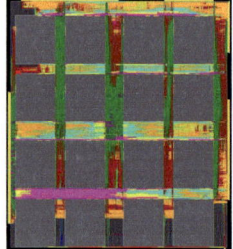

(b) MemPool$^{3D}_{8\,MiB}$.

Figure 5.4: MemPool$^{2D}_{8\,MiB}$ and MemPool$^{3D}_{8\,MiB}$ placed-and-routed designs, highlighting the group routing. Images to scale.

effect compounds with the reduced footprint of the 3D tiles, further reducing the footprint of the MemPool-3D groups. In Figure 5.4, we can also see the over-the-tile routing of the 2D designs—since the tiles are routed up to M6 and the group up to M8. Even though the 3D runs have a more aggressive BEOL than the 2D runs, M6M6, the lack of over-the-tile routing incurs extra congestion since all group interconnects have routing confined to the channels. The footprint of the MemPool-3D groups could be further reduced if routing resources of the tiles would be available to implement the group level.

Tables 5.2 and 5.3 summarize the implementation results of the eight considered groups normalized our baseline, $\mathrm{MemPool}^{2D}_{1\,\mathrm{MiB}}$. In terms of footprint, the 3D groups are much smaller than the 2D groups. For example, the largest 3D group, $\mathrm{MemPool}^{3D}_{8\,\mathrm{MiB}}$, has a footprint 14% smaller than the smallest 2D group, $\mathrm{MemPool}^{2D}_{1\,\mathrm{MiB}}$. The 3D MemPool groups also have a footprint much smaller than their 2D counterparts. For instance, the $\mathrm{MemPool}^{3D}_{8\,\mathrm{MiB}}$ group has a footprint 46% smaller than $\mathrm{MemPool}^{2D}_{8\,\mathrm{MiB}}$, as seen in Figure 5.4.

Table 5.2: Group's 2D and 3D PPA results of instances with 1 MiB and 2 MiB of SPM L1 memory, normalized by the results of the baseline 2D design with 1 MiB of SPM. The numbers in parentheses show the difference relative to the 2D counterpart design.

L1 SPM Capacity	1 MiB		2 MiB	
Implementation Flow	2D	3D	2D	3D
BEOL	M8	M6M6	M8	M6M6
Footprint	1.000	0.665 (−33%)	1.074	0.665 (−38%)
Combined Die Area	1.000	1.330 (+33%)	1.074	1.330 (+23%)
Wire Length	1.000	0.803	1.036	0.803
Density [%]	53.0	54.5	54.0	54.8
#Buffers	182.9E3	151.5E3	190.3E3	151.2E3
#F2F Bumps	—	78.3E3	—	78.9E3
Eff. Frequency	1.000	1.040 (+4.0%)	0.930	0.979 (+5.2%)
Total Negative Slack	−1.000	−0.184	−2.080	−0.458
#Failing Paths	1140	1046	1636	1332
Total Power	1.000	0.913	1.045	0.958
Power-delay product	1.000	0.877 (−12%)	1.129	0.981 (−13%)

Table 5.3: Group's 2D and 3D PPA results of instances with 4 MiB and 8 MiB of SPM L1 memory, normalized by the results of the baseline 2D design with 1 MiB of SPM. The numbers in parentheses show the difference relative to the 2D counterpart design.

L1 SPM Capacity	4 MiB		8 MiB	
Implementation Flow	2D	3D	2D	3D
BEOL	M8	M6M6	M8	M6M6
Footprint	1.299	0.737 (−43%)	1.572	0.857 (−46%)
Combined Die Area	1.299	1.474 (+13%)	1.572	1.714 (+9.0%)
Wire Length	1.131	0.844	1.294	0.888
Density [%]	53.4	53.2	56.9	54.4
#Buffers	212.5E3	166.5E3	217.6E3	156.1E3
#F2F Bumps	—	84.4E3	—	86.2E3
Eff. Frequency	0.875	0.955 (+9.1%)	0.885	0.930 (+5.1%)
Total Negative Slack	−5.887	−0.604	−5.212	−0.962
#Failing Paths	4396	1747	4352	2403
Total Power	1.129	1.041	1.299	1.173
Power-delay product	1.290	1.089 (−16%)	1.469	1.261 (−14%)

The combined area of the memory and logic dies of the MemPool-3D groups is larger than the area of the MemPool-2D groups. The area overhead of the MemPool-3D groups, however, decreases with increasing SPM capacity. The combined die area of the largest 3D group, $\text{MemPool}^{3D}_{8\,\text{MiB}}$, is only 9% larger than the $\text{MemPool}^{2D}_{8\,\text{MiB}}$ group area, indicating that the partitioning is closer to ideal. Although the footprint is the most important metric for analyzing PPA gains of the 3D integration thanks to reduced interconnect lengths, the combined area is more relevant for an implementation cost analysis of the 3D designs. This work focuses on the physical implementation of the groups, MemPool's most critical hierarchical level since the cluster only has four identical groups and some glue logic. However, it can be noted that the 12-layer mirrored BEOL of the MemPool-3D designs implies that the channels between groups needed to route the cluster-level connections can be made shorter than the equivalent channels of the MemPool-2D cluster. This means that we can expect an even more favorable area ratio at the cluster level.

Power and Operating Frequency

MemPool's sensibility to the footprint size can be seen in the normalized wire length results of Tables 5.2 and 5.3. The wire length of the MemPool-2D groups grows by 29.4% from $\text{MemPool}^{2D}_{1\,\text{MiB}}$ to $\text{MemPool}^{2D}_{8\,\text{MiB}}$, accompanied by an 18.9% increase in the number of buffers. The effect compounds to other PPA metrics. For example, the 2D groups achieve an operating frequency up to 12.5% slower, a power consumption up to 29.9% higher, and a Power-Delay Product (PDP) up to 46.9% higher than the baseline $\text{MemPool}^{2D}_{1\,\text{MiB}}$ group.

The MemPool-3D groups have a significantly smaller PPA degradation with increasing SPM capacity than the MemPool-2D groups. The low utilization of the $\text{MemPool}^{3D}_{1\,\text{MiB}}$ design (Figure 5.2a) implies it is possible to implement the $\text{MemPool}^{3D}_{2\,\text{MiB}}$ group without increasing the footprint. Even the largest MemPool-3D group, with 8 MiB of SPM, has a footprint only 10.6% larger than the $\text{MemPool}^{3D}_{1\,\text{MiB}}$ group. This smaller footprint variation leads to a PPA degradation which is less drastic than the one affecting the MemPool-2D groups. As a result, the MemPool-3D groups achieve an operating frequency only 11.8% slower and a power consumption only 28.4% higher than the baseline.

The benefits of 3D integration on MemPool are clearer when comparing instances with the same SPM capacity across 2D and 3D implementation flows. In general, the MemPool-3D designs have a smaller footprint, achieve a higher operating frequency, and consume less power than their 2D counterparts. In terms of footprint, the largest gains are found on the groups of the 8 MiB configuration, with $\text{MemPool}^{3D}_{8\,\text{MiB}}$ having a footprint 46% smaller than $\text{MemPool}^{2D}_{8\,\text{MiB}}$. In terms of frequency and PDP, the $\text{MemPool}^{3D}_{4\,\text{MiB}}$ group achieves an operating frequency 9.1% higher and a PDP 16% lower than the $\text{MemPool}^{2D}_{4\,\text{MiB}}$ group. It is also interesting that there is an operating frequency drop of 6.2% between the $\text{MemPool}^{3D}_{2\,\text{MiB}}$ and $\text{MemPool}^{3D}_{1\,\text{MiB}}$ groups, despite having the same footprint. This is due to the longer SRAMs' delay, which impacts the timing of the tile's input-to-register and register-to-output paths. In general, the MemPool-3D groups have a higher operating frequency, consume less power, and have a lower PDP than the MemPool-2D groups with the same SPM capacity thanks to their smaller footprint and wire length.

5.4 Performance Analysis

We use a matrix multiplication kernel as a representative application for MemPool's target domain to quantify the algorithmic benefits of increasing the memory capacity even for compute-bound kernels. Benefits on memory bound kernels are obviously larger, but we believe the analysis in a compute-bound regime allows us to gather more interesting insights on MemPool-3D's performance.

5.4.1 Cycle Count

We measure the cycle count of computing the matrix multiplication of two $M \times M$ matrices, $M = 326\,400$, that do not fit into the SPM but reside in global memory through a cycle-accurate register-transfer level simulation of the MemPool cluster. The matrix size is chosen to be the least common multiple of the tile sizes $t \times t$, with t one of 256, 384, 544, and 800, that fully utilize the available SPM in each configuration, enabling optimal tiling and maximizing data reuse. The cores load the input tiles and synchronize in a memory phase before computing on the output tile in a compute phase. Those phases are repeated until the output tile is fully computed. At this point, the output tile is stored back into the main memory, and the process repeats for the subsequent output tiles. Since different output tiles require the same input data, each input element is loaded exactly M/t times. Therefore, having a bigger SPM allows for more data reuse and less memory overhead. The second benefit of increased tile size is the increased length of the compute phase minimizing repeated static overhead due to loop setup and synchronization.

We calculate the cycle count of the memory phase for different off-chip memory bandwidths. A Double Data Rate (DDR) Synchronous Dynamic Random Access Memory (SDRAM) stick has a data width of 8 B, which means a single DDR channel clocked at the same frequency as MemPool could deliver at most 16 B/cycle. Therefore, we analyze bandwidths around this realistic case, ranging from a worst-case bandwidth of 4 B/cycle to a very optimistic 64 B/cycle. Our model idealizes the latency into the off-chip global memory. We measure the duration of the compute phase with a hot instruction cache and calculate the total cycle count by accumulating all phases. The results in Figure 5.5 show a speedup of 43% for the 8 MiB case over the baseline for the worst-case bandwidth, where the memory transfers make up a significant portion of the runtime. For the off-chip memory bandwidth of one DDR channel, the configuration with 8 MiB of SPM achieves a cycle count speedup of 16% over the baseline. Even for the optimistic off-chip memory bandwidth of 64 B/cycle, the largest configuration still generates an 8% benefit over the baseline, showing that larger memories are beneficial from an algorithmic point of view.

5.4.2   Performance and Energy-Efficiency

The increased SPM capacity impacts the PPA of the design, as seen in Section 5.3.3. Here, we combine those effects to analyze how MemPool's performance and energy efficiency evolve across all considered configurations. We chose an off-chip memory bandwidth of 16 B/cycle to represent our memory subsystem.

Figure 5.6 shows the performance of the matrix multiplication kernel on MemPool, as a function of the SPM capacity, for the

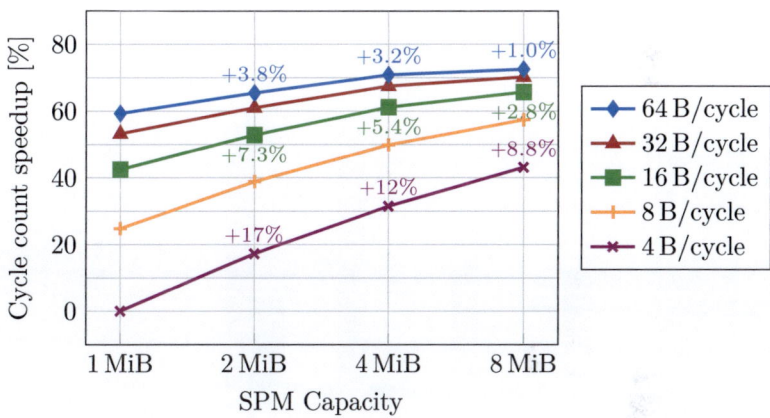

Figure 5.5: Cycle count speedup of the matrix multiplication kernel with larger SPM capacity, as a function of the off-chip memory bandwidth, relative to the 1 MiB configuration with an off-chip memory bandwidth of 4 B/cycle. The percentages by the data points indicate the speedup relative to the instance with the same off-chip memory bandwidth but half of the SPM capacity.

MemPool-2D and MemPool-3D designs. Thanks to their higher operating frequencies, the MemPool-3D groups achieve a performance up to 9.1% higher than the MemPool-2D groups. The MemPool-2D groups achieve small performance gains with increasing SPM capacity, reaching a gain of at most 3.1% for the $\text{MemPool}^{\text{2D}}_{8\,\text{MiB}}$ case. Due to a particularly low operating frequency, the $\text{MemPool}^{\text{2D}}_{4\,\text{MiB}}$ has a performance drop compared to the $\text{MemPool}^{\text{2D}}_{1\,\text{MiB}}$ design. The MemPool-3D designs, on the other hand, achieve consistently higher performances with increasing SPMs, outperforming their 2D counterparts. $\text{MemPool}^{\text{3D}}_{8\,\text{MiB}}$ achieves the highest performance, 8.4% above the baseline.

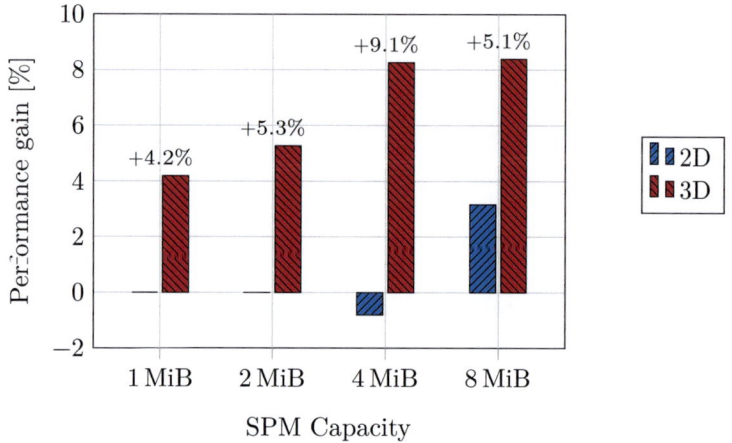

Figure 5.6: Performance gain of the matrix multiplication kernel with larger SPM capacity, relative to $\text{MemPool}^{\text{2D}}_{1\,\text{MiB}}$ with a $16\,\text{B/cycle}$ off-chip memory bandwidth. The percentages indicate the speedup of the MemPool-3D instance compared to the MemPool-2D with the same SPM capacity.

The energy efficiency, as expected, shows the opposite trend than the performance. As shown in Figure 5.7, the energy efficiency of the MemPool designs tends to decrease with an increasing SPM capacity. The $\text{MemPool}^{\text{2D}}_{8\,\text{MiB}}$ group achieves the worst energy efficiency, 21% below the efficiency of the $\text{MemPool}^{\text{2D}}_{1\,\text{MiB}}$ design. In addition, the 3D designs consistently outperform their 2D counterparts. For example, the MemPool$_{4\,\text{MiB}}^{3D}$ design achieves an efficiency 18.4% higher than the 2D design with the same SPM capacity.

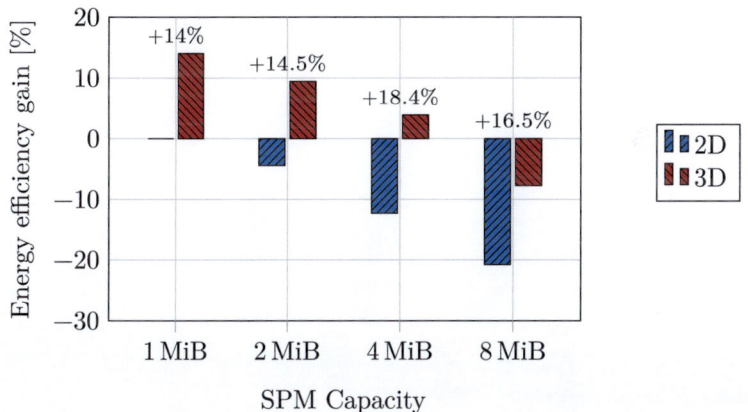

Figure 5.7: Energy efficiency gain with larger SPM capacity, relative to MemPool$_{1\,\text{MiB}}^{2D}$ with a 16 B/cycle off-chip memory bandwidth, when running the matrix multiplication kernel. The percentages indicate the energy efficiency gain of the MemPool-3D instance compared to the MemPool-2D with the same SPM capacity. Higher is better.

The results of Figure 5.7 indicate that the MemPool$_{1\,\text{MiB}}^{3D}$ is the optimal design from the energy efficiency point of view, 14% higher than MemPool$_{1\,\text{MiB}}^{2D}$. In addition, three-dimensional integration allows for the implementation of MemPool$_{4\,\text{MiB}}^{3D}$—a design with four times as much SPM capacity as the baseline design, MemPool$_{1\,\text{MiB}}^{2D}$—on an energy budget 3.7% smaller. This intrinsic tradeoff between performance and energy efficiency can be better analyzed with the Energy-Delay Product (EDP) results of Figure 5.8, the EDP defined as the product of the total energy consumption by the runtime. The MemPool$_{1\,\text{MiB}}^{3D}$ configuration has the lowest EDP, 15.6% below the baseline.

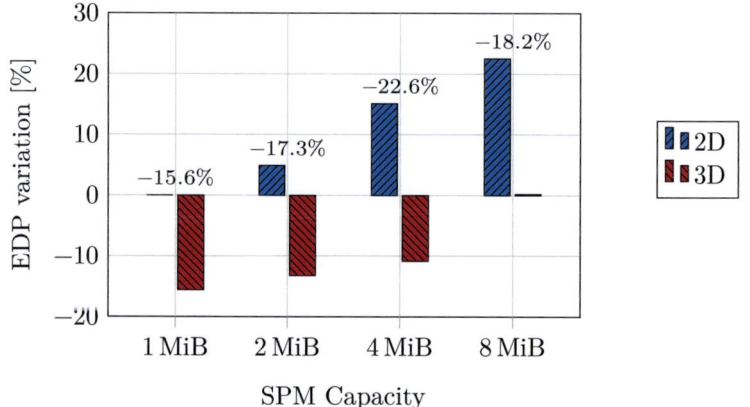

Figure 5.8: EDP variation with larger SPM capacity, relative to MemPool$^{2D}_{1\,MiB}$ with a $16\,B/cycle$ off-chip memory bandwidth, when running the matrix multiplication kernel. The percentages indicate the EDP variation of the MemPool-3D instance compared to the MemPool-2D with the same SPM capacity. Lower is better.

5.5 Conclusions

In this chapter, we analyzed the power, performance, area, and energy efficiency of MemPool, through a co-exploration of its architectural and technological parameter spaces. We implemented MemPool with 1 MiB, 2 MiB, 4 MiB, and 8 MiB of SPM, using 2D and 3D implementation flows, on a modern commercial 28 nm technology node. We explored MemPool's performance while running a large matrix multiplication kernel as a function of the L1 SPM capacity and the off-chip memory bandwidth. For a bandwidth of 16 B/cycle, we observe a cycle count reduction of 16% when increasing the SPM from 1 MiB to 8 MiB.

Despite the operating frequency degradation with increasing SPM capacity, the 3D designs can still achieve an operating frequency up to 9.1% higher than their 2D counterparts. The $\text{MemPool}_{8\,\text{MiB}}^{3D}$ design achieves a performance 8.4% higher than the $\text{MemPool}_{1\,\text{MiB}}^{2D}$ baseline. The 3D designs consistently outperform their 2D counterparts by up to 9.1%. Regarding energy efficiency, the 3D designs outperform their 2D counterparts by up to 18.4%. While increasing the SPM size in the 2D case leads to worse energy efficiency, all but the largest 3D designs achieve a better energy efficiency than the 2D baseline. We are able to implement the $\text{MemPool}_{4\,\text{MiB}}^{3D}$ design with an energy budget 3.7% smaller than the 2D instance with only one-fourth of the SPM capacity, $\text{MemPool}_{1\,\text{MiB}}^{2D}$. To summarize, in this chapter we showed the need for a co-exploration approach with full 3D implementations to optimize modern designs constrained by their interconnect subsystems.

Chapter 6

Spatz meets MemPool: A High-Performance, Energy-Efficient, Large-Scale Shared-L1 Cluster

6.1 Introduction

The ever-growing need for computing performance under an increasingly limited power budget is the defining characteristic of modern computer architecture. As an answer to the phase-out of Moore's Law [2] and Dennard's scaling [3], computer architects must strive for improved scalability and energy efficiency to propel performance scaling in the post-Moore era [126]. This challenge has led to an architectural shift from exploiting high ILP towards the exploitation of on-chip MIMD parallelism [127].

A common architectural pattern comprises clusters of PEs that share tightly-coupled L1 memory through a low-latency interconnect [14]. GPUs, which dominate most of the Top500 list [5], follow this architectural pattern. For example, NVIDIA Hopper GPUs are composed of several SMs with four tensor cores and 256 KiB of shared L1 data cache. Each tensor core controls several FMA units, with the whole SM capable of 1024 FP16/FP32 FMA operations per cycle [87].

Despite the diffusion of shared-L1 PE clusters, there is no consensus on how small their PE should be. However, evidence shows that ultra-small cores controlling large functional units can be energetically efficient [92]. Manticore [86] took this approach, using the tiny (22 kGE) Snitch core [92] to build a 4096-core system composed of four compute chiplets. Each chiplet contains 128 clusters, each featuring 128 KiB of tightly-coupled L1 memory and eight small Snitch cores equipped with large double-precision FPUs. Another example is MemPool, Chapter 4, a scaled-up Snitch-based system with 256 cores sharing 1 MiB of L1 SPM accessible by all cores within at most five cycles of zero-load latency. However, there is a fundamental trade-off between the number of PEs and the VNB, i.e., the memory traffic and energy overhead due to the instruction fetching mechanism and related logic [1]. Therefore, maximizing the PE's instruction fetch efficiency is the key challenge for improving the overall system's energy efficiency.

Instead of scaling by exploiting MIMD, the SIMD parallelism tackles the VNB by executing the same instruction on several chunks of data. In particular, the vector-SIMD approach promises to reach very high performance and energy efficiency numbers without requiring the ultra-wide datapaths of packed-SIMD-based architectures [89]. Moreover, by exploiting DLP, vector engines are potentially the most efficient approach to tackle the VNB.

From its inception with the Cray-1 machine to A64FX [4], vector processing has always been associated with supercomputers. Vector processors usually include all microarchitectural tricks to increase ILP, e.g., renaming, out-of-order execution, speculation, and branch prediction, which increase the area and energy overhead of classical high-performance vector processors. However, the defining characteristic of a vector processor is not ILP but DLP. This key observation has led to the design of more streamlined vector cores where most hardware resources are dedicated to DLP support, i.e., a wide VRF with parallel execution lanes [7]. In this vein, the idea of an embedded vector machine is gaining traction with modern vector ISAs. Arm's MVE [59] and the `Zve*` subset of the RVV [6] both target small vector machines for edge data-parallel processing.

Ultimately, the key benefit of a vector ISA is that the fetch and decode cost of a single vector instruction can be amortized over many data-processing cycles. In this chapter, we use Spatz, Section 3.3, as a small and efficient PEs for large-scale clusters with tightly-coupled L1 memory. We limit Spatz' ISA support to the embedded subset of the RISC-V "V" extension version 1.0 [6].

6.2 Architecture

Spatz is a small parametric vector unit based on the RVV ISA version 1.0, supporting instructions from its `Zve32x` subset for embedded vector machines. This section describes Spatz' architecture. Figure 6.1 details the microarchitecture of Spatz_N, a Spatz instance with N IPUs, and its integration within the MemPool tile. Spatz has a latch-based VRF, divided into two 3R1W banks. Snitch and Spatz form a CC.

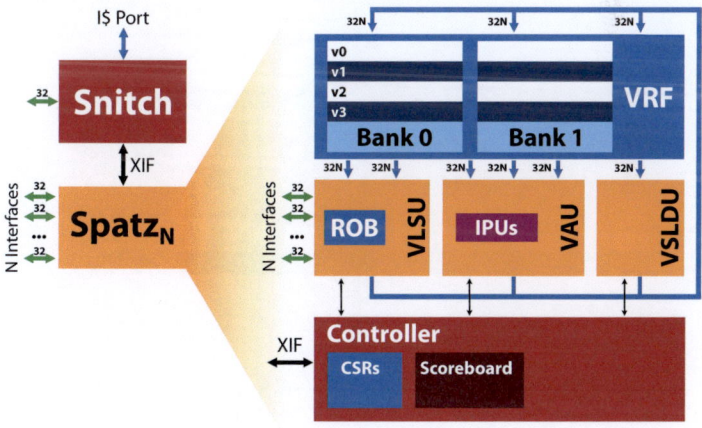

Figure 6.1: Microarchitecture of Spatz_N, a Spatz instance with N IPUs, and its integration with the Snitch core.

Spatz$_N$ is integrated within a small-scale shared-L1 cluster with 16 KiB of local SPM, divided into 16 SRAM banks with 1 KiB each. Each CC has a private latch-based L0 I$ of 128 B and share 2 KiB of L1 I$. An address-based demultiplexer decides whether the CC memory requests are forwarded to the AXI interface or the logarithmic crossbar between the CCs and L1 SPM banks.

By and large, Spatz' architecture is much similar to that presented in Section 3.3. However, since this Spatz does not support floating-point computations, there are no FPUs in its VAU nor there is an FPU sequencer to handle scalar floating-point memory requests that interface with the FPR. Furthermore, while the Spatz instance we presented in Section 3.3 had a 64-bit datapath, the Spatz instances considered in this Chapter have a 32-bit datapath.

The IPU supports 8-bit, 16-bit, and 32-bit elements. Each IPU has a throughput of 32 bit/cycle, regardless of the element width. Within one IPU, execution happens in a packed-SIMD fashion. Figure 6.2 shows the architecture of one of those IPUs. For area saving purposes, the IPU has four datapaths, one 32-bit wide, one 16-bit wide, and two 8 bit wide. Narrow operations reuse the wide datapaths.

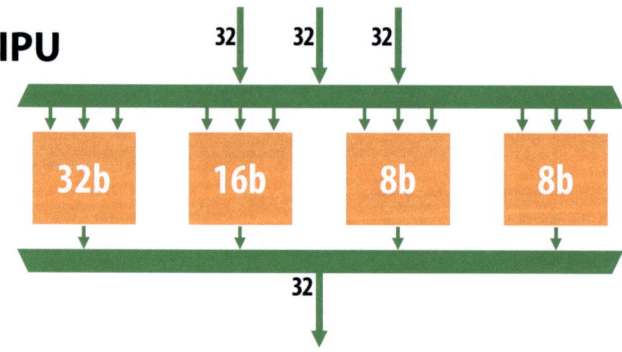

Figure 6.2: Architecture of Spatz' IPU.

Each datapath implements a multiplier, an adder, comparators, and shifters. The most complex operation supported by the IPU's datapaths is `vmacc`, a multiply-accumulate operation.

6.3 Spatz-based Processing Element

In this section, we analyze the performance of a Spatz-based PE with key data-parallel kernels. We consider two differently-sized Spatz configurations, $Spatz_2$ and $Spatz_4$. Their design parameters are summarized in Table 6.1. All Spatz configurations were designed for a peak operation per memory bandwidth ratio of 0.5 OP/B.

Table 6.1: Spatz configurations.

	$Spatz_2$	$Spatz_4$
#IPUs	2	4
Vector length [bit]	256	512
VRF size [KiB]	1	2
Peak performance [OP/cycle]	4	8
Memory bandwidth [B/cycle]	8	16

We used the shared-L1 cluster of Figure 6.1 as the smallest cluster with which we can analyze Spatz' PPA. All considered clusters have four IPUs in total, either in a single $Spatz_4$ CC, two $Spatz_2$ CCs, or four scalar Snitch CCs.

6.3.1 Performance

We benchmark a single Spatz unit with key compute-bound signal processing kernels. Those kernels operate on matrices stored in local low-latency L1 memory. A DMA engine copies data from higher memory levels into the L1 memory, while Spatz operates on local data.

The `matmul` kernel, the multiplication of two $n \times n$ matrices, is the prime example of a compute-bound kernel for large matrices. In fact, its arithmetic intensity is $\mathcal{O}(n)$. Spatz' VRF allows us to tile the matrix multiplication in blocks much larger than the blocks that would fit in the register file of a scalar core. For example, using RVV's LMULs, we can group up to eight logical vector registers into a single one, i.e., $\ell = 8$. In $Spatz_4$, this is a physical vector of 4096 bits, enough to fit 128 32-bit matrix elements.

We also benchmarked our system with `conv2d`, the 2D integer convolution kernel. This kernel also has a large amount of data reuse, with its arithmetic intensity a function of the kernel size $f \times f$. On a multi-core environment, each scalar core has its copy of the convolution kernel K to avoid unnecessary banking conflicts in the L1 memory. Spatz implements the `conv2d` algorithm with optimized vector slides.

The performance results were extracted with a cycle-accurate RTL simulation of the target kernels. The roofline plot of Figure 6.3 shows Spatz_2's and Spatz_4's performance on the `matmul` and `conv2d` kernels, together with their maximum achievable performance. Spatz_2 reaches an almost-ideal IPU utilization for the considered benchmarks. The peak performance for the `matmul` benchmark is 3.84 OP/cycle (96.0%), and the peak performance for the `conv2d` benchmark is 3.95 OP/cycle (98.8%). Large kernels also reach very high performance on Spatz_4. Its peak performance on the `matmul` kernel is 7.67 OP/cycle (95.8%) and 7.78 OP/cycle (97.2%) on the `conv2d` kernel.

Figure 6.3 also shows how gracefully the performance of the vector unit scales for small problems. On Spatz_2, even matmul_8 reaches 3.54 OP/cycle (88.6%). In contrast, on Spatz_4, we remark a performance degradation for this kernel size, reaching 5.17 OP/cycle. This IPU utilization of 64% is a consequence of the short execution time of the `vmacc` instructions, which take two cycles to process a matrix row of eight elements. As a result, Snitch must issue a new `vmacc` every two cycles to keep Spatz' pipelines full. However, bookkeeping scalar instructions limit the `vmacc` issue rate to once every three cycles. This limitation translates into an additional performance boundary [7].

The roofline shows that a Spatz-based PE can reach high performance and functional unit utilization even for very small kernels. Moreover, Spatz achieves this without needing a superscalar or out-of-order core. The vector abstraction allows a pseudo-double-issue behavior, with the VAU, VLSU, and VSLDU working in parallel, without the scalar core issuing more than one instruction per cycle. Section 6.4 will analyze how Spatz performs in a manycore system, with several instances competing for L1 memory bandwidth.

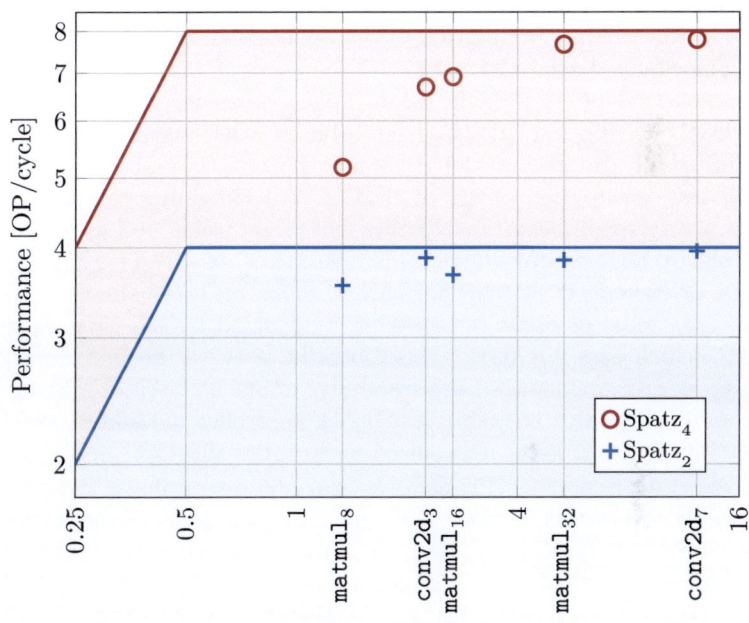

Figure 6.3: Roofline plot for $Spatz_2$ and $Spatz_4$ PEs running the `matmul` and `conv2d` benchmarks. The subscript numbers beside the benchmark names indicate the matrix sizes n for `matmul` and the kernel size f for `conv2d`.

6.3.2 Synthesis Results

We used Synopsys' Fusion Compiler 2022.03 to synthesize the Spatz-
and Snitch-based small-sized shared-L1 clusters of Figure 6.1 using
GlobalFoundries' 22FDX FD-SOI technology. We target 500 MHz
in worst-case conditions (SS, 0.72 V, 125 °C). Figure 6.4 shows the
post-synthesis area distribution of the $Spatz_2$ and $Spatz_4$ CCs.

The $Spatz_2$-based CC is 193 kGE large, or 97 kGE/IPU. Snitch
occupies 12% of it, 23 kGE, while $Spatz_2$ occupies the remaining
170 kGE. $Spatz_2$'s 1 KiB-large latch-based VRF occupies most of
its footprint, 101 kGE. The IPUs are the next largest component
of $Spatz_2$, occupying a total of 47 kGE. All remaining components
have a very small footprint. Notably, Spatz' controller and associated
scoreboard logic occupy only 6 kGE. The $Spatz_4$-based CC is 355 kGE
large, or 89 kGE/IPU. This normalized footprint is 8% smaller than
$Spatz_2$'s. Most of $Spatz_4$'s footprint is occupied by the 2 KiB-large
VRF, which uses 201 kGE. This footprint is twice the footprint of
$Spatz_2$'s VRF, evidence of the scalability of our architecture. $Spatz_4$
amortizes the footprint overhead of Spatz' controller and Snitch, which
contributes to the lower normalized footprint of this CC.

We used Synopsys' PrimePower 2022.03 to estimate the post-
synthesis energy consumption per elementary operation of the $Spatz_4$-
based cluster in typical conditions (TT, 0.80 V, 25 °C), using switching
activities extracted from a gate-level simulation. Both $Spatz_2$-based
and $Spatz_4$-based clusters are more efficient than the scalar Snitch-
based cluster. Figure 6.5 compares the energy consumption per
elementary operation of those clusters. For example, the $Spatz_4$-based
cluster consumes 5.2 pJ less energy than the Snitch-based cluster
with four scalar cores to run a multiply-accumulate instruction. This
40% reduction in energy consumption highlights the feasibility of
embedded vector engines to mitigate the VNB in small shared-L1
clusters. Even for very simple arithmetic instructions, such as an
addition, the Spatz-based cluster requires 14% less energy than the
equivalent Snitch-based cluster.

The $Spatz_2$-based and $Spatz_4$-based MemPool tiles have similar
energy consumption for the considered instructions. However, the
$Spatz_2$-based tile has a footprint 8% larger, which might impact its
integration and replication at a higher hierarchy level.

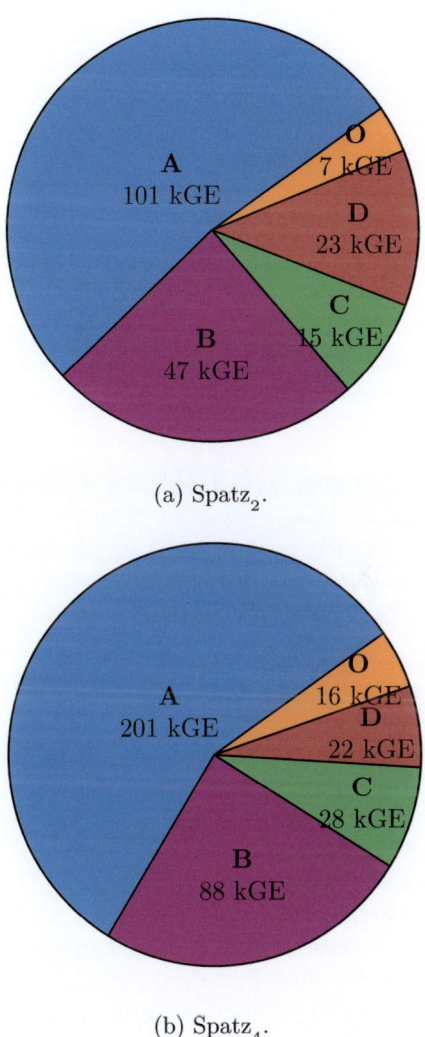

(a) Spatz$_2$.

(b) Spatz$_4$.

Figure 6.4: Post-synthesis area distribution of Spatz$_2$ and Spatz$_4$ CCs. The labels correspond to (A) VRF; (B) VAU; (C) VLSU; (D) Snitch; (O) other smaller blocks, e.g., VSLDU and controller.

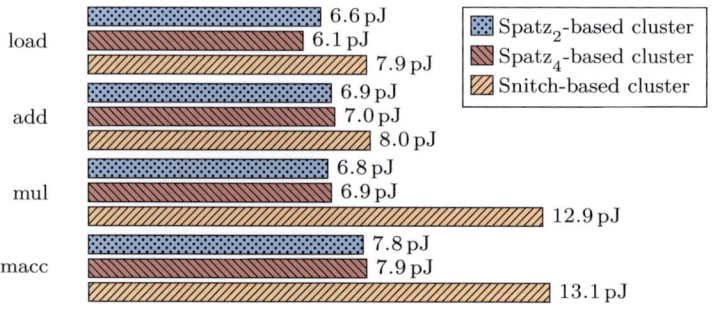

Figure 6.5: Energy consumption per elementary operation of Spatz$_2$-based, Spatz$_4$-based, and Snitch-based clusters running common instructions. All clusters instantiate 4 IPUs.

6.4 Spatz-based MemPool Cluster

We used Spatz as the PE used to build up the MemPool manycore system. In this section, we analyze this system's performance, in OP/cycle, on key data-parallel kernels.

6.4.1 MemPool Configurations

MemPool is a highly-parametric design. Its smallest unit, the tile (Figure 4.1), contains four Snitch cores, 2 KiB of L1 I$, 16 KiB of SPM divided into 16 SRAM banks, and a fully-connected logarithmic crossbar between the cores and memories. This tile can be replicated to build systems with as low as 16 cores (the "*minpool*" configuration) to as high as 256 cores (the "*mempool*" configuration). We analyze Spatz' impact on the PPA of several MemPool configurations, representing a wide range of shared-L1 cluster sizes.

We name a specific MemPool configuration as MemPool$_c$Spatz$_i$, where c is the number of Snitch + Spatz cores in the system, and i is the number of IPUs that each Spatz controls. A MemPool configuration with scalar cores only is called MemPool$_c$, where c is the number of Snitches in the system, each controlling a single IPU. First, we define *minpool* configurations, all with a peak performance of 32 OP/cycle:

MemPool$_{16}$ Configuration with 16 Snitch cores;

MemPool$_8$Spatz$_2$ Configuration with 8 Snitch + Spatz$_2$ cores;

MemPool$_4$Spatz$_4$ Configuration with 4 Snitch + Spatz$_4$ cores.

Each Spatz instance has a VRF with a vector length of 128 bit/IPU. In total, all VRFs amount to 8 KiB of L0 storage. We also define *mempool* configurations, all with a peak performance of 512 OP/cycle:

MemPool$_{256}$ Configuration with 256 Snitch cores;

MemPool$_{128}$Spatz$_2$ Configuration with 128 Snitch + Spatz$_2$ cores;

MemPool$_{64}$Spatz$_4$ Configuration with 64 Snitch + Spatz$_4$ cores.

Each Spatz instance has a VRF with a vector length of 128 bit/IPU. In total, all VRFs amount to 128 KiB of L0 storage.

6.4.2 Benchmarks

We benchmark the MemPool instances with the `matmul` and `conv2d` compute-bound signal processing kernels. Our analysis is performed assuming matrices stored in MemPool's low-latency L1 memory, which is 64 KiB large for the small *minpool* configurations, and 1 MiB for the larger *mempool* configurations. Figure 6.6 shows the rooflines of the considered MemPool configurations. The Spatz-based MemPool systems reach equal or higher performance than the Snitch-based MemPool systems for both the *mempool* and *minpool* configurations and with all benchmarks.

Spatz' high performance and efficiency is fully confirmed in the small MemPool configurations. The MemPool$_8$Spatz$_2$ instance reaches 30.6 OP/cycle (95.6%) on `matmul`$_{64}$. This performance is much higher than MemPool$_{16}$'s, 18.6 OP/cycle (58.1%). Spatz' performance degrades slightly for small matrices. MemPool$_8$Spatz$_2$ achieves up to 22.0 OP/cycle (68.8%) on the `matmul`$_{16}$ kernel, with the performance being limited by Snitch's issue rate. Despite reaching similar performance for large problems, MemPool$_4$Spatz$_4$ performs slightly worse than MemPool$_8$Spatz$_2$ on `matmul`$_{16}$, reaching 20.0 OP/cycle (62.4%) due to a different `matmul` tiling. The convolution also performs

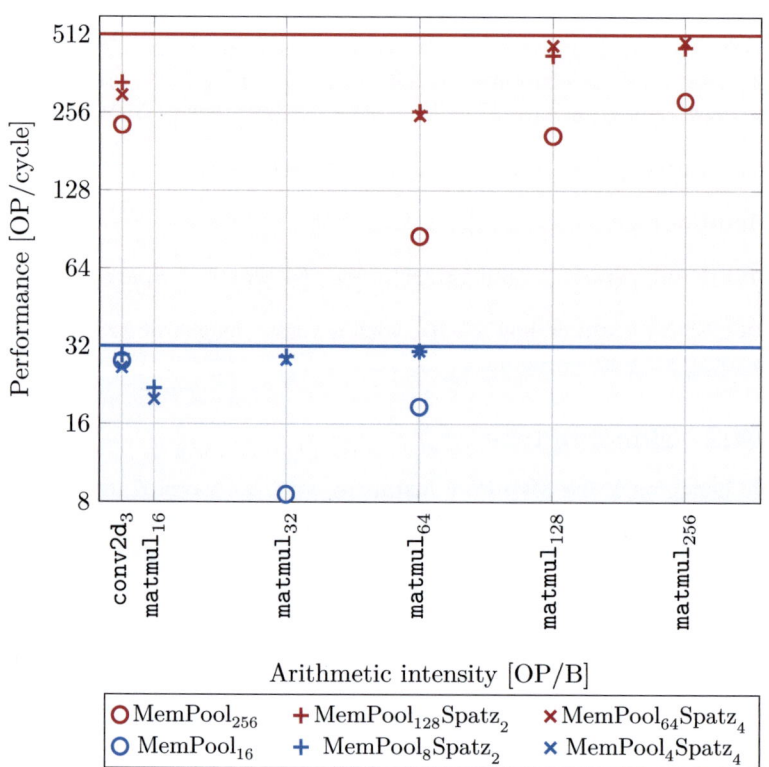

Figure 6.6:   Roofline plot for MemPool instances running the `matmul` and `conv2d` benchmarks.   The subscript numbers besides the benchmark names indicate the matrix size n for `matmul` and the kernel size f for `conv2d`.

well on Spatz, with $\text{MemPool}_8\text{Spatz}_2$ reaching $29.5\,\text{OP/cycle}$ (92.2%) on `conv2d`$_3$. MemPool_{16}'s performance is competitive with Spatz' performance, thanks to a handwritten implementation of `conv2d`$_3$.

The advantage of a vector PE grows with large MemPool configurations. On MemPool_{256}, for example, the `matmul`$_{256}$ kernel reaches $284\,\text{OP/cycle}$ (55.4%). Performance is limited by the data reuse and the `matmul` tiling, which is bounded by Snitch's scalar register file. The VRF allows for increased data reuse on Spatz, which significantly improves Spatz' performance. Moreover, vector chaining allows both the VLSU and the VAU to work concurrently, in a pseudo-double-issue behavior. Thanks to that, $\text{MemPool}_{64}\text{Spatz}_4$ reaches $480.2\,\text{OP/cycle}$ (93.1%) when running `matmul`$_{256}$. While there is some performance degradation for smaller matrices—the $\text{MemPool}_{128}\text{Spatz}_2$ instance reaches $258.3\,\text{OP/cycle}$ (50.4%) on `matmul`$_{64}$—this is still much higher than MemPool_{256}'s performance on the same kernel, which reaches $85.2\,\text{OP/cycle}$ (16.6%). With the convolution kernel, $\text{MemPool}_{128}\text{Spatz}_2$ reaches $332.8\,\text{OP/cycle}$ (65.0%) on `conv2d`$_3$, higher than MemPool_{256}'s $229\,\text{OP/cycle}$ (44.7%).

6.5 Physical Implementation

This section analyzes the post-place-and-route PPA metrics of MemPool group instances that use either Snitch or Spatz as their PEs. We used Synopsys' Fusion Compiler 2022.03 to synthesize, place, and route the MemPool groups using GlobalFoundries' advanced 22FDX FD-SOI technology. All designs target an operating frequency of $500\,\text{MHz}$ in worst-case conditions (SS, $0.72\,\text{V}$, $125\,°\text{C}$).

6.5.1 Area and Performance

Table 6.2 summarizes the area and performance results of MemPool groups derived from the MemPool_{256}, $\text{MemPool}_{128}\text{Spatz}_2$, and $\text{MemPool}_{64}\text{Spatz}_4$ configurations.

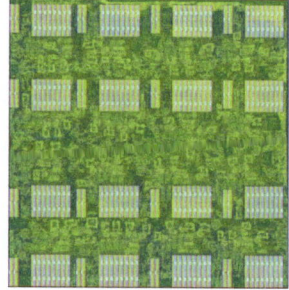

(a) MemPool$_{64}$Spatz$_4$.   (b) MemPool$_{256}$.

Figure 6.7:   Placed-and-routed MemPool group instances of MemPool$_{64}$Spatz$_4$ and MemPool$_{256}$. Images to scale.

Table 6.2: Post-place-and-route PPA results of MemPool$_{256}$, MemPool$_{128}$Spatz$_2$, and MemPool$_{64}$Spatz$_4$.

	MemPool$_{256}$	MemPool$_{128}$Spatz$_2$	MemPool$_{64}$Spatz$_4$
Area [mm^2]	15.8	21.0	20.1
Area (Group) [mm^2]	2.75	3.65	3.50
Cell Area Utilization (Group) [%]	68%	67%	66%
Operating Frequency (w.c.) [MHz]	485	471	472
Operating Frequency (typ.) [MHz]	587	591	594
Peak performance [GOPS]	167	270	285
Area efficiency [GOPS/mm^2]	10.6	12.0	14.2
Power consumption [W]	1.30	1.15	1.07
Energy efficiency [GOPS/W]	128	234	266

The MemPool$_{64}$Spatz$_4$ group is 27% larger than the MemPool$_{256}$ group. As discussed in Section 6.3.2, Spatz' extra footprint is due to its VRF. Figure 6.7 shows the placed-and-routed MemPool$_{64}$Spatz$_4$ and MemPool$_{256}$ groups. The MemPool$_{64}$Spatz$_4$ group of Figure 6.7a was implemented as a 1.87 mm × 1.87 mm macro, and the MemPool$_{256}$ group of Figure 6.7b is a 1.66 mm × 1.66 mm macro. The larger footprint has a small impact on MemPool's maximum operating frequency, which drops from 485 MHz for MemPool$_{256}$ to 471 MHz for MemPool$_2$Spatz$_{128}$. In typical conditions, the three analyzed groups achieve the same operating frequency of around 590 MHz. The critical path of MemPool$_4$Spatz$_{64}$ is 53 gates long, going from a register at the VLSU boundary, through the VRF's read interface, and through the VAU, until reaching a register at the VRF's write port. Overall, Spatz reaches similar frequencies to the rest of the MemPool group despite the length of its critical path and does not limit MemPool's frequency. Moreover, it is possible to pipeline Spatz' critical path by adding a pipeline stage at the VRF read interface. MemPool$_{128}$Spatz$_2$ and MemPool$_{64}$Spatz$_4$ perform similarly in terms of footprint. Due to the reduced size of the Spatz$_4$ PEs, MemPool$_{64}$Spatz$_4$'s area is 5% smaller than MemPool$_{128}$Spatz$_2$'s.

Thanks to comparable operating frequencies and much-improved IPU utilization, the Spatz-based MemPool systems achieve a peak performance much higher than the Snitch-based MemPool. In particular, MemPool$_{64}$Spatz$_4$ reaches the highest performance, 285 GOPS, when running a `matmul`$_{256}$, 71% higher than MemPool$_{256}$'s performance, 167 GOPS. Even considering the larger footprint of the Spatz-based groups, MemPool$_{64}$Spatz$_4$ reaches an area efficiency of 14.2 GOPS/mm^2, which is 33% higher than the 10.6 GOPS/mm^2 of MemPool$_{256}$. Concerning the Spatz-based MemPool instances, the MemPool$_{128}$Spatz$_2$ design reaches a slightly lower area efficiency, 12.0 GOPS/mm^2, due to its lower `matmul`$_{256}$ performance and larger footprint compared to MemPool$_{64}$Spatz$_4$.

6.5.2   Power and Energy Efficiency

We used Synopsys' PrimePower 2022.03 to extract post-place-and-route power results of the MemPool group in typical operating conditions

(TT, 0.80 V, 25 °C), using switching activities extracted from a gate-level simulation of `matmul`$_{256}$. Table 6.2 summarizes the power results for the considered MemPool instances. MemPool$_{256}$ consumes 1.30 W, which is higher than the consumption of both MemPool$_{128}$Spatz$_2$ and MemPool$_{64}$Spatz$_4$. Figure 6.8 shows their power breakdown.

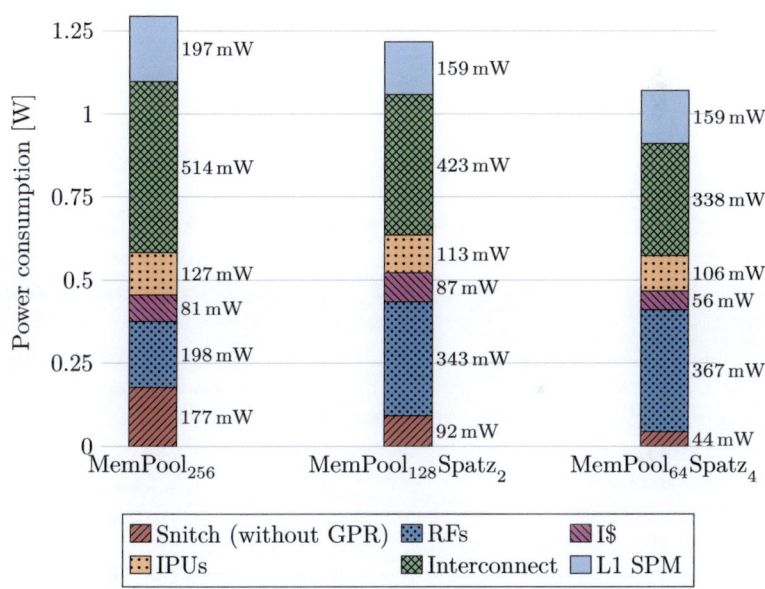

Figure 6.8: Power consumption breakdown of MemPool$_{256}$, MemPool$_{128}$Spatz$_2$, and MemPool$_{64}$Spatz$_4$ running the `matmul`$_{256}$ kernel on typical conditions.

Snitch is a major contributor to of MemPool$_{256}$'s power consumption, being responsible for 375 mW, 29% of the system's overall power consumption. More than half (198 mW, 53%) of the power is consumed by the register file alone. On the other hand, MemPool$_{256}$'s IPUs consume only 127 mW, comparable to the power consumption of its instruction cache, 81 mW. This shows how the VNB translates into a large energy overhead for dispatching instruction. The unbalance in the power consumption breakdown is even more striking because of the low power consumption of the IPUs, which consume only 10% of MemPool$_{256}$'s overall energy consumption. Finally, Snitch's data reuse is limited by the size of its scalar register file. The largest matrix blocks we could fit in the register file is 4×4, i.e., the kernel loads eight elements from L1 for every 16 multiply-accumulate operations. Due to this high L1 memory traffic, the interconnects and L1 SPM SRAM banks are responsible for most of MemPool$_{256}$'s power consumption.

Vector processing amortizes much of the power overheads spotted on MemPool$_{256}$. Snitch's power consumption is only $92\,\mathrm{mW}$ on MemPool$_{128}$Spatz$_2$ and $44\,\mathrm{mW}$ on MemPool$_{64}$Spatz$_4$, 8% and 4% of their overall power consumption. Spatz' VRF consumes a large portion of the total power. On MemPool$_{128}$Spatz$_2$, the VRF consumes $343\,\mathrm{mW}$, 30% of the overall power consumption. That number increases to $367\,\mathrm{mW}$ on MemPool$_{64}$Spatz$_4$, 34% of its total power consumption. Although Spatz' VRF consumes 85% more power than Snitch's register files, its capacity is also four times larger. Therefore, the largest matrix blocks we could fit in the VRF are 8×8, i.e., the kernel loads 16 elements from L1 for every 64 multiply-accumulate operations. As a result, the VRF acts as an L0 memory level, improving the locality and reducing the rate at which the PEs do expensive memory accesses into the L1 SRAM banks. In turn, this decreases the power consumed by the interconnects and L1 SPM banks, which consume $497\,\mathrm{mW}$ (46%) on MemPool$_{64}$Spatz$_4$.

In terms of energy efficiency, Spatz is an highly viable PE option to build a shared-L1 cluster. It more than doubled the energy efficiency of MemPool$_{256}$, with MemPool$_{128}$Spatz$_2$ reaching $234\,\mathrm{GOPS/W}$ and MemPool$_{64}$Spatz$_4$ reaching $266\,\mathrm{GOPS/W}$. Even considering Spatz' increased footprint, for an area increase of 27% (mostly due to the VRF), compared to MemPool$_{256}$, we increased the peak performance by 70% and the energy efficiency by 107%.

6.6   Conclusion

Here, we explored for the first time vector processing as an option to build small and efficient PEs for large-scale clusters with tightly-coupled shared-L1 memory. We adapted Spatz to act as a compact vector processing unit based on the `Zve32x` embedded integer subset of RISC-V's RVV extension version 1.0. The most efficient Spatz configuration, Spatz_4, has four IPUs, and a centralized 2 KiB VRF.

We implemented Spatz_4 with GlobalFoundries' 22FDX FD-SOI technology and measured its energy consumption when running simple arithmetic and memory operations. Spatz amortizes much of Snitch's energy consumption on instruction fetching and decoding thanks to the vector processing induced instruction fetch reduction, i.e., by mitigating the VNB. While a small Spatz_4-based cluster needs 7.9 pJ to execute a multiply-accumulate elementary operation, a Snitch-based cluster requires 13.1 pJ, 66% more energy for the same elementary operation, the difference mainly due to the scalar core.

We also explored Spatz' PPA when it is used as a PE on MemPool, a large-scale shared-L1 cluster with 256 IPUs and 1 MiB of L1. On a multi-core Spatz_4 environment, $\text{MemPool}_{64}\text{Spatz}_4$ reaches up to 480 OP/cycle, a IPU utilization of 94%. This performance is much higher than the performance achieved by the Snitch-based MemPool_{256} cluster, 284 OP/cycle, i.e., a IPU utilization of 55%. On the same kernel, $\text{MemPool}_{64}\text{Spatz}_4$ consumes 1.07 W, 18% less than the 1.30 W consumed by MemPool_{256} running the same kernel and operating conditions. Spatz amortizes Snitch's power requirements, responsible for 29% of MemPool_{256}'s consumption. Moreover, its VRF improves locality and reduces accesses to the L1 SPM.

In terms of energy efficiency, $\text{MemPool}_{64}\text{Spatz}_4$ reaches up to 266 GOPS/W, more than twice the energy efficiency reached by the MemPool_{256} instance, 128 GOPS/W. Even considering Spatz' impact on the design's footprint, for an area increase of 27% (mostly attributed to the VRF), compared to MemPool_{256}, we increased performance by 70% and energy efficiency by 116%. Spatz' agile vector architecture allows a highly efficient PE, which improves the energy efficiency of a vast array of architectures and ensures that it is computation and not instruction fetch and decode to consume most of the power.

Chapter 7

Conclusions

7.1 Summary

This thesis has investigated many techniques to tackle the rapidly growing computational needs of current AI and ML embarrassingly parallel workloads while working under a strict power budget. More precisely, we improved the performance and energy efficiency of computing systems by developing computer architectures that exploit DLP and deploying them on modern and emerging VLSI technologies.

Common to the many threads of this work, we focus on a cluster of small PEs sharing access to some low-latency L1 SPM. The shared-L1 cluster is a simple but ubiquitous architectural pattern. However, despite its simplicity, it is possible to build large and flexible computing systems by replicating and interconnecting many such clusters with a latency-tolerant NoC. As such, optimizing the key metrics of the shared-L1 cluster is a key challenge to enable large-scale, high-performance, energy-efficient programmable computing architectures. Throughout this work, we will focus on many aspects of the shared-L1 cluster, e.g., its PE, the interconnection between the PEs and the L1 SPM, its scalability, and how it can exploit non-planar integration techniques.

Vector architectures promise to tackle the inherent limitations of the word-at-a-time programming style of von Neumann's architecture. We investigated such promises with an open-source 64-bit vector processor and a large application-class scalar core. Its long vectors amortize the expensive cost of fetching and decoding instructions, which percolate through the complex pipeline of the scalar core. As such, our vector processor's almost-ideal performance and state-of-the-art energy efficiency demonstrate that vector processing has its place as a technique to exploit DLP. However, our vector processor fails to achieve good performance with small problems since it starves waiting for the single-issue instruction fetch of its scalar core. Furthermore, although a superscalar issue mechanism would improve the system's performance for a wide range of data-parallel workloads, it would also exacerbate the VNB and degrade its energy efficiency.

The defining characteristic of a vector processor is its ability to exploit DLP and not ILP. This key observation motivated us to design a streamlined vector core that exploits DLP. First, we coupled a small embedded vector unit with a tiny single-stage scalar core, thereby maximizing the cluster area occupied by the double-precision FPUs. Then, we investigated how well this vector-capable CC performs as the PE of the shared-L1 cluster. We achieved this by developing a model of the energy efficiency of the shared-L1 cluster considering the traffic balance tradeoff between the L0 VRF and the L1 SPMs. Thanks to the small instruction fetching and decoding cost of the scalar core, a very small VRF is needed to maximize the cluster's energy efficiency. By exploring the vector abstraction to build compact PEs, we were able to improve the area and energy efficiency of a shared-L1 cluster.

Despite its flexibility, the shared-L1 cluster typically only scales to the low tens of cores. We challenged this through a hierarchical interconnection mechanism, which connects up to 256 cores to 1 MiB of SRAM within at most five cycles (in the absence of contention) at 700 MHz in a modern 22 nm FD-SOI technology node. As a result, we reach up to 60% utilization of the FUs and almost unitary IPC when running a data-parallel workload across this cluster. However, having scalar cores as PEs makes the design a prime target for VNB-related shortcomings. We tackled those through both architectural and physical implementation techniques.

On the physical implementation side, we used 3DICs to relax the wiring congestion and decrease the footprint of the scaled-up cluster. As a result, a 3DIC version of our design consistently achieves higher PPA than the planar equivalent. Furthermore, since the cluster allows for an easy parameterization of the SPM capacity, we can tune the L1 capacity so that the SRAM macros occupy a similar area to the cluster's logic. Therefore, we can have even larger L1 memories under the same footprint, which improves the amount of data reuse within the 3DIC cluster with negligible impact on its operating frequency.

Finally, we improved the cluster's performance and energy efficiency through an architectural exploration. First, we adapted our compact vector PE into a 32-bit integer PE. Replacing scalar cores with this compact PE increases scaled-up cluster's footprint, mainly due to the addition of the VRFs. However, for a small area cost, we achieve almost full utilization of the scaled-up cluster's FUs and more than double its energy efficiency due to the reduction in costly L1 SPM accesses thanks to the increased data reuse enabled by the PE's VRFs.

7.2 Summary of the Contributions

The main results and contributions of this thesis can be summarized as follows.

Design of an Application-Class Vector Unit: Ara is a 64-bit vector processor based on RISC-V's "V" Extension version 1.0. With this design, we analyzed the intrinsic limitations of the vector programming model. As a result, we discovered that the high performance promised by such an architectural model is only feasible for "large-enough" problems. Furthermore, we placed and routed Ara in a modern FD-SOI 22 nm technology node, achieving an energy efficiency of up to $41\,\mathrm{GFLOPS_{DP}/W}$ on a 256×256 double-precision matrix multiplication kernel.

Energy Consumption Model of the Shared-L1 Cluster: Shared-L1 clusters are a common architectural model which comprises small PEs, each with private L0 memory, sharing access to some low-latency L1 memory. We modeled the cluster's energy efficiency as a function of the L0 memory of the PEs, considering that we can trade off larger L0 capacity against lower L1 bandwidth. We discovered that only a very small L0 memory is required to optimally balance such energy costs while also amortizing the VNB related to the fetching and decoding of individual instructions.

Design of an Embedded Vector Unit: Spatz is a compact, parametric, 64-bit vector processor based on RISC-V's "V" Extension version 1.0. Assuming that Spatz is the PE of a small shared-L1 cluster and its VRF is the L0 memory, our results indicate that only a very small VRF is required to achieve high performance and energy efficiency. Unlike Ara, Spatz is extremely simple and focuses solely on exploiting DLP. Therefore, the design is much leaner, particularly since its VRF is much smaller than typical large vector processors. We implemented the Spatz-based shared-L1 cluster in a modern FinFET 12 nm node. Spatz achieves up to 87 $\mathrm{GFLOPS_{DP}}$/W on a 64×64 double-precision matrix multiplication kernel.

Scale-Out of the Shared-L1 Cluster: Despite the ubiquity of this architectural model, the shared-L1 cluster was thought only to scale to the low tens of cores. With MomPool, we pushed this boundary further to the hundreds. MemPool comprises 256 cores sharing access to 1 MiB of L1 SPM, accessible within five cycles of latency in the absence of contention. We achieve this through a hierarchical interconnect, grouping cores physically close to a neighborhood with lower latency and higher throughput. Despite the challenges associated with programming 256 cores, MemPool's PEs achieve an average IPC of 0.96 for a peak performance of 229 GOPS and an energy efficiency of 192 GOPS/W on a large 32-bit integer matrix multiplication kernel.

Co-Optimization of the Shared-L1 Cluster: This work is two-fold, as we tried to improve MemPool's PPA through architectural improvements and by exploiting emerging VLSI technologies. First, using Spatz as the PE of such a large-scale shared-L1 cluster proved highly beneficial since it increased MemPool's performance by 70% and more than doubled its energy efficiency for a moderate area increase of 27%. Then, we investigated whether 3DIC integration could help with the routing congestion of MemPool. In general, the 3DIC MemPool designs achieved higher operating frequency, performance, and energy efficiency than their 2DIC counterparts. Furthermore, we integrated 8 MiB of L1 SPM under a footprint smaller than the 2DIC design with only 1 MiB of L1.

7.3 Outlook and Future Work

In this section, we discuss some possible future research topics, and conclude the thesis with an outlook.

7.3.1 Future Work

Sparsity: Exploiting sparsity is a challenge for many computer architectures, particularly those which exploit DLP. For example, the traditional methods to exploit sparsity in a vector machine turn a sparse vector in memory into a dense vector in the VRF. This is, however, only appropriate for a few sparse workloads. As such, other solutions which depart from the vector programming model reach much higher performance at the cost of a complex memory interconnect. Extending the vector abstraction might help achieve high sparse performance with a vector processor while not sacrificing its leanness.

Low-Precision: Many modern arithmetically-intensive workloads do not require the high precision provided by a 64-bit FPU, for example. RISC-V's "V" ISA supports down to 16-bit half-precision floating-point computations. However, the vector ISA proves to be inadequate whenever there is a need to convert between precision modes. Reaching high performance and full utilization of the FPUs on a vector processor might require the extension of the vector ISA to contemplate this use case.

Scale-Out of the Shared-L1 Cluster: Despite MemPool's flexibility, its scalability breaks when we push its core count even further. Therefore, we must deploy novel physical design techniques to integrate thousands of cores sharing high-bandwidth access to a large swath of L1 SPM. Furthermore, the energy cost of this L1 interconnect is prohibitively expensive. Particularly, extending our shared-L1 cluster energy model might give insights into the optimal bandwidth that the cluster's interconnects should provide, possibly across many memory levels.

7.3.2 Outlook

Those are exciting times for computer architecture. Despite the challenges imposed by the breakdown of Moore's Law and Dennard's scaling—or thanks to them—computing systems still keep up with the ever-increasing needs of modern workloads. Moreover, there is an interesting prospect of co-optimization between architecture and physical design through architectural innovation and the exploitation of emerging VLSI technologies. The systems developed throughout this thesis hint at the performance and energy efficiency gains allowed by physically-driven architectures for the post-Moore era.

Appendix A

Chip Gallery

This appendix lists all chips the author has contributed to in the form of technical work or supervision. A complete, up-to-date list of chips with the author's involvement can be found online at `http://asic.ethz.ch/authors/Matheus_Cavalcante.html`.

A.1   Hedwig

Hedwig is the interposer for the final 2.5D integrated Occamy system and is designed to host two Occamy dies and two 16 GiB High-Bandwidth Memory Gen2E (HBM2E) dies. It provides high speed connectivity with ground shielding between each Occamy die and their dedicated HBM2E die as well as the connectivity of our custom serial die-to-die link. The interposer has been designed to support 3.2 Gbit/s/pin HBM2E connectivity as well as providing up to 150 A of current for the entire system. The interposer has only interconnections, and no active or passive devices are integrated on it.

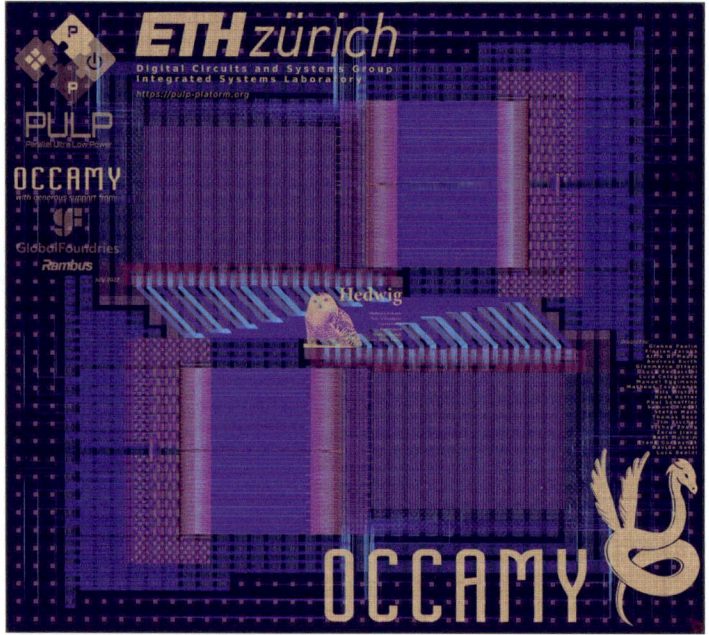

Figure A.1: Hedwig.

The interposer has 40×35 C4 bumps arrayed at the bottom as a Ball Grid Array (BGA) and has been designed to be mounted on a Printed Circuit Board (PCB) directly. This project has been very generously sponsored by GlobalFoundries and Rambus and has received support from Synopsys and Micron. Staying with the Harry Potter theme, the interposer has been named after Harry Potter's owl.

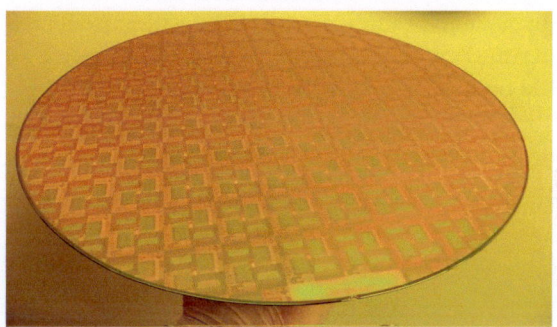

Figure A.2: Hedwig 300-mm-diameter wafer sample.

Name	Hedwig
Designers	Matheus Cavalcante, Sina Arjmandpour, Gianna Paulin, Zerun Jiang, Beat Muheim, Frank K. Gürkaynak, Alfonso Fontao
Application/Publication	HPC/Research Project
Technology/Package	GF-SI65/BGA1400
Dimensions	26.3 mm × 23.05 mm
Voltage	0.8 V, 1.2 V, 1.8 V, 2.5 V
Clock	1 GHz Occamy, 1.6 GHz HBM2E, 125 MHz Die-to-Die (D2D)

A.2   Occamy

Occamy is the compute die of an ambitious project that has been very generously sponsored by GlobalFoundries and Rambus. It was also supported by Synopsys and Micron. The compute die contains 216 RISC-V cores and an HBM2E controller by Rambus. Two such dies are connected on the Hedwig interposer, Appendix A.1. Furthermore, each compute die has access to its dedicated HBM2E memory module, also assembled together on top of Hedwig.

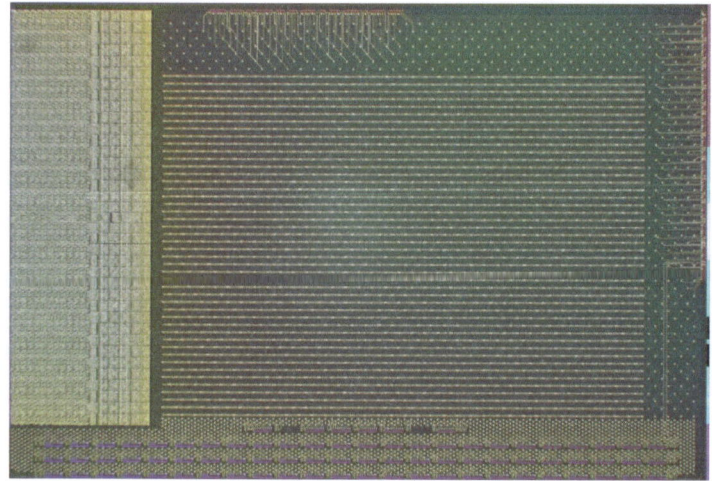

Figure A.3: Occamy.

Name	Occamy
Designers	Gianna Paulin, Florian Zaruba,
	Alfio Di Mauro, Andreas Kurth, Gianmarco
	Ottavi, Luca Bertaccini, Luca Colagrande,
	Manuel Eggimann, Matheus Cavalcante,
	Nils Wistoff, Noah Huetter,
	Paul Scheffler, Samuel Riedel,
	Stefan Mach, Thomas Benz,
	Tim Fischer, Yichao Zhang,
	Zerun Jiang, Beat Muheim, Frank K.
	Gürkaynak, Davide Rossi, Luca Benini
Application/Publication	HPC/Research Project
Technology/Package	GF12/Custom
Dimensions	10.5 mm × 6.95 mm
Voltage	0.8 V
Clock	1 GHz

A.3   Yun

Yun is the first tape-out of Ara, Chapter 2, a RISC-V-based vector
processing engine attahed to the CVA6 core. It includes a minimal
configuration with four lanes supporting double precision floating-point
computation with a total of 16 KiB of Ara VRF, 16 KiB of CVA6 caches,
and a 64 KiB L2 SRAM for the system.

Figure A.4: Yun.

The name "Yun" is a Chinese character for the Sun. It also uses
the symbol for the Four Horsemen from the movie Now You See Me.
The logo incorporates all these elements, with a Macaw (or Ara), the
Yun character, and the Four Horsemen logo embedded into the "N."

Name	Yun
Designers	Jiantao Liu, Matheus Cavalcante
	Matteo Perotti, Alessandro Ottaviano
Application/Publication	PULP
Technology/Package	TSMC65/QFN56
Dimensions	$2000\,\mu m \times 3000\,\mu m$
Voltage	$1.2\,V$
Clock	$250\,MHz$

A.4 MinPool

MinPool is based on the MemPool architecture, Chapter 4. MemPool aims to place a high number of cores in one chip. This is done with a special interconnect through which all cores can access the scratchpad memory of any other core. MinPool is a scaled down version of MemPool with 16 cores.

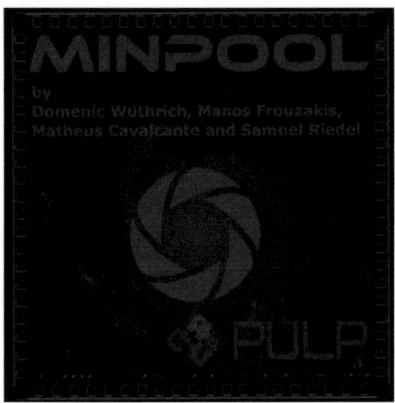

Figure A.5: MinPool.

MinPool is a manycore computer architecture with the purpose of incorporating a high number of CPU cores on a chip die. One of the main issues with scaling multicore clusters to high core counts is the intercore latency. MinPool demonstrates an approach to scale up the L1-interconnect, while ensuring that the average memory access latency stays below 6 cycles. The CPU cores used in MinPool are the highly-flexible, general-purpose Snitch cores.

In total MinPool has a modest 64 KiB scratchpad memory, 8 KiB of I$ and 64 KiB of L2 memory. MinPool runs at 200 MHz. The internal name of the project is also Pinwheel, and the logo shows such a stylized pinwheel galaxy embedded within MemPool's logo.

Name	MinPool
Designers	Domenic Wüthrich, Emmanouil Frouzakis, Matheus Cavalcante, Samuel Riedel
Application/Publication	PULP
Technology/Package	TSMC65/QFN56
Dimensions	2400 µm × 2400 µm
Voltage	1.2 V
Clock	200 MHz

Appendix B

Notation and Acronyms

Symbols

ELEN	Maximum size in bits of a vector element that any vector instruction can produce or consume.
EW	Current SEW configuration, $EW \in \{8, 16, 32, 64\}$ bit, describing the width of each element in a vector register.
Φ	Arithmetic intensity, in OP/B.
ℓ	Current LMUL configuration, $\ell \in \{1, 2, 4, 8\}$, used to trade available vector registers against longer vectors at runtime.
λ	Injected load, in request/core/cycle.
Π	Peak performance, in OP/cycle.
π	Achieved performance, in OP/cycle.
ρ	Probability of the traffic generator to generate a request in its local tile's sequential memory region.
VLENB	Number of bytes in a vector register.

VLMAX   Maximum number of elements that can be operated with a single vector instruction, given the current SEW and LMUL settings.

Acronyms

1RW	Single-Ported Read and Write
2DIC	Two-Dimensional Integrated Circuit
2.5DIC	Two-and-a-Half-Dimensional Integrated Circuit
3DIC	Three-Dimensional Integrated Circuit
3R1W	Three Read Ports and one Write Port
AI	Artificial Intelligence
ALU	Arithmetic and Logic Unit
ASIC	Application-Specific Integrated Circuit
AVX	Advanced Vector Extension
AXI	Advanced eXtended Interface
BB	Body Biasing
BEOL	Back End of the Line
BGA	Ball Grid Array
BLAS	Basic Linear Algebra Subprograms
C4	Controlled Collapse Chip Connection
CC	Core Complex
CMOS	Complementary Metal-Oxide-Semiconductor
CNN	Convolutional Neural Network
CPU	Central Processing Unit
CSR	Control and Status Register
D2D	Die-to-Die
DCT	Discrete Cosine Transform
DDR	Double Data Rate
DLP	Data Level Parallelism
DMA	Direct Memory Access

DRV	Design Rule Violation
DSP	Digital Signal Processing
ECL	Emitter-Coupled Logic
EDA	Electronic Design Automation
EDP	Energy-Delay Product
EUV	Extreme Ultraviolet Lithography
F2F	Face-to-Face
FBB	Forward Body Biasing
FD-SOI	Fully-Depleted Silicon-on-Insulator
FFT	Fast Fourier Transform
FinFET	Fin Field-Effect Transistor
FMA	Fused Multiply-Add
FO4	Fan-Out Four
FPGA	Field-Programmable Gate Array
FPR	Floating-Point Register File
FPU	Floating Point Unit
FU	Functional Unit
GP-GPU	General-Purpose computing on Graphics Processing Units
GPR	General-Purpose Register File
GPU	Graphics Processing Unit
HB	Hybrid Bonding
HBM2E	High-Bandwidth Memory Gen2E
HPC	High-Performance Computing
I$	Instruction Cache
ICG	Integrated Clock Gating
ILP	Instruction Level Parallelism
IoT	Internet-of-Things
IPC	Instructions per Cycle
IPU	Integer Processing Unit
ISA	Instruction Set Architecture
LMUL	Vector Length Multiplier
LSU	Load/Store Unit

LVT	Low Voltage Threshold
MAC	Multiply-Accumulate
MCM	Multi-Chip Module
MIMD	Multiple Instruction, Multiple Data
ML	Machine Learning
MVE	M-Profile Vector Extension
NoC	Network-on-Chip
NUMA	Non-Uniform Memory Access
PC	Program Counter
PCB	Printed Circuit Board
PDP	Power-Delay Product
PE	Processing Element
PG	Power Gating
PPA	Power, Performance, and Area
RAM	Random Access Memory
RAW	Read After Write
RBB	Reverse Body Biasing
RF	Register File
ROB	Reorder Buffer
RTL	Register Transfer Level
RVV	RISC-V Vector Extension
SCM	Standard Cell Memory
SDRAM	Synchronous Dynamic Random Access Memory
SEW	Selected Element Width
SIMD	Single Instruction, Multiple Data
SIMT	Single Instruction, Multiple Thread
SLVT	Super-Low Voltage Threshold
SM	Streaming Multiprocessor
SoC	System-on-Chip
SPM	Scratchpad Memory
SRAM	Static Random-Access Memory
SSE	Streaming SIMD Extension
SSR	Stream Semantic Register

STA	Static Timing Analysis
SVE	Scalable Vector Extension
TLP	Thread Level Parallelism
TTM	Time-to-Market
VALU	Vector Arithmetic and Logic Unit
VAU	Vector Arithmetic Unit
VLA	Vector Length Agnostic
VLIW	Very Long Instruction Word
VLSI	Very-Large-Scale Integration
VLSU	Vector Load/Store Unit
VMASKU	Vector Mask Unit
VMFPU	Vector Multiplier and Floating Point Unit
VNB	von Neumann Bottleneck
VPU	Vector Processing Unit
VRF	Vector Register File
VSLDU	Vector Slide Unit
VT	Vector Thread
WAR	Write After Read
WAW	Write After Write
XIF	CORE-V's X-Interface

Bibliography

[1] J. Backus, "Can Programming Be Liberated from the von Neumann Style? A Functional Style and Its Algebra of Programs," *Communications of ACM*, vol. 21, no. 8, pp. 613–641, Aug. 1978.

[2] G. Moore, "Progress in digital integrated electronics," *International Electron Devices Meeting, IEEE*, vol. 21, pp. 11–13, 1975.

[3] R. Dennard, F. Gaensslen, V. Rideout, E. Bassous, and A. LeBlanc, "Design of ion-implanted MOSFET's with very small physical dimensions," *IEEE Journal of Solid-State Circuits*, vol. 9, no. 5, pp. 256–268, Oct. 1974.

[4] T. Yoshida, "Fujitsu high performance CPU for the Post-K computer," in *Proceedings of the 2018 IEEE Hot Chips 30 Symposium (HC30)*, ser. HC30, Cupertino, CA, USA: IEEE, Aug. 2018.

[5] Top500, *Top500 list - November 2022*, Nov. 2022. [Online]. Available: https://www.top500.org/lists/top500/2022/11/ (visited on Mar. 1, 2023).

[6] RISC-V International, *RISC-V "V" Vector Extension, version 1.0*, 2022. [Online]. Available: https://github.com/riscv/riscv-v-spec/releases/tag/v1.0 (visited on Jun. 18, 2022).

[7] M. Cavalcante, F. Schuiki, F. Zaruba, and L. Benini, "Ara: A 1-GHz+ scalable and energy-efficient RISC-V vector processor with multiprecision floating-point support in 22-nm FD-SOI,"

IEEE Transactions on Very Large Scale Integration (VLSI) Systems, vol. 28, no. 2, pp. 530–543, 2020.

[8] X. Lin, J. Li, R. Baldemair, J.-F. T. Cheng, S. Parkvall, D. C. Larsson, H. Koorapaty, M. Frenne, S. Falahati, A. Grovlen, and K. Werner, "5G new radio: Unveiling the essentials of the next generation wireless access technology," *IEEE Communications Standards Magazine*, vol. 3, no. 3, pp. 30–37, 2019.

[9] M. Bertuletti, Y. Zhang, A. Vanelli-Coralli, and L. Benini, "Efficient parallelization of 5G-PUSCH on a scalable RISC-V many-core processor," in *Proceedings of the 2023 Design, Automation, & Test in Europe Conference & Exhibition (DATE)*, Antwerp, Belgium: IEEE, Mar. 2023.

[10] Green500, *Green500 list – June 2022*, Jun. 2022. [Online]. Available: https://www.top500.org/green500/lists/2022/06/ (visited on Mar. 1, 2023).

[11] M. Cavalcante, D. Wüthrich, M. Perotti, S. Riedel, and L. Benini, "Spatz: A compact vector processing unit for high-performance and energy-efficient shared-L1 clusters," in *Proceedings of the 41st International Conference on Computer-Aided Design*, San Diego, CA, USA: IEEE/Association for Computing Machinery, Oct. 2022.

[12] F. Minervini and O. Palomar, "Vitruvius: And area-efficient RISC-V decoupled vector accelerator for high performance computing," in *Proceedings of the RISC-V Summit 2021*, RISC-V International, San Francisco, CA, USA, Dec. 2021.

[13] A. Ivanov, N. Dryden, T. Ben-Nun, S. Li, and T. Hoefler, "Data movement is all you need: A case study on optimizing transformers," in *Proceedings of 4th Conference on Machine Learning and Systems (MLSys 2021)*, vol. 3, Virtual conference, Apr. 2021, pp. 711–732.

[14] M. Cavalcante, S. Riedel, A. Pullini, and L. Benini, "MemPool: A shared-L1 memory many-core cluster with a low-latency interconnect," in *Proceedings of the 2021 Design, Automation, & Test in Europe Conference & Exhibition (DATE)*, Grenoble, France: IEEE, Mar. 2021, pp. 701–706.

[15] T. Li, J. Hou, J. Yan, R. Liu, H. Yang, and Z. Sun, "Chiplet heterogeneous integration technology: Status and challenges," *Electronics*, vol. 9, no. 4, p. 670, Apr. 2020.

[16] J. Redgrave, A. Meixner, N. Goulding-Hotta, A. Vasilyev, and O. Shacham, "Pixel Visual Core: Google's fully programmable image, vision and AI processor for mobile devices," in *Proceedings of the 2018 IEEE Hot Chips 30 Symposium (HC30)*, IEEE Technical Committee on Microprocessors and Microcomputers, Cupertino, CA, USA, Aug. 2018.

[17] E. Talpes, D. Williams, and D. Das Sarma, "Dojo: The Microarchitecture of Tesla's Exa-Scale Computer," in *Proceedings of the 2022 IEEE Hot Chips 34 Symposium (HC34)*, IEEE Technical Committee on Microprocessors and Microcomputers, Cupertino, CA, USA, Aug. 2022.

[18] Apple Corp., *Apple unveils M1 Ultra, the world's most powerful chip for a personal computer*, 2022. [Online]. Available: `https://nr.apple.com/d2I1v3s8D5` (visited on Dec. 2, 2022).

[19] S. Mirabbasi, L. C. Fujino, and K. C. Smith, "Through the looking glass—the 2022 edition: Trends in solid-state circuits from ISSCC," *IEEE Solid-State Circuits Magazine*, vol. 14, no. 1, pp. 54–72, 2022.

[20] Synopsys Corp., *3DIC Compiler*, Datasheet, Mountain View, CA, USA, 2022. [Online]. Available: `https://www.synopsys.com/implementation-and-signoff/3dic-design.html` (visited on Dec. 2, 2022).

[21] Cadence Corp., *3D-IC Design Solutions*, Datasheet, San Jose, CA, USA, 2023. [Online]. Available: `https://www.cadence.com/en_US/home/solutions/3dic-design-solutions.html` (visited on Mar. 6, 2023).

[22] S. Panth, K. Samadi, Y. Du, and S.-K. Lim, "High-density integration of functional modules using monolithic 3D-IC technology," in *Proceedings of the 2013 18th Asia and South Pacific Design Automation Conference (ASP-DAC)*, 2013, pp. 681–686.

[23] V. Pavlidis and E. Friedman, "Interconnect-Based Design Methodologies for Three-Dimensional Integrated Circuits," *Proceedings of the IEEE*, vol. 97, no. 1, pp. 123–140, 2009.

[24] X. Dong, J. Zhao, and Y. Xie, "Fabrication cost analysis and cost-aware design space exploration for 3-D ICs," *IEEE Transactions on Computer-Aided Design of Integrated Circuits and Systems*, vol. 29, no. 12, pp. 1959–1972, 2010.

[25] A. Agnesina, M. Brunion, A. García-Ortiz, F. Catthoor, D. Milojevic, M. Komalan, M. Cavalcante, S. Riedel, L. Benini, and S.-K. Lim, "Hier-3D: A hierarchical physical design methodology for face-to-face-bonded 3D ICs," in *Proceedings of the ACM/IEEE International Symposium on Low Power Electronics and Design*, ser. ISLPED '22, Boston, MA, USA: Association for Computing Machinery, 2022.

[26] L. Bamberg, A. García-Ortiz, L. Zhu, S. Pentapati, D. Shim, and S.-K. Lim, "Macro-3D: A physical design methodology for face-to-face-stacked heterogeneous 3D ICs," in *Proceedings of the 2020 Design, Automation & Test in Europe Conference & Exhibition (DATE)*, Grenoble, France, Mar. 2020, pp. 37–42.

[27] L. Yang, R. M. Radway, Y.-H. Chen, T. F. Wu, H. Liu, E. Ansari, V. Chandra, S. Mitra, and E. Deigné, "Three-dimensional stacked neural network accelerator architectures for AR/VR applications," *IEEE Micro*, vol. 42, no. 6, pp. 116–124, 2022.

[28] M. Cavalcante, A. Agnesina, S. Riedel, M. Brunion, A. García-Ortiz, D. Milojevic, F. Catthoor, S.-K. Lim, and L. Benini, "MemPool-3D: Boosting performance and efficiency of shared-L1 memory many-core clusters with 3D integration," in *Proceedings of the 2022 Design, Automation & Test in Europe Conference & Exhibition (DATE)*, Antwerp, Belgium: IEEE, Mar. 2022, pp. 394–399.

[29] M. Perotti, M. Cavalcante, N. Wistoff, R. Andri, L. Cavigelli, and L. Benini, "A 'new Ara' for vector computing: An open source highly efficient RISC-V V 1.0 vector processor design," in *Proceedings of the 33rd IEEE International Conference on Application-specific Systems, Architectures and Processors*, Gothenburg, Sweden: IEEE, Jul. 2022.

[30] G. Paulin, M. Cavalcante, P. Scheffler, L. Bertaccini, Y. Zhang, F. Gürkaynak, and L. Benini, "Soft tiles: Capturing physical implementation flexibility for tightly-coupled parallel processing

clusters," in *Proceedings of the IEEE Computer Society Annual Symposium on VLSI 2022*, Pafos, Cyprus: IEEE, Jul. 2022.

[31] M. Cavalcante, A. Kurth, F. Schuiki, and L. Benini, "Design of an open-source bridge between non-coherent burst-based and coherent cache-line-based memory systems," in *Proceedings of the 17th ACM International Conference on Computing Frontiers*, (Catania, Italy), ser. CF '20, New York, NY, USA: Association for Computing Machinery, 2020, pp. 81–88.

[32] A. Kurth, W. Rönninger, T. Benz, M. Cavalcante, F. Schuiki, F. Zaruba, and L. Benini, "An Open-Source Platform for High-Performance Non-Coherent On-Chip Communication," *IEEE Transactions on Computers*, pp. 1794–1809, 2021.

[33] S. Riedel, G. H. Khov, S. Mazzola, M. Cavalcante, R. Andri, and L. Benini, "MemPool meets systolic: Flexible systolic computation in a large shared-memory processor cluster," in *Proceedings of the 2023 Design, Automation & Test in Europe Conference & Exhibition (DATE)*, Antwerp, Belgium: IEEE, Mar. 2023.

[34] P. Iff, M. Besta, M. Cavalcante, T. Fischer, L. Benini, and T. Hoefler, "Sparse hamming graph: A customizable network-on-chip topology," in *Proceedings of the 60th Design Automation Conference*, ser. DAC '23, San Francisco, CA, USA: Association for Computing Machinery, Jun. 2023.

[35] P. Iff, M. Besta, M. Cavalcante, T. Fischer, L. Benini, and T. Hoefler, "HexaMesh: Scaling to hundreds of chiplets with an optimized chiplet arrangement," in *Proceedings of the 60th Design Automation Conference*, ser. DAC '23, San Francisco, CA, USA: Association for Computing Machinery, Jun. 2023.

[36] V. Jain, M. Cavalcante, N. Bruschi, M. Rogenmoser, T. Benz, A. Kurth, D. Rossi, L. Benini, and M. Verhelst, "PATRONoC: Parallel AXI transport reducing overhead for networks-on-chip targeting multi-accelerator DNN platforms at the edge," in *Proceedings of the 60th Design Automation Conference*, ser. DAC '23, San Francisco, CA, USA: Association for Computing Machinery, Jun. 2023.

[37] M. Perotti, M. Cavalcante, A. Ottaviano, J. Liu, and L. Benini, "Yun: An open-source, 64-bit RISC-V-Based vector processor with multi-precision integer and floating-point support in 65-nm CMOS," *IEEE Transactions on Circuits and Systems II: Express Briefs*, 2023.

[38] R. Dreslinski, M. Wieckowski, D. Blaauw, D. Sylvester, and T. Mudge, "Near-threshold computing: Reclaiming Moore's law through energy efficient integrated circuits," *Proceedings of the IEEE*, vol. 98, no. 2, pp. 253–266, Feb. 2010.

[39] I. Hwang and M. Pedram, "A comparative study of the effectiveness of CPU consolidation versus dynamic voltage and frequency scaling in a virtualized multicore server," *IEEE Transactions on Very Large Scale Integration (VLSI) Systems*, vol. 24, no. 6, pp. 2103–2116, Jun. 2016.

[40] S. Kiamehr, M. Ebrahimi, M. Golanbari, and M. Tahoori, "Temperature-aware dynamic voltage scaling to improve energy efficiency of near-threshold computing," *IEEE Transactions on Very Large Scale Integration (VLSI) Systems*, vol. 25, no. 7, pp. 2017–2026, Jul. 2017.

[41] V. Sze, Y. Chen, T. Yang, and J. Emer, "Efficient processing of deep neural networks: A tutorial and survey," *Proceedings of the IEEE*, vol. 105, no. 12, pp. 2295–2329, Dec. 2017.

[42] D. Dabbelt, C. Schmidt, E. Love, H. Mao, S. Karandikar, and K. Asanović, "Vector processors for energy-efficient embedded systems," in *Proceedings of the Third ACM International Workshop on Many-core Embedded Systems*, ser. MES '16, New York, NY, USA: ACM, 2016, pp. 10–16.

[43] J. Owens, M. Houston, D. Luebke, S. Green, J. Stone, and J. Phillips, "GPU computing," *Proceedings of the IEEE*, vol. 96, no. 5, pp. 879–899, May 2008.

[44] E. Lindholm, J. Nickolls, S. Oberman, and J. Montrym, "NVIDIA Tesla: A unified graphics and computing architecture," *IEEE Micro*, vol. 28, no. 2, pp. 39–55, Mar. 2008.

[45] M. Bojarski, D. Del Testa, D. Dworakowski, B. Firner, B. Flepp, P. Goyal, L. Jackel, M. Monfort, U. Muller, J. Zhang, X. Zhang, J. Zhao, and K. Zieba, "End to end learning for self-driving cars," *CoRR*, 2016. arXiv: 1604.07316.

[46] R. Russell, "The CRAY-1 computer system," *Communications of ACM*, vol. 21, no. 1, pp. 63–72, Jan. 1978.

[47] S. Beldianu and S. Ziavras, "Performance-energy optimizations for shared vector accelerators in multicores," *IEEE Transactions on Computers*, vol. 64, no. 3, pp. 805–817, Mar. 2015.

[48] J. Choquette, W. Gandhi, O. Giroux, N. Stam, and R. Krashinsky, "NVIDIA A100 tensor core GPU: Performance and innovation," *IEEE Micro*, vol. 41, no. 2, pp. 29–35, 2021.

[49] M. Morris, C. Kime, and T. Martin, *Logic and Computer Design Fundamentals*, 5th. Hoboken, NJ, USA: Pearson High Education, 2015.

[50] J. Hennessy and D. Patterson, *Computer Architecture: A Quantitative Approach*, 5th. San Francisco, CA, USA: Morgan Kaufmann Publishers Inc., 2011.

[51] F. Zaruba and L. Benini, "The cost of application-class processing: Energy and performance analysis of a Linux-ready 1.7-GHz 64-Bit RISC-V core in 22-nm FDSOI technology," *IEEE Transactions on Very Large Scale Integration (VLSI) Systems*, vol. 27, no. 11, pp. 2629–2640, 2019.

[52] A. Peleg and U. Weiser, "MMX technology extension to the Intel architecture," *IEEE Micro*, vol. 16, no. 4, pp. 42–50, Aug. 1996.

[53] M. Flynn, "Some computer organizations and their effectiveness," *IEEE Transactions on Computers*, vol. C-21, no. 9, pp. 948–960, Sep. 1972.

[54] J. Reinders, "Intel AVX-512 instructions," *Intel Software Developer Zone*, Jun. 2017. [Online]. Available: `https://software. intel . com / en - us / blogs / 2013 / avx - 512 - instructions` (visited on Mar. 1, 2023).

[55] Arm Corp., *Neon programmer's guide*, Version 1.0, Cambridge, UK, 2013. [Online]. Available: `https://developer.arm.com/documentation/den0018/a/?lang=en` (visited on Mar. 1, 2023).

[56] M. Gautschi, P. Schiavone, A. Traber, I. Loi, A. Pullini, D. Rossi, E. Flamand, F. Gürkaynak, and L. Benini, "Near-threshold RISC-V core with DSP extensions for scalable IoT endpoint devices," *IEEE Transactions on Very Large Scale Integration (VLSI) Systems*, vol. 25, no. 10, pp. 2700–2713, Oct. 2017.

[57] K. Asanović, "Vector microprocessors," Ph.D. dissertation, University of California, Berkeley, 1998.

[58] N. Stephens, S. Biles, M. Boettcher, J. Eapen, M. Eyole, G. Gabrielli, M. Horsnell, G. Magklis, A. Martinez, N. Premillieu, A. Reid, A. Rico, and P. Walker, "The ARM Scalable Vector Extension," *IEEE Micro*, vol. 37, no. 2, pp. 26–39, Mar. 2017.

[59] Arm Corp., *Introduction to Armv8.1-M architecture*, Revision r1p1, Arm Corp., Cambridge, UK, Feb. 2019.

[60] Arm Corp., *Arm Cortex-M55 processor datasheet*, Arm Corp., Cambridge, UK, 2020. [Online]. Available: `https://developer.arm.com/documentation/102833/0100/?lang=en` (visited on Mar. 1, 2023).

[61] Y. Lee, R. Avizienis, A. Bishara, R. Xia, D. Lockhart, C. Batten, and K. Asanović, "Exploring the tradeoffs between programmability and efficiency in data-parallel accelerators," *SIGARCH Computer Architecture News*, vol. 39, no. 3, pp. 129–140, 2011.

[62] R. Krashinsky, C. Batten, M. Hampton, S. Gerding, B. Pharris, J. Casper, and K. Asanović, "The vector-thread architecture," *SIGARCH Computer Architecture News*, vol. 32, no. 2, p. 52, Mar. 2004.

[63] C. Schmidt, A. Ou, and K. Asanović, "Hwacha: A data-parallel RISC-V extension and implementation," in *Inaugural RISC-V Summit Proceedings*, RISC-V International, Santa Clara, CA, USA, Dec. 2018.

[64] F. Schuiki, F. Zaruba, T. Hoefler, and L. Benini, "Stream semantic registers: A lightweight RISC-V ISA extension achieving full compute utilization in single-issue cores," *IEEE Transactions on Computers*, vol. 70, no. 2, pp. 212–227, 2021.

[65] P. Scheffler, F. Zaruba, F. Schuiki, T. Hoefler, and L. Benini, "Indirection stream semantic register architecture for efficient sparse-dense linear algebra," in *Proceedings of the 2021 Design, Automation & Test in Europe Conference & Exhibition (DATE)*, Grenoble, France, Mar. 2021, pp. 1787–1792.

[66] C. Schmidt, A. Ou, Y. Lee, and K. Asanović, "Vector extension proposal," in *Proceedings of the 2nd RISC-V Workshop*, Berkeley, CA, USA, Jun. 2015.

[67] M. Cavalcante, "Low-energy cluster-coupled vector coprocessor for special-purpose PULP acceleration," M.Sc. thesis, ETH Zürich, Zürich, Switzerland, Jun. 2018.

[68] RISC-V International, *The RISC-V Instruction Set Manual: Unprivileged ISA*, ed. by A. Waterman and K. Asanović, Version 20191213, CS Division, EECS Department, University of California, Berkeley, CA, USA, Dec. 2019.

[69] S. Mach, F. Schuiki, F. Zaruba, and L. Benini, "FPnew: An open-source multiformat floating-point unit architecture for energy-proportional transprecision computing," *IEEE Transactions on Very Large Scale Integration (VLSI) Systems*, vol. 29, no. 4, pp. 774–787, 2021.

[70] S. Mach, D. Rossi, G. Tagliavini, A. Marongiu, and L. Benini, "A transprecision floating-point architecture for energy-efficient embedded computing," in *Proceedings of the 2018 IEEE International Symposium on Circuits and Systems (ISCAS)*, May 2018, pp. 1–5.

[71] S. Williams, A. Waterman, and D. Patterson, "Roofline: An insightful visual performance model for multicore architectures," *Communications of ACM*, vol. 52, no. 4, pp. 65–76, Apr. 2009.

[72] G. Ofenbeck, R. Steinmann, V. Caparros, D. G. Spampinato, and M. Pueschel, "Applying the roofline model," in *Proceedings of the IEEE International Symposium on Performance Analysis of Systems and Software (ISPASS)*, Mar. 2014, pp. 76–85.

[73] C. Szegedy, W. Liu, Y. Jia, P. Sermanet, S. Reed, D. Anguelov, D. Erhan, V. Vanhoucke, and A. Rabinovich, "Going deeper with convolutions," in *Computer Vision and Pattern Recognition (CVPR)*, 2015. arXiv: 1409.4842.

[74] S. Beldianu and S. Ziavras, "ASIC design of shared vector accelerators for multicore processors," in *Proceedings of the 2014 IEEE 26th International Symposium on Computer Architecture and High Performance Computing*, Oct. 2014, pp. 182–189.

[75] Arm Corp., *Arm Cortex-A77 Core*, Revision r1p1, Cambridge, UK, Oct. 2019.

[76] Y. Lu, S. Rooholamin, and S. Ziavras, "Vector coprocessor virtualization for simultaneous multithreading," *ACM Transactions on Embedded Computing Systems*, vol. 15, no. 3, 57:1–57:25, May 2016.

[77] Y. Lee, A. Ou, C. Schmidt, S. Karandikar, H. Mao, and K. Asanović, "The Hwacha microarchitecture manual," University of California at Berkeley, Berkeley, CA, USA, Tech. Rep. UCB/EECS-2015-263, version 3.8.1, Dec. 2015.

[78] Y. Lee, C. Schmidt, S. Karandikar, D. Dabbelt, A. Ou, and K. Asanović, "Hwacha preliminary evaluation results," University of California at Berkeley, Berkeley, CA, USA, Tech. Rep. UCB/EECS-2015-264, version 3.8.1, Dec. 2015.

[79] S. Naffziger, "Cross-disciplinary innovations required for the future of computing," in *Proceedings of the 58th Design Automation Conference*, IEEE/ACM, San Francisco, CA, USA, Jan. 2022.

[80] J. Wuu, "Memory solutions for HPC & AI," in *Proceedings of the 2022 International Electron Devices Meeting*, San Francisco, CA, USA: IEEE, Dec. 2022.

[81] E. Flamand, D. Rossi, F. Conti, I. Loi, A. Pullini, F. Rotenberg, and L. Benini, "GAP-8: A RISC-V SoC for AI at the edge of the IoT," in *Proceedings of the 2018 IEEE 29th International Conference on Application-specific Systems, Architectures and Processors (ASAP)*, 2018, pp. 1–4.

[82] N. Verma, "Future prospects of in- and near-memory computing," in *Proceedings of the 2022 International Electron Devices Meeting*, San Francisco, CA, USA: IEEE, Dec. 2022.

[83] Y. Wu *et al.*, "A 3nm CMOS FinFlex platform technology with enhanced power efficiency and performance for mobile SoC and high performance computing applications (Late News)," in *Proceedings of the 2022 International Electron Devices Meeting*, San Francisco, CA, USA: IEEE, Dec. 2022.

[84] M. Scherer, G. Rutishauser, L. Cavigelli, and L. Benini, "CUTIE: Beyond PetaOp/s/W ternary DNN inference acceleration with better-than-binary energy efficiency," *IEEE Transactions on Computer-Aided Design of Integrated Circuits and Systems*, vol. 41, no. 4, pp. 1020–1033, 2022.

[85] R. Brain, "Interconnect scaling: Challenges and opportunities," in *Proceedings of the 2016 International Electron Devices Meeting*, San Francisco, CA, USA, Dec. 2016, pp. 232–235.

[86] F. Zaruba, F. Schuiki, and L. Benini, "Manticore: A 4096-core RISC-V chiplet architecture for ultra-efficient floating-point computing," in *Proceedings of the 2020 IEEE Hot Chips 32 Symposium (HC32)*, IEEE Technical Committee on Microprocessors and Microcomputers, Cupertino, CA, USA: IEEE, Aug. 2020, pp. 36–42.

[87] NVIDIA Corp., *Nvidia H100 tensor core GPU architecture*, 1.02, NVIDIA Corp., 2022. [Online]. Available: `https://resources.nvidia.com/en-us-tensor-core` (visited on Mar. 1, 2023).

[88] H. T. Kung, "Memory requirements for balanced computer architectures," *SIGARCH Computer Architecture News*, vol. 14, no. 2, pp. 49–54, May 1986.

[89] C. Kozyrakis and D. Patterson, "Scalable vector processors for embedded systems," *IEEE Micro*, vol. 23, no. 6, pp. 36–45, 2003.

[90] N. Stephens, S. Biles, M. Boettcher, J. Eapen, M. Eyole, G. Gabrielli, M. Horsnell, G. Magklis, A. Martinez, N. Premillieu, A. Reid, A. Rico, and P. Walker, "The ARM scalable vector extension," *IEEE Micro*, vol. 37, no. 2, pp. 26–39, 2017.

[91] F. Minervini, O. Palomar, O. Unsal, E. Reggiani, J. Quiroga, J. Marimon, C. Rojas, R. Figueras, A. Ruiz, A. Gonzalez, J. Mendoza, I. Vargas, C. Hernandez, J. Cabre, L. Khoirunisya, M. Bouhali, J. Pavon, F. Moll, M. Olivieri, M. Kovac, M. Kovac, L. Dragic, M. Valero, and A. Cristal, "Vitruvius+: An area-efficient RISC-V decoupled vector coprocessor for high performance computing applications," *ACM Trans. Archit. Code Optim.*, Dec. 2022, Just Accepted.

[92] F. Zaruba, F. Schuiki, T. Hoefler, and L. Benini, "Snitch: A tiny pseudo dual-issue processor for area and energy efficient execution of floating-point intensive workloads," *IEEE Transactions on Computers*, vol. 70, no. 11, pp. 1845–1860, 2020.

[93] A. Teman, D. Rossi, P. Meinerzhagen, L. Benini, and A. Burg, "Power, area, and performance optimization of standard cell memory arrays through controlled placement," *ACM Transactions on Design Automation of Electronic Systems*, vol. 21, no. 4, May 2016.

[94] J. Shlomi, T. Ishihara, and H. Onodera, "Fully digital on-chip memory using minimum height standard cells for near-threshold voltage computing," in *Proceedings of the 2016 26th International Workshop on Power and Timing Modeling, Optimization and Simulation (PATMOS)*, 2016, pp. 44–49.

[95] J. W. Choi, D. Bedard, R. Fowler, and R. Vuduc, "A roofline model of energy," in *2013 IEEE 27th International Symposium on Parallel and Distributed Processing*, May 2013, pp. 661–672.

[96] K. Czechowski, C. Battaglino, C. McClanahan, A. Chandramowlishwaran, and R. Vuduc, "Balance principles for algorithm-architecture co-design," in *Proceedings of the 3rd USENIX Conference on Hot Topic in Parallelism*, ser. HotPar'11, Berkeley, CA, USA: USENIX Association, 2011, p. 9.

[97] OpenHW Corp., *OpenHW Group eXtension Interface*, Commit hash a3bcdd76, OpenHW Corp., Apr. 2022. [Online]. Available: https://docs.openhwgroup.org/projects/openhw-group-core-v-xif (visited on Mar. 1, 2023).

[98]   L. Bertaccini, G. Paulin, T. Fischer, S. Mach, and L. Benini, "MiniFloat-NN and ExSdotp: An ISA extension and a modular open hardware unit for low-precision training on RISC-V cores," in *2022 IEEE 29th Symposium on Computer Arithmetic (ARITH)*, Los Alamitos, CA, USA: IEEE Computer Society, Sep. 2022.

[99]   SiFive Corp., *SiFive performance P270*, 21G3, SiFive Corp., San Mateo, CA, USA, 2022. [Online]. Available: `https : / / sifive . cdn . prismic . io / sifive / 859c28c0 - 8bd5 - 4fc4 - 9113-a25a2a89bf9c_P270+Data+Sheet.pdf` (visited on Mar. 1, 2023).

[100]   SiFive Corp., *SiFive intelligence X280*, 21G3, SiFive Corp., San Mateo, CA, USA, 2022. [Online]. Available: `https : / / sifive . cdn . prismic . io / sifive / 62e0df53 - be02 - 4b50 - b211-aa55b7042fc8_x280-datasheet-21G3.pdf` (visited on Mar. 1, 2023).

[101]   M. Platzer and P. Puschner, "Vicuna: A Timing-Predictable RISC-V Vector Coprocessor for Scalable Parallel Computation," in *Proceedings of the 33rd Euromicro Conference on Real-Time Systems (ECRTS 2021)*, B. B. Brandenburg, Ed., vol. 196, Dagstuhl, Germany: Schloss Dagstuhl – Leibniz-Zentrum für Informatik, 2021, 1:1–1:18.

[102]   I. Al Assir, M. El Iskandarani, H. Al Sandid, and M. Saghir, *Arrow: A RISC-V vector accelerator for machine learning inference*, 2021. arXiv: 2107.07169.

[103]   M. Johns and T. Kazmierski, "A minimal risc-v vector processor for embedded systems," in *Proceedings of the 2020 Forum for Specification and Design Languages (FDL)*, Kiel, Germany: IEEE, 2020, pp. 1–4.

[104]   H. Esmaeilzadeh, E. Blem, R. Amant, K. Sankaralingam, and D. Burger, "Dark silicon and the end of multicore scaling," in *Proceedings of the 2011 38th Annual International Symposium on Computer Architecture (ISCA)*, Sep. 2011, pp. 365–376.

[105]   S. Eggers, J. Emer, H. Levy, J. Lo, R. Stamm, and D. Tullsen, "Simultaneous multithreading: A platform for next-generation processors," *IEEE Micro*, vol. 17, no. 5, pp. 12–19, 1997.

[106] J.-Y. Tsai, J. Huang, C. Amlo, D. Lilja, and P.-C. Yew, "The superthreaded processor architecture," *IEEE Transactions on Computers*, vol. 48, no. 9, pp. 881–902, 1999.

[107] M. Lam and R. Wilson, "Limits of control flow on parallelism," in *Proceedings of the 19th Annual International Symposium on Computer Architecture*, ser. ISCA '92, Queensland, Australia: Association for Computing Machinery, 1992, pp. 46–57.

[108] N. Nassif, A. Munch, C. Molnar, G. Pasdast, S. Lyer, Z. Yang, O. Mendoza, M. Huddart, S. Venkataraman, S. Kandula, R. Marom, A. Kern, B. Bowhill, D. Mulvihill, S. Nimmagadda, V. Kalidindi, J. Krause, M. Haq, R. Sharma, and K. Duda, "Sapphire Rapids: The next-generation Intel Xeon scalable processor," in *Proceedings of the 2022 IEEE International Solid-State Circuits Conference (ISSCC)*, vol. 65, 2022, pp. 44–46.

[109] D. Ditzel, R. Espasa, N. Aymerich, A. Baum, T. Berg, J. Burr, E. Hao, J. Iyer, M. Izquierdo, S. Jayaratnam, *et al.*, "Accelerating ML recommendation with over a thousand RISC-V/tensor processors on Esperanto's ET-SoC-1 chip," in *2021 IEEE Hot Chips 33 Symposium (HCS)*, IEEE, 2021, pp. 1–23.

[110] S. Mazzola, S. Riedel, M. Cavalcante, L. Benini, and A. Macii, "ISA extensions in the Snitch processor for signal processing," M.S. thesis, Politecnico di Torino, Apr. 2021, pp. 1–98.

[111] W. J. Dally and B. P. Towles, *Principles and Practices of Interconnection Networks*. San Francisco, CA, USA: Morgan Kaufmann Publishers Inc., 2004.

[112] R. Muralidhar, R. Borovica-Gajic, and R. Buyya, "Energy efficient computing systems: Architectures, abstractions and modeling to techniques and standards," *ACM Computing Surveys*, vol. 54, no. 11s, pp. 1–37, Sep. 2022. arXiv: 2007.09976.

[113] H. Ayed, J. Ermont, J.-L. Scharbarg, and C. Fraboul, "Towards a unified approach for worst-case analysis of Tilera-like and KalRay-like NoC architectures," in *2016 IEEE World Conference on Factory Communication Systems (WFCS)*, May 2016.

[114] GreenWaves Technologies Corp., *GAP8 hardware reference manual*, Version 1.5.5, Grenoble, France, Jan. 2019. [Online]. Available: `https://gwt-website-files.s3.amazonaws.com/gap8_datasheet.pdf` (visited on Jun. 18, 2022).

[115] R. Ginosar, P. Aviely, T. Israeli, and H. Meirov, "RC64: High performance rad-hard manycore," in *Proceedings of the 2016 IEEE Aerospace Conference*, Mar. 2016.

[116] B. Dupont de Dinechin, "A qualitative approach to many-core architecture," in *Multi-Processor System-on-Chip 1: Architectures*, L. Andrade and F. Rousseau, Eds., Hoboken, NJ, USA: Wiley, Apr. 2021, ch. 2, pp. 27–51.

[117] S. Bell, B. Edwards, J. Amann, R. Conlin, K. Joyce, V. Leung, J. MacKay, M. Reif, L. Bao, J. Brown, M. Mattina, C. Miao, C. Ramey, D. Wentzlaff, W. Anderson, E. Berger, N. Fairbanks, D. Khan, F. Montenegro, J. Stickney, and J. Zook, "TILE64 processor: A 64-core SoC with mesh interconnect," in *Proceedings of the 2018 IEEE International Solid-State Circuits Conference*, Feb. 2008, pp. 88–90.

[118] S. Davidson, S. Xie, C. Torng, K. Al-Hawai, A. Rovinski, T. Ajayi, L. Vega, C. Zhao, R. Zhao, S. Dai, A. Amarnath, B. Veluri, P. Gao, A. Rao, G. Liu, R. K. Gupta, Z. Zhang, R. Dreslinski, C. Batten, and M. B. Taylor, "The Celerity open-source 511-core RISC-V tiered accelerator fabric: Fast architectures and design methodologies for fast chips," *IEEE Micro*, vol. 38, no. 2, pp. 30–41, Mar. 2018.

[119] B. Bohnenstiehl, A. Stillmaker, J. J. Pimentel, T. Andreas, B. Liu, A. T. Tran, E. Adeagbo, and B. M. Baas, "KiloCore: A 32-nm 1000-processor computational array," *IEEE Jornal on Solid-State Circuits*, vol. 52, no. 4, pp. 891–902, Apr. 2017.

[120] A. Olofsson, T. Nordström, and Z. Ul-Abdin, "Kickstarting high-performance energy-efficient manycore architectures with Epiphany," in *Proceedings of the 2014 48th Asilomar Conference on Signals, Systems and Computers*, 2014, pp. 1719–1726.

[121] W. S. Tsai, C. Y. Huang, C. K. Chung, K. H. Yu, and C. F. Lin, "Generational changes of flip chip interconnection technology," in *Proceedings of the 2017 12th International Microsystems, Packaging, Assembly and Circuits Technology Conference (IMPACT)*, 2017, pp. 306–310.

[122] E. Beyne, S.-W. Kim, L. Peng, N. Heylen, J. De Messemaeker, O. Okudur, A. Phommahaxay, T.-G. Kim, M. Stucchi, D. Velenis, A. Miller, and G. Beyer, "Scalable, sub 2 µm pitch, Cu/SiCN to cu/sicn hybrid wafer-to-wafer bonding technology," in *Proceedings of the 2017 IEEE International Electron Devices Meeting (IEDM)*, 2017, pp. 32.4.1–32.4.4.

[123] M. Healy, K. Athikulwongse, R. Goel, M. Hossain, D. Kim, Y.-J., D. Lewis, T.-W. Lin, C. Liu, M. Jung, B. Ouellette, M. Pathak, H. Sane, G. S., D. Woo, X. Z., G. Loh, H.-H. Lee, and S.-K. Lim, "Design and analysis of 3D-MAPS: A many-core 3D processor with stacked memory," in *Proceedings of the IEEE Custom Integrated Circuits Conference 2010*, 2010, pp. 1–4.

[124] S. Pentapati, L. Zhu, L. Bamberg, D. E. Shim, A. Garcia-Ortiz, and S.-K. Lim, "A logic-on-memory processor-system design with monolithic 3-D technology," *IEEE Micro*, vol. 39, no. 6, pp. 38–45, 2019.

[125] PULP Platform, *MemPool*, GitHub repository, 2021. [Online]. Available: https://github.com/pulp-platform/mempool/ (visited on Mar. 2, 2023).

[126] J. Vetter, E. DeBenedictis, and T. Conte, "Architectures for the Post-Moore Era," *IEEE Micro*, vol. 37, no. 04, pp. 6–8, Jul. 2017.

[127] J. Domke, E. Vatai, B. Gerofi, Y. Kodama, M. Wahib, A. Podobas, S. Mittal, M. Pericàs, L. Zhang, P. Chen, A. Drozd, and S. Matsuoka, *At the locus of performance: A case study in enhancing CPUs with copious 3D-Stacked cache*, Apr. 2022. arXiv: 2204.02235.

Curriculum Vitæ

Matheus de Araújo Cavalcante was born the 6th November, 1995 in Campina Grande, Paraíba, Brazil. He received the M.Sc. degree in Integrated Electronic Systems from the Grenoble Institute of Technology (Phelma), Grenoble, France in 2018. Mr. Cavalcante successively joined the research group of Prof. Dr. Luca Benini at the Integrated Systems Laboratory (IIS) as a Ph.D. candidate. His research interests  include high-performance computing systems, with particular interest in vector processors and manycore systems. He furthermore works in architectural co-optimization with emerging VLSI technologies, such as two-and-a-half and three-dimensional integrated circuits.

SERIES IN MICROELECTRONICS

#170: Melanie Etherton, Charged Device Model (CDM) ESD in ICs: Physics, Modeling, and Circuit Simulation. ISBN 3-86628-067-X

171: Christian Kromer, 10 Gb/s to 40 Gb/s Receiver for High-Density Optical Interconnects in 80-nm CMOS. ISBN 3-86628-069-6

#172: Corrado Carta, BiCMOS Radio-Frequency Front-Ends for Wireless-LAN Receivers. ISBN 3-86628-071-8

#173: Timm Höhr, Quantum-Mechanical Modeling of Transport Parameters for MOS-Devices. ISBN 3-86628-087-4

#174: Ilian Kouchev, Design of a Highly Linear Direct-Conversion Receiver for Third-Generation Mobile Communi-cations. ISBN 3-86628-093-9

#175: Chiara Martelli, Multi-Standard Low-Power Base-Band Digital Receiver, Enhanced for HSDPA. ISBN 3-86628-094-7

#176: Walter Oesch, Controlling Software for EMF Laboratory Studies. ISBN 3-86628-097-1

#177: Stefan Odermatt, Physics and Simulation of Semiconductor Lasers: Static and Dynamic Characteristics. ISBN 3-86628-111-0

#178: José Miguel Ruiz Palmero, Physical InP-Based HBT Models for Ultimate Digital Circuit Optimization. ISBN 3-86628-117-X

#179: Lutz Schneider, Multidimensional Modeling and Simulation of Wavelength-Tunable Semiconductor Lasers. ISBN 3-86628-122-6

#180: Marco Buzzo, Dopant Imaging and Profiling of Wide Bandgap Semiconductor Devices. ISBN 3-86628-124-2

#181: Beat Sahli, Ab Initio Molecular Dynamics Simulation of Diffusion in Silicon. ISBN 3-86628-133-1

#182: Ulrich Glaser, Complex ESD Protection Elements and Issues in Decananometre CMOS Technologies. ISBN 3-86628-135-8

#183: Chiara Corvasce, Mobility and Impact Ionization in Silicon at High Temperature. ISBN 3-86628-136-6

#184: Stefan Benkler, Robust Conformal Subcell Modeling for Electromagnetic Simulations in Time Domain. ISBN 3-86628-137-4

#185: Gion Sialm, VCSEL Modeling and CMOS Trans-mitters up to 40 Gb/s for High-Density Optical Links. ISBN 3-86628-143-9

#186: Mathieu Luisier, Quantum Transport Beyond the Effective Mass Approximation. ISBN 3-86628-149-8

#187: Flavio Carbognani, Low-Power Techniques for Low-Frequency VLSI Applications. ISBN 3-86628-161-7

#188: Marc Simon Wegmüller, Intra-Body Communication for Biomedical Sensor Networks. ISBN 3-86628-162-5

189: Valerio Laino, Performance Analysis of Edge Emitting Lasers in the Mid Infra-Red and Visible Spectrum. ISBN 3-86628-169-2

190: Christoph David Perels, Frame-Based MIMO-OFDM Systems: Impairment Estimation and Compensation. ISBN 3-86628-172-2

191: Verónica J. Berdinas Torres, Exposure Systems and Dosimetry of Large-Scale In Vivo Studies. ISBN 3-86628-180-3

192: Simon Häne, VLSI Circuits for MIMO-OFDM Physical Layer. ISBN 3-86628-196-X

193: Felix Bürgin, Low-Power Circuit Architectures and Clocking Strategies for Digital Hearing Aids. ISBN 3-86628-211-7

194: Luca Sponton, From manu-facturing variability to process-aware circuit simulation. 3-86628-230-3

195: Yves Saad, TCAD-Based Three-Dimensional Modeling of Non-Volatile Memories. ISBN 3-86628-237-0

196: Stefan Schild, Advanced Material Modeling in EM-FDTD ISBN 3-86628-238-9

197: Sebastian Steiger, Modelling Nano-LEDs. ISBN 3-86628-257-5

198: Alexandra Baecker, A TCAD Analysis of Long-Wavelength Vertical-Cavity Surface-Emitting Lasers. ISBN 3-86628-258-3

199: Martin Loeser, Theory and Design of Broadband Active Opto-electronic Devices. ISBN 3-86628-276-1

200: Stefan Eberli, Application-Specific Processor for MIMO-OFDM Software-Defined Radio. ISBN 3-86628-285-0

201: Ratko G. Veprek, omputational Modeling of Semiconductor Nanostructures for Optoelectronics. ISBN 3-86628-286-9

202: Christoph Studer, Iterative MIMO Decoding: Algorithms and VLSI Implementation Aspects. ISBN 3-86628-288-5

203: Peter Jan Lüthi, VLSI Circuits for MIMO Preprocessing. ISBN 3-86628-295-8

204: Urs Hammer, Sub-micron InP/GaAsSb/InP Double Hetero-junction Bipolar Transistors for Ultra High-Speed Digital Integrated Circuits. ISBN 3-86628-301-6

205: Sven Kühn, EMF Risk Assessment: Exposure Assessment and Compliance Testing in Complex Environments. ISBN 3-86628-309-1

206: Jürg Treichler, Preserving High Resolution in Deep-Submicron CMOS Pipelined A/D. ISBN 3-86628-316-4

207: Philipp Kreuter, Modeling of Electrically Pumped Vertical-External-Cavity Surface-Emitting Lasers. ISBN 978-3-86628-317-6

208: Thomas Christen, Multi-Mode Delta-Sigma A/D-Converters for Multi-Standard Wireless Receivers. ISBN 978-3-86628-318-3

209: Christian Benkeser, Power Efficiency and the Mapping of

Communication Algorithms into VLSI.
ISBN 978-3-86628-323-7

210: Sven Ebert, EMF Risk
Assessment: Exposure Systems for
Large-Scale Laboratory and
Experimental Provocation Studies.
ISBN 978-3-86628-331-2

211: Martin Frey, Scattering in
Nanoscale Devices.
ISBN 978-3-86628-353-4

212: Kilian Vollenweider, Dopant
Clustering and Diffusion in Silicon.
ISBN 978-3-86628-354-1

213: Markus Wenk, MIMO-OFDM
Testbed: Challenges, Implemen-
tations, and Measurement Results.
ISBN 978-3-86628-366-4

214: Luca Henzen, VLSI Circuits for
Cryptographic Authentication.
ISBN 978-3-86628-367-1

215: Aniello Esposito, Band
Structure Effects and Quantum
Transport. ISBN 978-3-86628-378-7

216: Holctor Meier, Design,
Characterization and Simulation of
Avalanche Photodiodes.
ISBN 978-3-86628-380-0

217: Denis Dolgos, Full-Band Monte
Carlo Simulation of Single Photon
Avalanche Diodes.
ISBN 978-3-86628-421-0

218: Neviana Nikoloski, EMF Risk
Assessment: Exposure Assessment
and Specialized Exposure Setups.
ISBN 978-3-86628-422-7

219: Patrick Mächler, VLSI
Architectures for Compressive Sensing
and Sparse Signal Recovery.
ISBN 978-3-86628-446-3

220: Marcus Deppner, Design of
Nanorod-LEDs using Computational
Modelling. ISBN 978-3-86628-459-3

221: Pierre Greisen, Hardware
Architectures for Real-Time Video
Processing and View Synthesis.
ISBN 978-3-86628-461-6

222: Vincent Peikert, Utilizing
Wavelets to Solve High-Dimensional
Transport Equations in Nano-Devices.
ISBN 978-3-86628-466-1

223: Cédric Bessire,
Semiconducting Nanowire Tunnel
Devices. ISBN 978-3-86628-471-3

224: Artur Scheinemann, Modelling
of Leakage Currents Induced by Extended Defects in Extra-Functionality
Devices. ISBN 978-3-86628-504-0

225: Zhelio Andreev, Physics-based
Simulation of III-V Nitride LEDs: The
Role of Polarization.
ISBN 978-3-86628-542-2

226: Reto Rhyner, Quantum
Transport Beyond The Ballistic Limit.
ISBN 978-3-86628-545-3

227: Philipp Mensch, Thermoelectric
Characterization of InAs Nanowires.
ISBN 978-3-86628-546-0

228: Aron Szabo, Dissipative
quantum transport simulations in two-
dimensional semiconductor devices
from first principles.
ISBN 978-3-86628-570-5

229: Harald Kröll,
An Evolved EDGE System-on-Chip for
the Cellular Internet of Things.
ISBN 978-3-86628-572-9

230: Philipp Christoph Schönle,
A Power Efficient Spectrophotometry &
PPG Integrated Circuit for Mobile
Medical Instruments.
ISBN 978-3-86628-590-3

231: Michael Andreas Gautschi,
Design of Energy-Efficient Processing
Elements for Near-Threshold Parallel
Computing.ISBN 978-3-86628-595-8

232: Benjamin Sporrer,
Integrated Broadband Receivers for
Magnetic. Resonance Imaging.
ISBN 978-3-86628-607-8

233: David Emanuel Bellasi,
Toward Energy-Proportional
Compressive Sensors.
ISBN 978-3-86628-618-4

234: Pirmin Robert Vogel, Shared
Virtual Memory for Heterogeneous
Embedded Systems on Chips.
ISBN 978-3-86628-623-8

235: Michael Schaffner, Energy-
Efficient VLSI Architectures for Real-
Time and 3D Video Processing
ISBN 978-3-86628-624-5

236: Sandro Steffano Belfanti,
Design and Implementation of Efficient
VLSI Solutions for 3G and 4G Mobile
Communications.
ISBN 978-3-86628-635-1

237: Pascal Alexander Hager,
Design of Fully-Digital Medical
Ultrasound Imaging Systems.
ISBN 978-3-86628-649-8

238: Lukas Cavigelli, Towards
Energy-Efficient Convolutional Neural
Network Inference.
ISBN 978-3-86628-651-1

239: Florian Michael Scheidegger,
The concept of transprecision
computing.
ISBN 978-3-86628-689-4

240: Renzo Andri, Machine Learning
Acceleration for Tightly Energy-
Constrained Devices.
ISBN 978-3-86628-693-1

241: Stefan Mach, Floating-Point
Architectures for Energy-Efficient
Transprecision Computing.
ISBN 978-3-86628-719-8

242: Florian Zaruba, Energy-Efficient
High-Performance Computing.
ISBN 978-3-86628-720-4

243: Fabian Schuiki, Streaming
Architectures for Extreme Energy
Efficiency in High-Performance
Computing. ISBN 978-3-86628-725-9

#244: Andreas Dominic Kurth, An
Open-Source Research Platform for
Heterogeneous Systems on Chip.
ISBN 978-3-86628-774-7

#245: Florian Stefan Glaser,
An Event-Driven Parallel-Processing
Subsystem for Energy-Efficient Mobile
Medical Instrumentation.
ISBN 978-3-86628-777-8

Hartung-Gorre Verlag, Konstanz
http://www.hartung-gorre.de